LEARN HOW TO DRAW

FOR THE NON-ARTIST™

EARL R. PHELPS

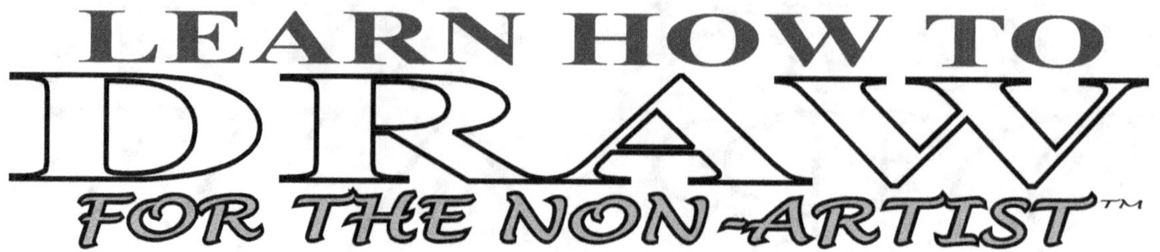

By Earl R. Phelps

Published by
Phelps Publishing
P.O. Box 22401
Cleveland, Ohio 44122

ISBN: 978-1-887627-12-2

Library of Congress Control Number:2019945969

Printed in the United States of American

Cover design and illustrations by Earl R. Phelps

Visit our website at: **https://www.phelpspublishing.com**

**I dedicate this book to my
Loving mother, *Edna* and my
Big personality son, *Marvell*.**

Table of Contents

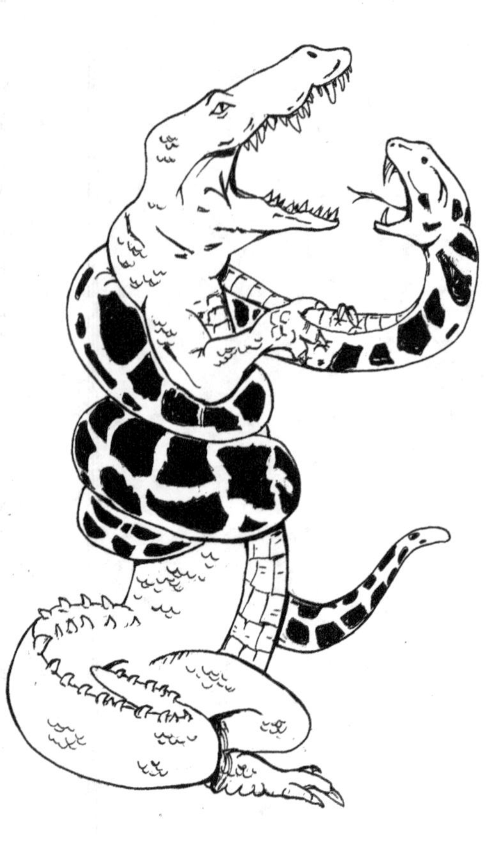

INTRODUCTION — 5
DRAWING SHAPES — 6
EYES — 7
NOSE AND LIPS — 8
HUMAN HEAD — 9
Lady With Hat — 10
Head Facing Front — 11
Head Facing Sideways — 12
Head Positions — 13
Large Head Sideways — 14
Big Hair Lady — 18
Classy Lady — 22
HUMAN FIGURE — 27
Arm Structure — 28
Hands — 29
Torso — 30
Female Figure — 31
Male Back — 32
Male Legs — 33
Feet — 34
STILL LIFE — 35
Apple and Banana — 36
Apple, Pear ,and Plum — 40
Apple, Banana, Orange, and Pear — 44
Lamp — 48
Banana, Orange, Grapes, and Apple — 52
BASIC PERSPECTIVE — 57
One-Point Perspective — 58
Two-Point Perspective — 59
Two-Point Perspective Building — 60
DRAWING REPTILES — 61
Turtle — 62
Lizard — 66
DRAWING MAMMALS — 71
Elephant — 72
Hippopotamus — 76
Horse — 80
DRAWING SPORTS — 85
Boxers — 86
Tennis Lady — 90
DRAWING SUPERCHARACTERS — 95
Ram-Man — 96
Space Eyeglass Lady — 100
Metal Rider — 104
C-Lady — 108
FANTASY DRAWING — 113
Alligator vs. Snake — 114
Man-Dragon — 118
COVER LADY — 123

Introduction

llo Artist,

ope you enjoy this book, not just on learning how to draw or drawing better. I want you
reward yourself in the process of learning, relax and free your mind. And there's no
tter way to do it than with this book.

earn How to Draw for the Non-Artist" is a book I created for those who want to learn
w to draw as well for those who want to improve their drawing skills. What I mean by
n-Artist is that any and everyone can learn how to draw.

ave included a combination of pencil and ink drawings in this book for your education.
r ink drawings, I started with a pencil and then draw over my pencils with markers. All
u need is a pencil and paper to get started. As in all of my books, I like to keep things
nple, and this one is no different.

u will learn to draw many different things in this book. After completing this book you
I have accomplished how to draw such things as Still Life, the Human Head, Human
jure, Mammals, Reptiles, Sports Figures, Supercharacters, Fantasy drawings and
sic Perspective drawing.

truly become great at anything in life, you have to study, visualize, and perform, in
her words, practice, practice, and more practice. Ain't nothing to it, but to do it!

t's get busy!!

rl R. Phelps

SHAPES

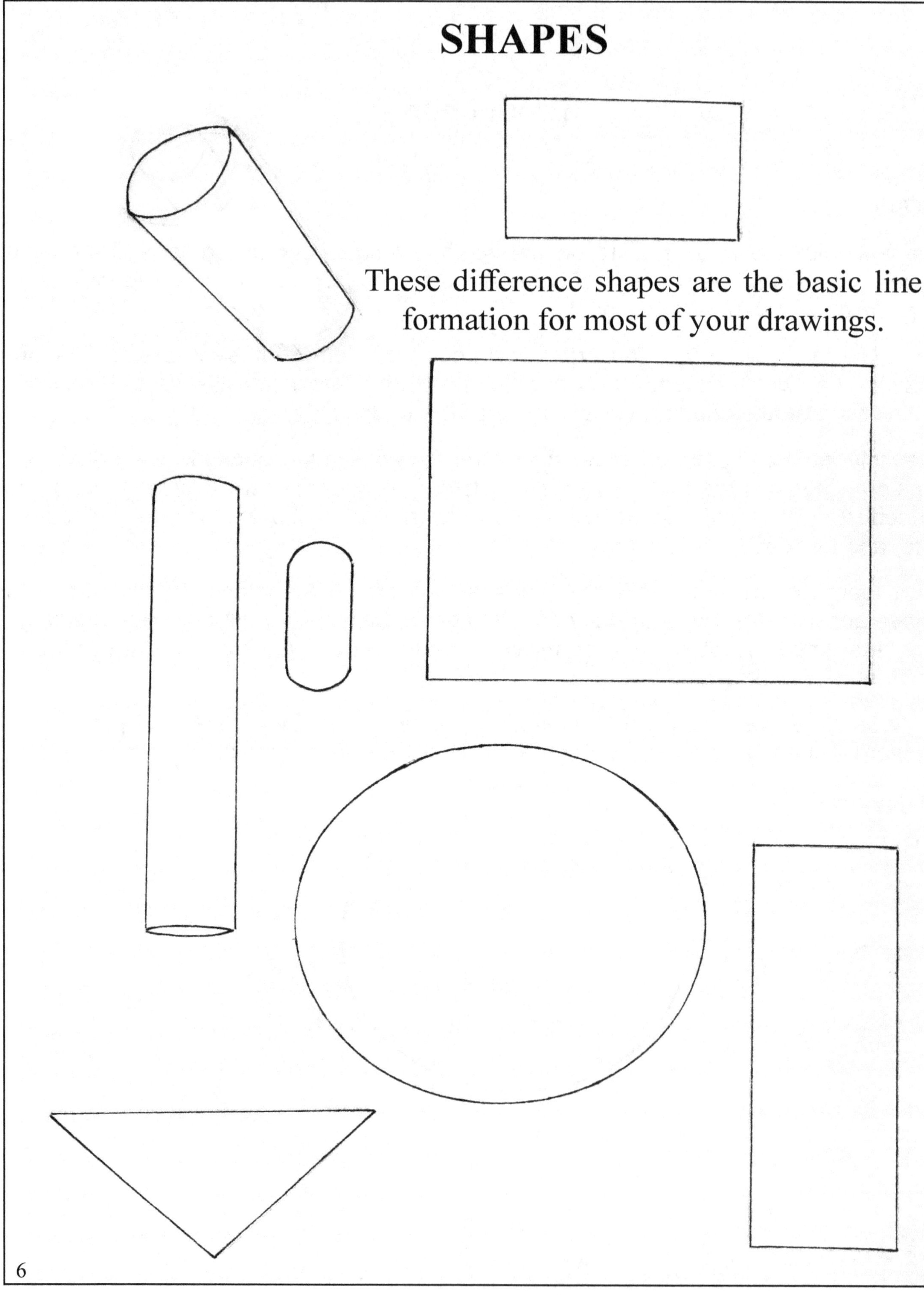

These difference shapes are the basic line formation for most of your drawings.

EYES

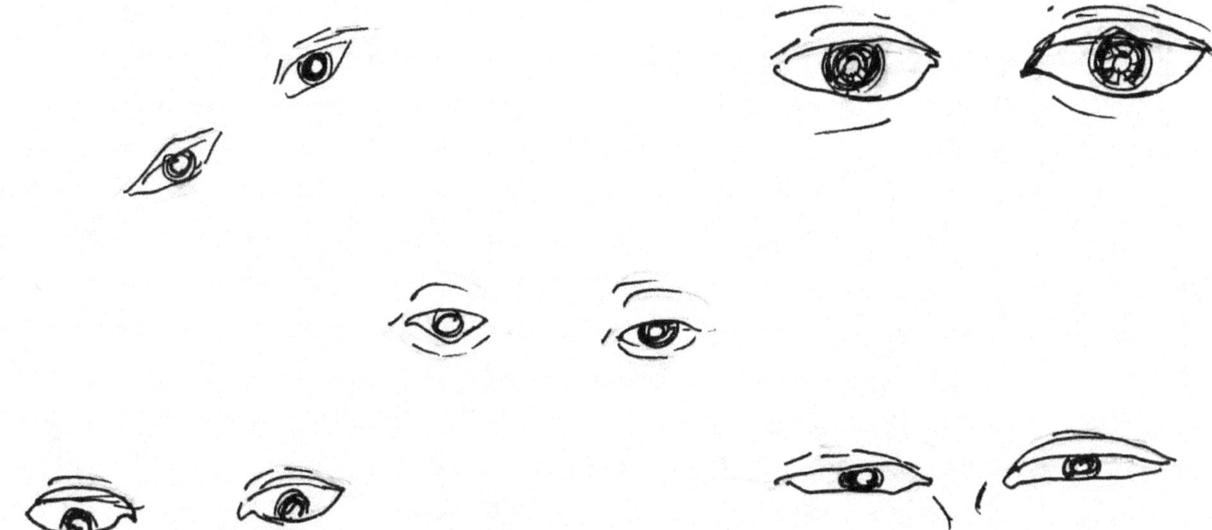

I drew some examples the men eyes above and
the women eyes below.

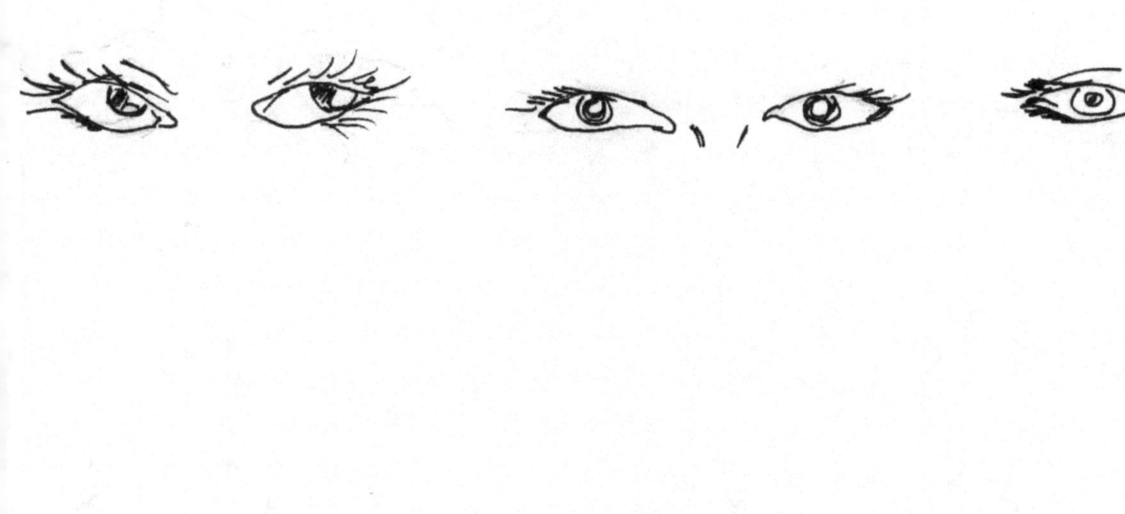

NOSES and LIPS

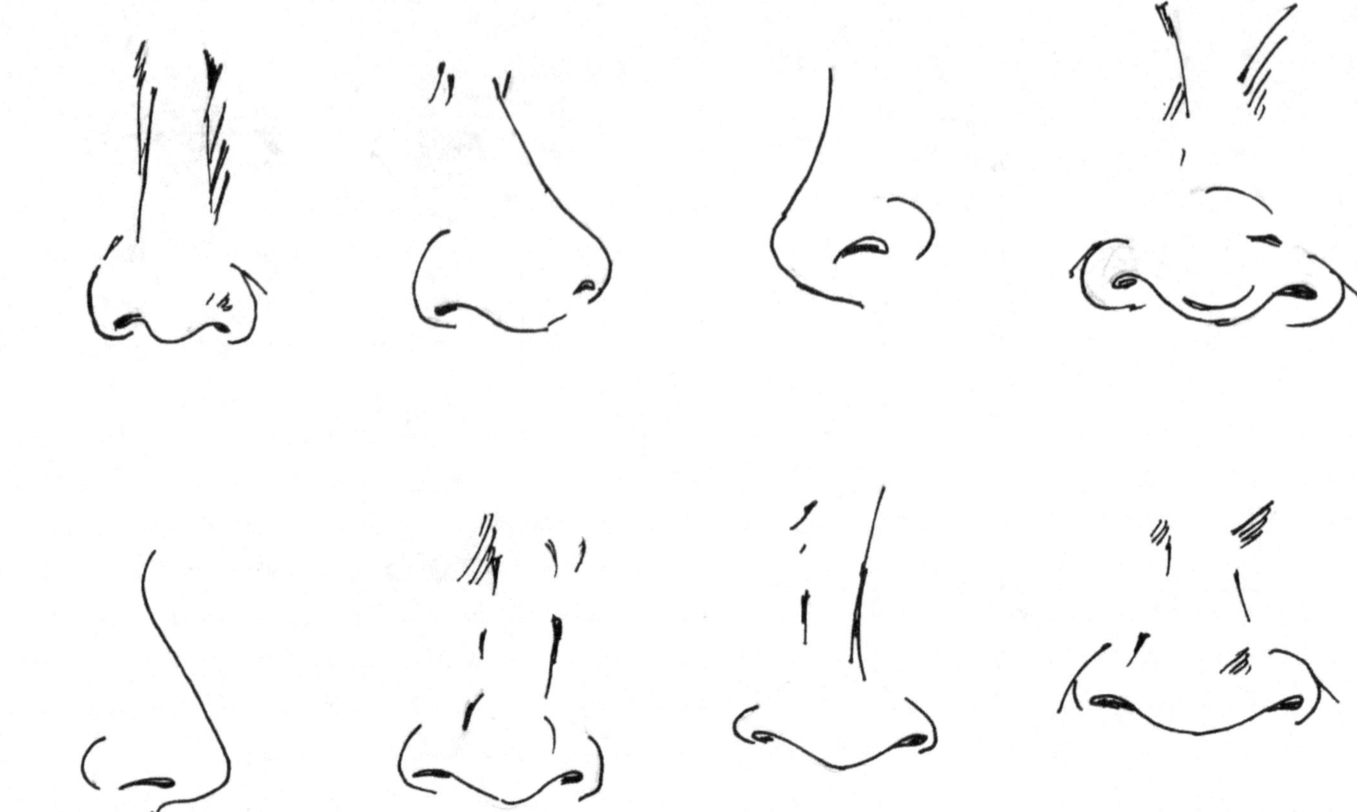

Look at yourself in the mirror and study the noses and lips of other people.

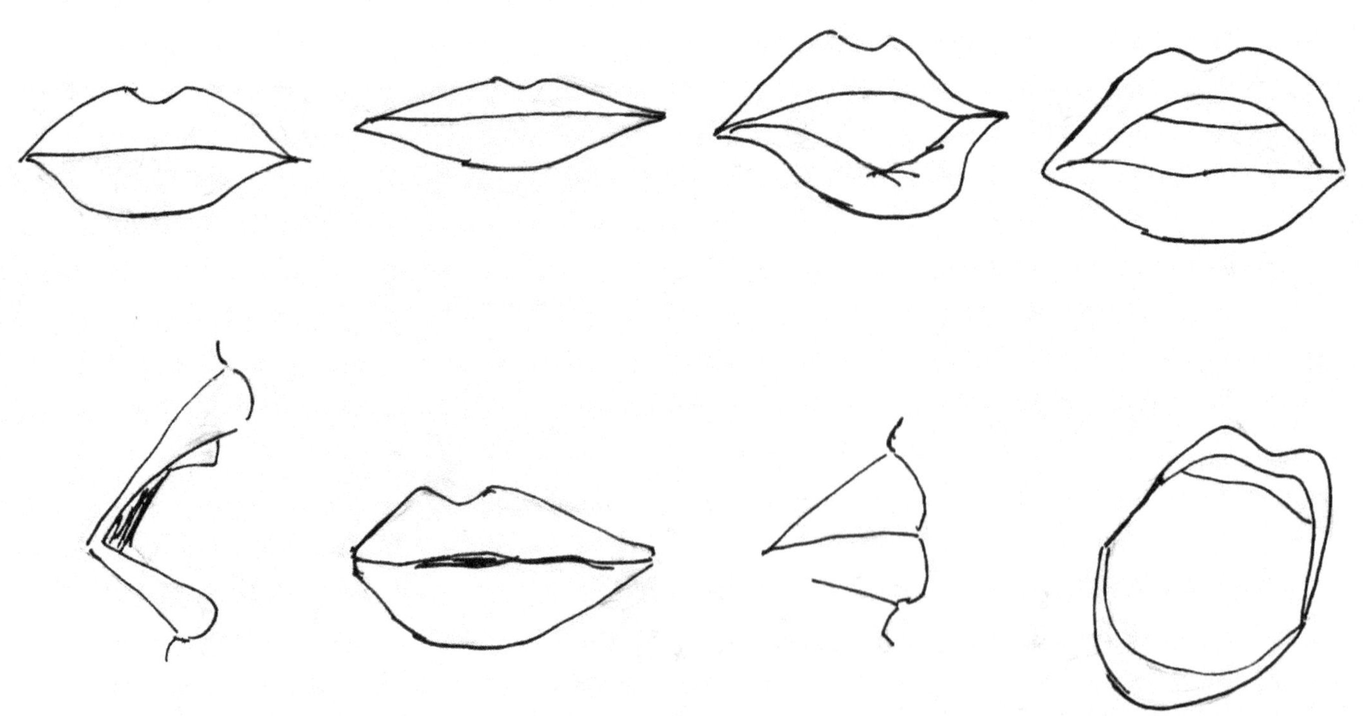

HUMAN HEAD

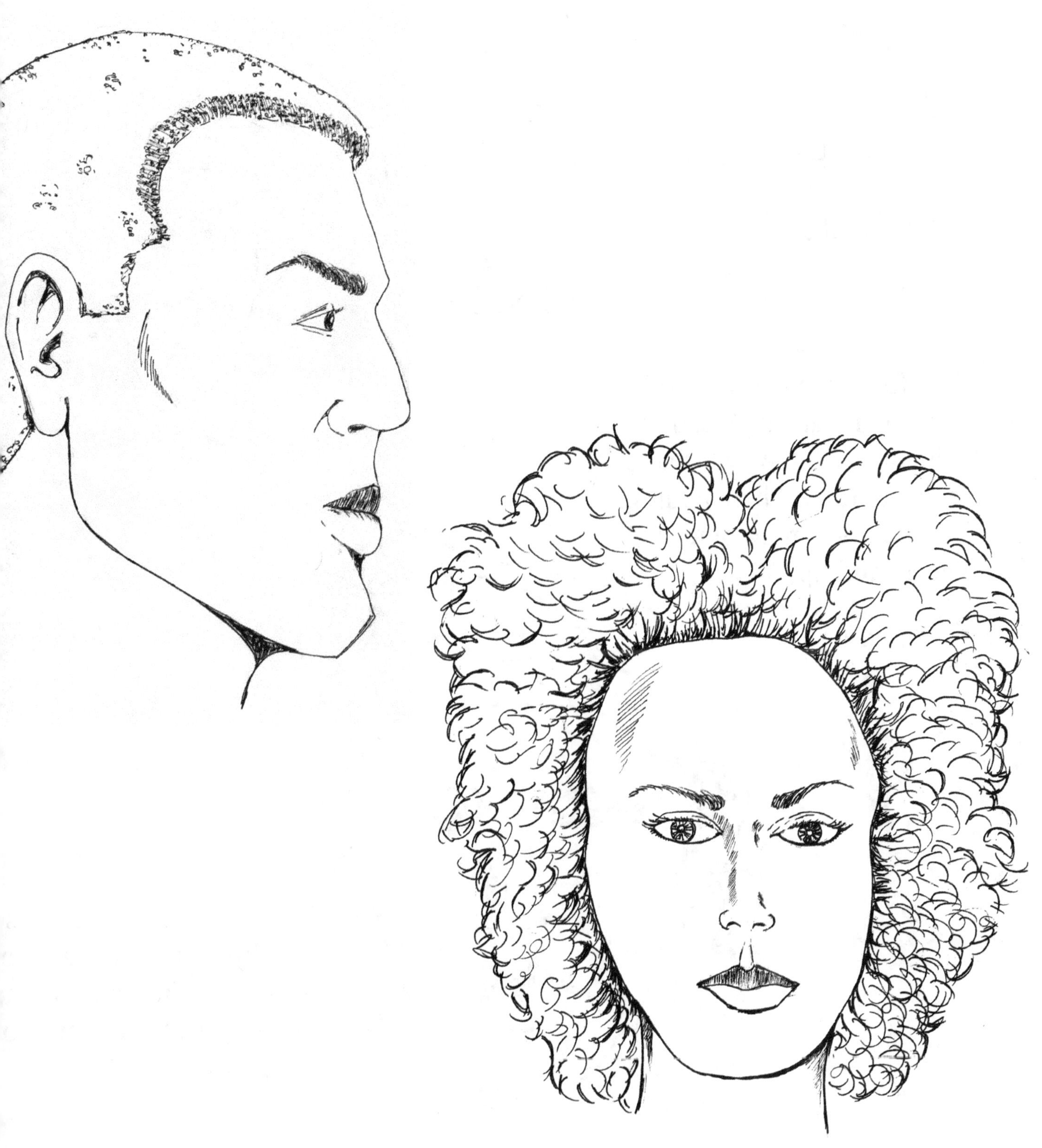

LADY with HAT

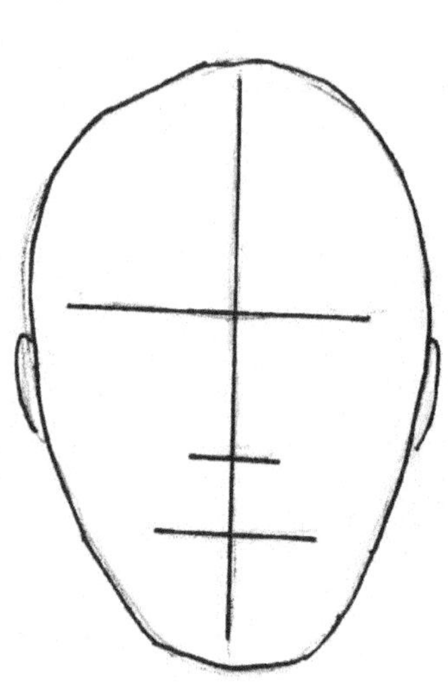

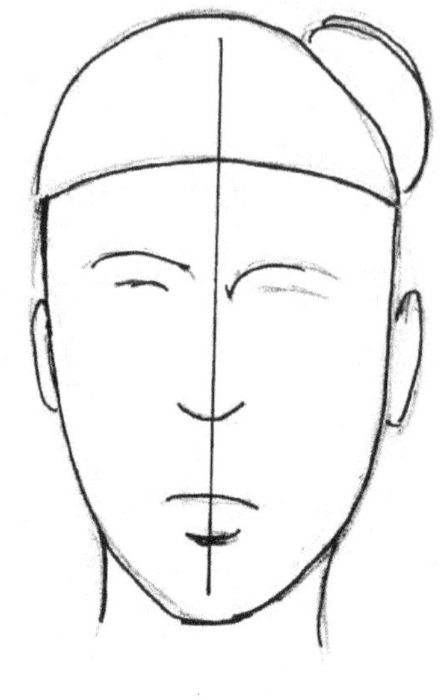

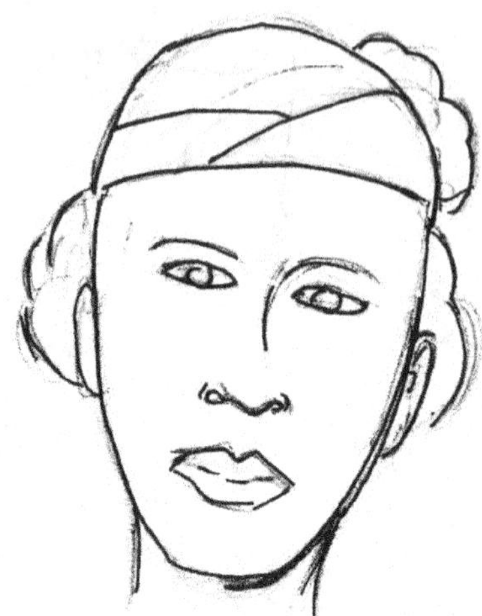

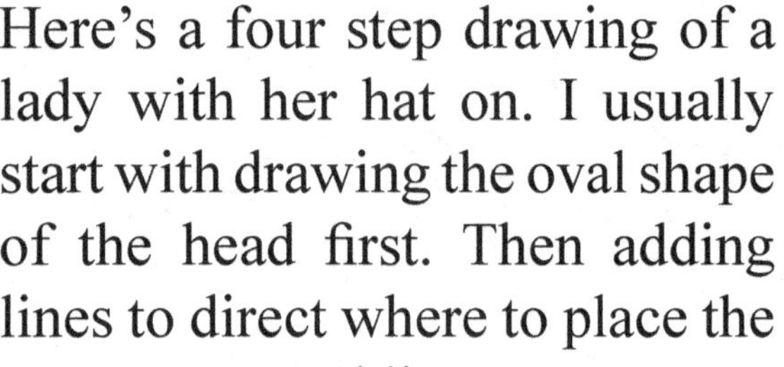

Here's a four step drawing of a lady with her hat on. I usually start with drawing the oval shape of the head first. Then adding lines to direct where to place the eyes, nose, and lips.

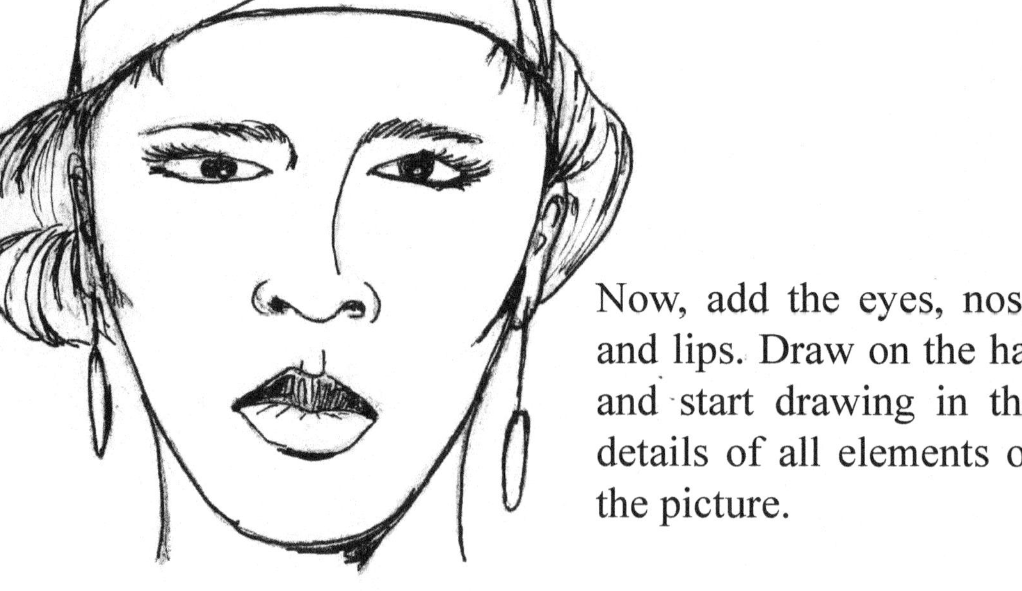

Now, add the eyes, nose, and lips. Draw on the hat and start drawing in the details of all elements of the picture.

HEAD FACING FRONT

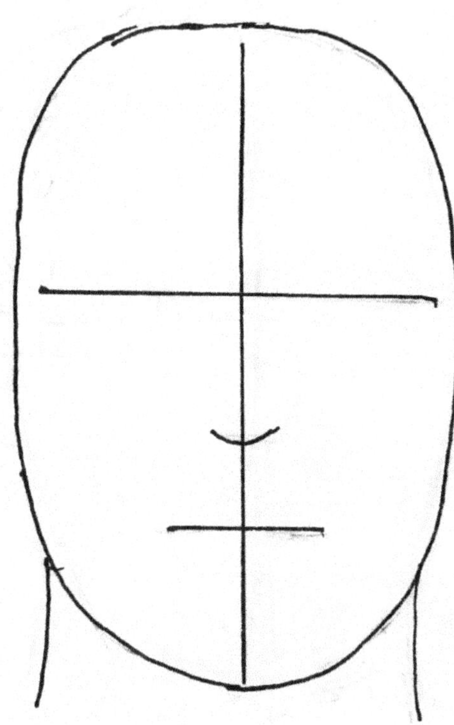

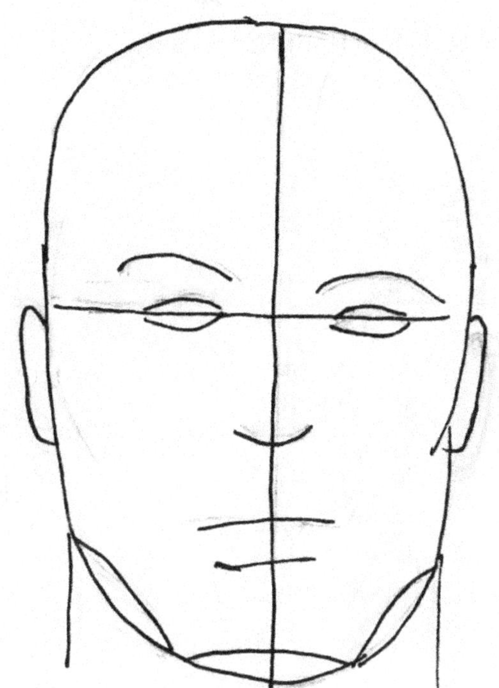

Start with drawing the shape of head, then proceed with putting in the lines to position the eyes, nose and mouth. The last step is drawing in the details. Whether you want a mustache, beard, hair or no hair, it's up to you.

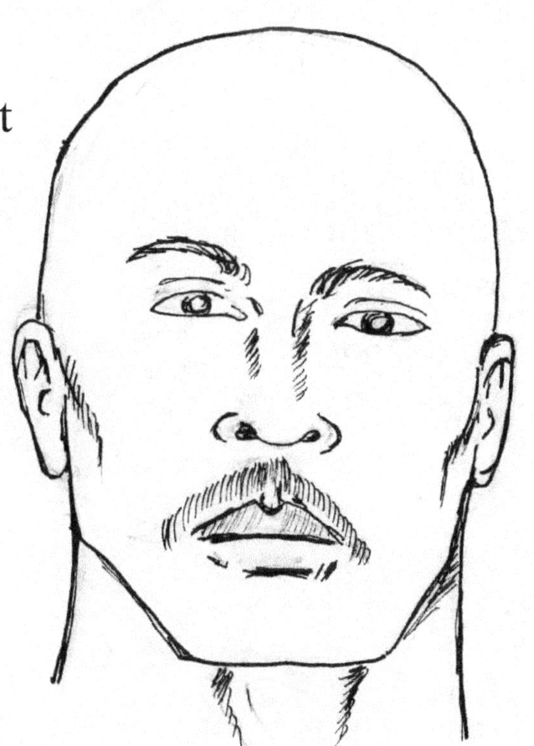

HEAD FACING SIDEWAYS

Let's start with drawing a oval shape, then add a triangle type shape below. Draw a straight line where the eyes will go as well the nose and lips.

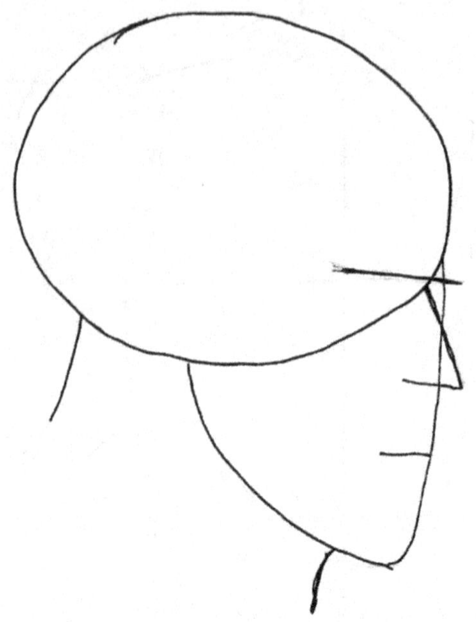

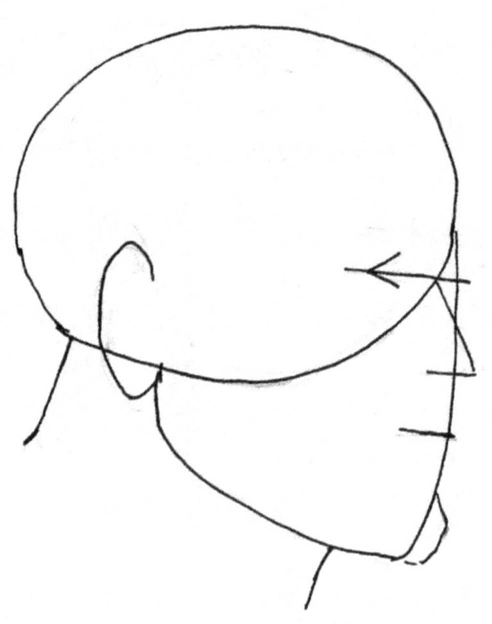

Draw the ear and draw a arrow shape for the eye. His chin needs to be little larger. let's extend the chin.

Now, define the drawing by drawing in more details for the ear, eye, nose and mouth. Here's your finish drawing.

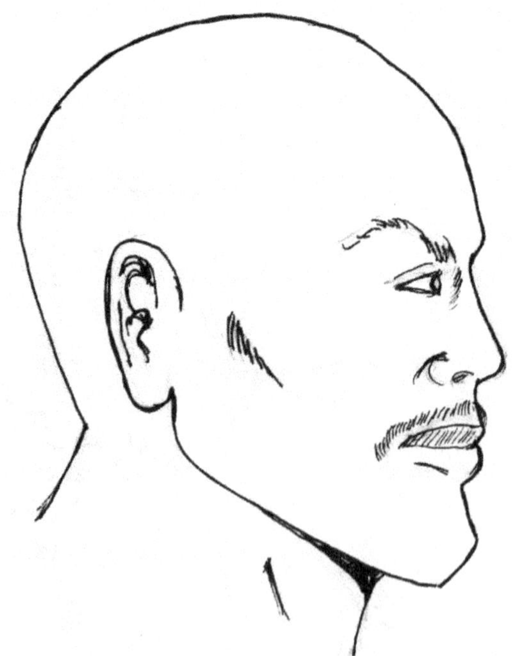

HEAD POSITIONS

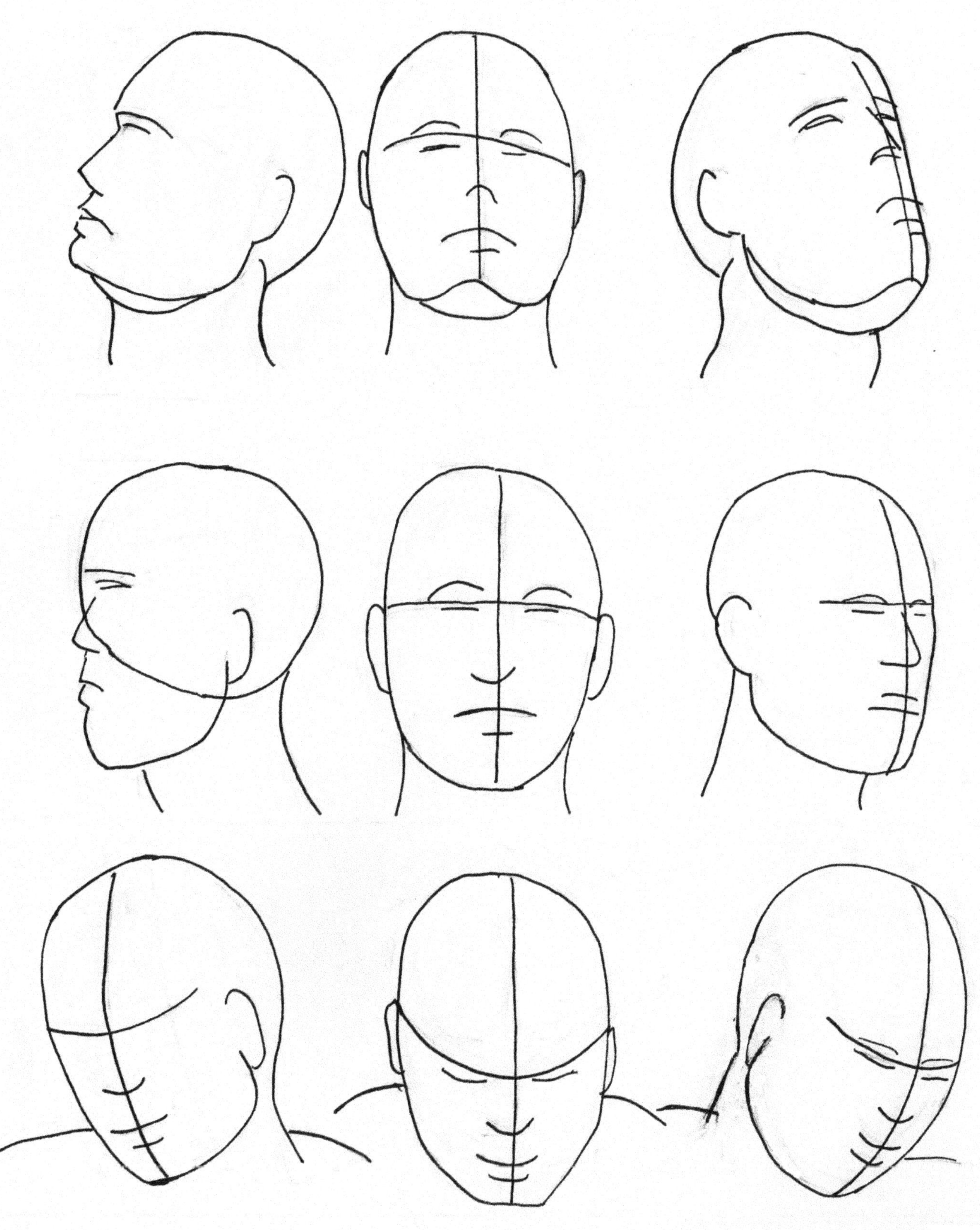

LARGE HEAD FACING SIDEWAYS

Not like the previous head drawing where I started with a oval and triple shape. I'm just drawing one egg shape to start this drawing.

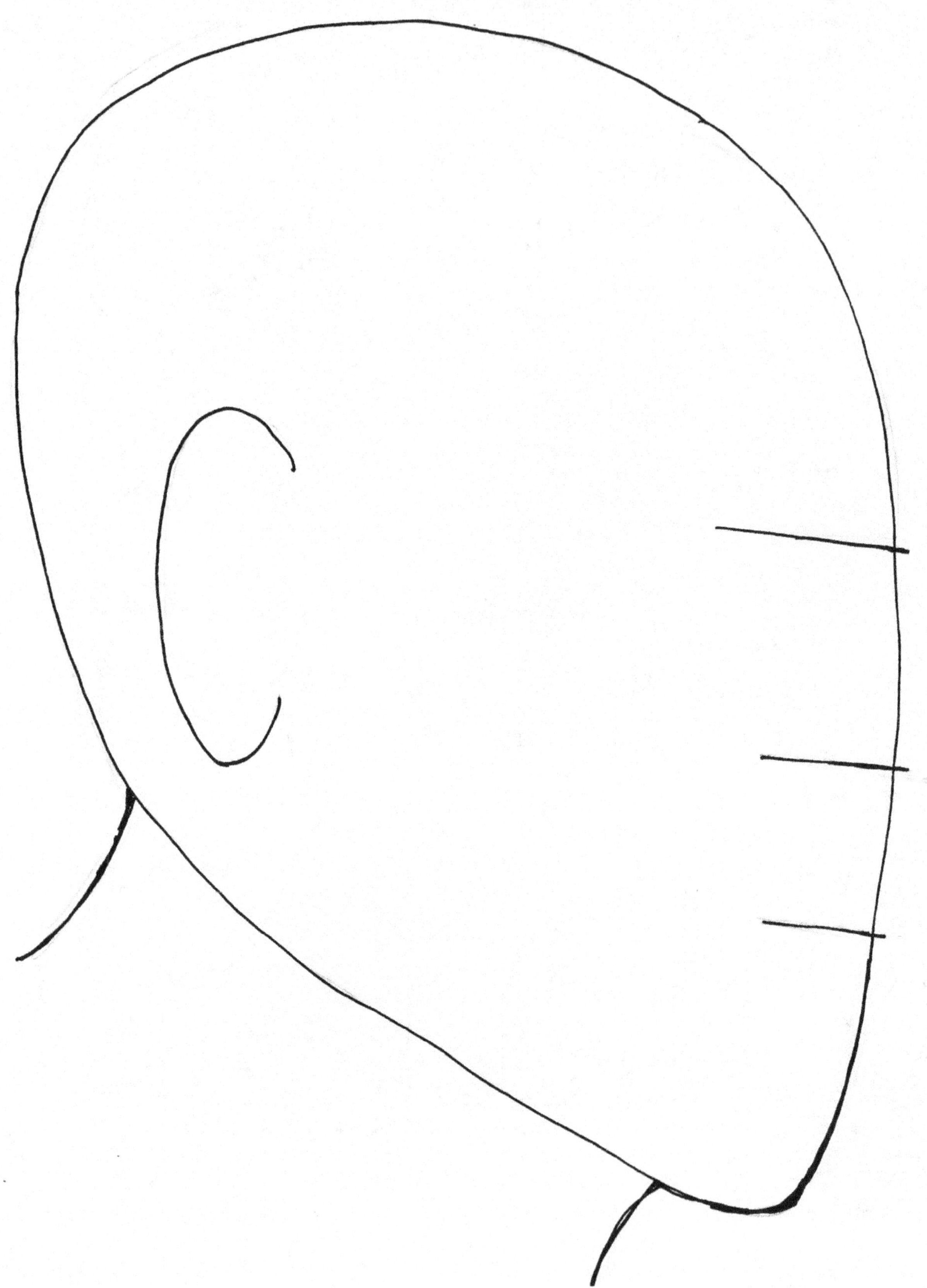

Now, lets draw in shapes for the hair, eye brows, eyes, nose, and chin.
Don't forget to draw a straight line down from the ear indicating the jaw.

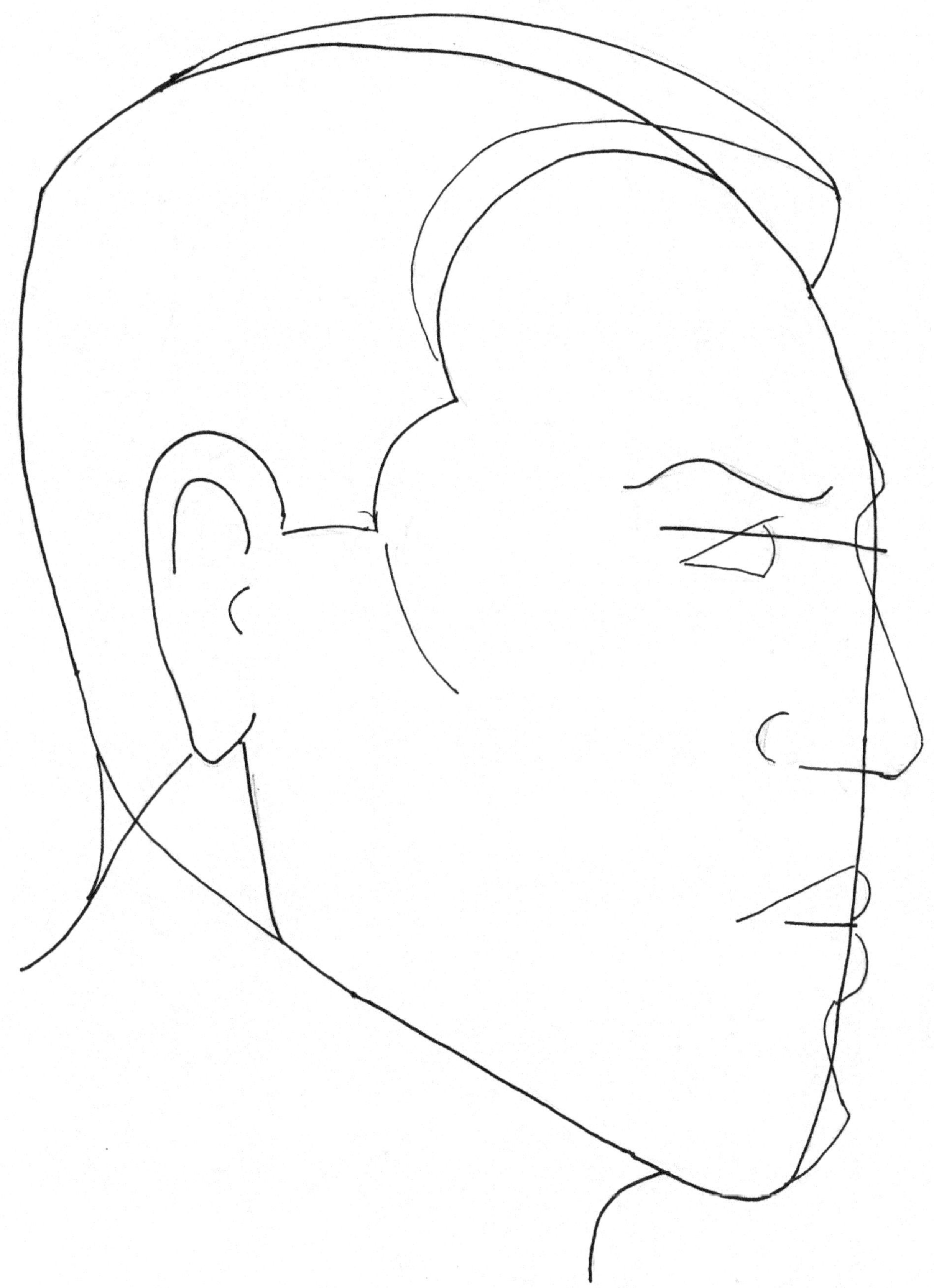

This is the drawing after erasing all guidelines and drawing in more details to the ears, eye brows, nose and mouth.

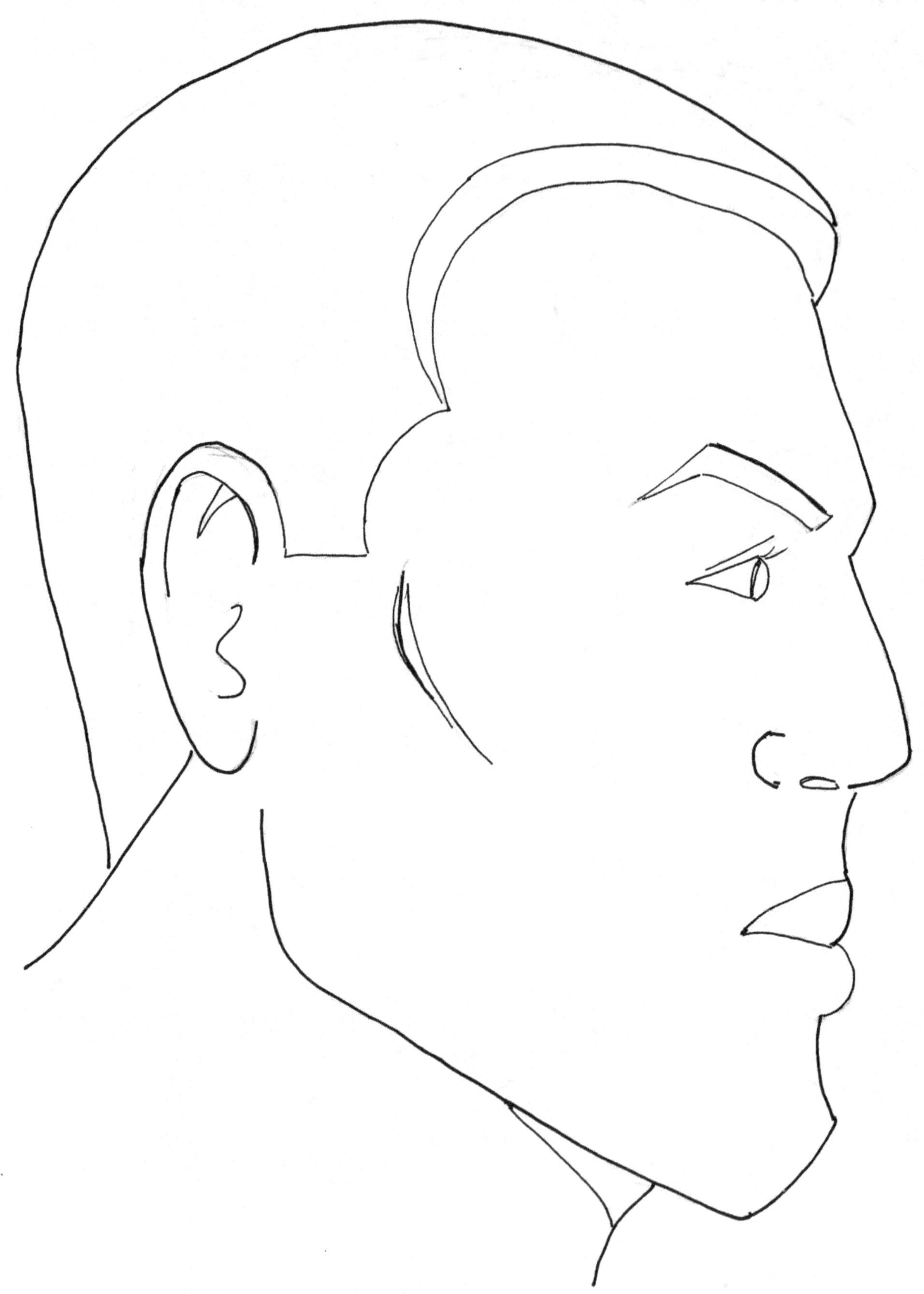

Draw in more details by shading in parts of the hair, ear, eyebrow, eye, nose and mouth to finish this head drawing.

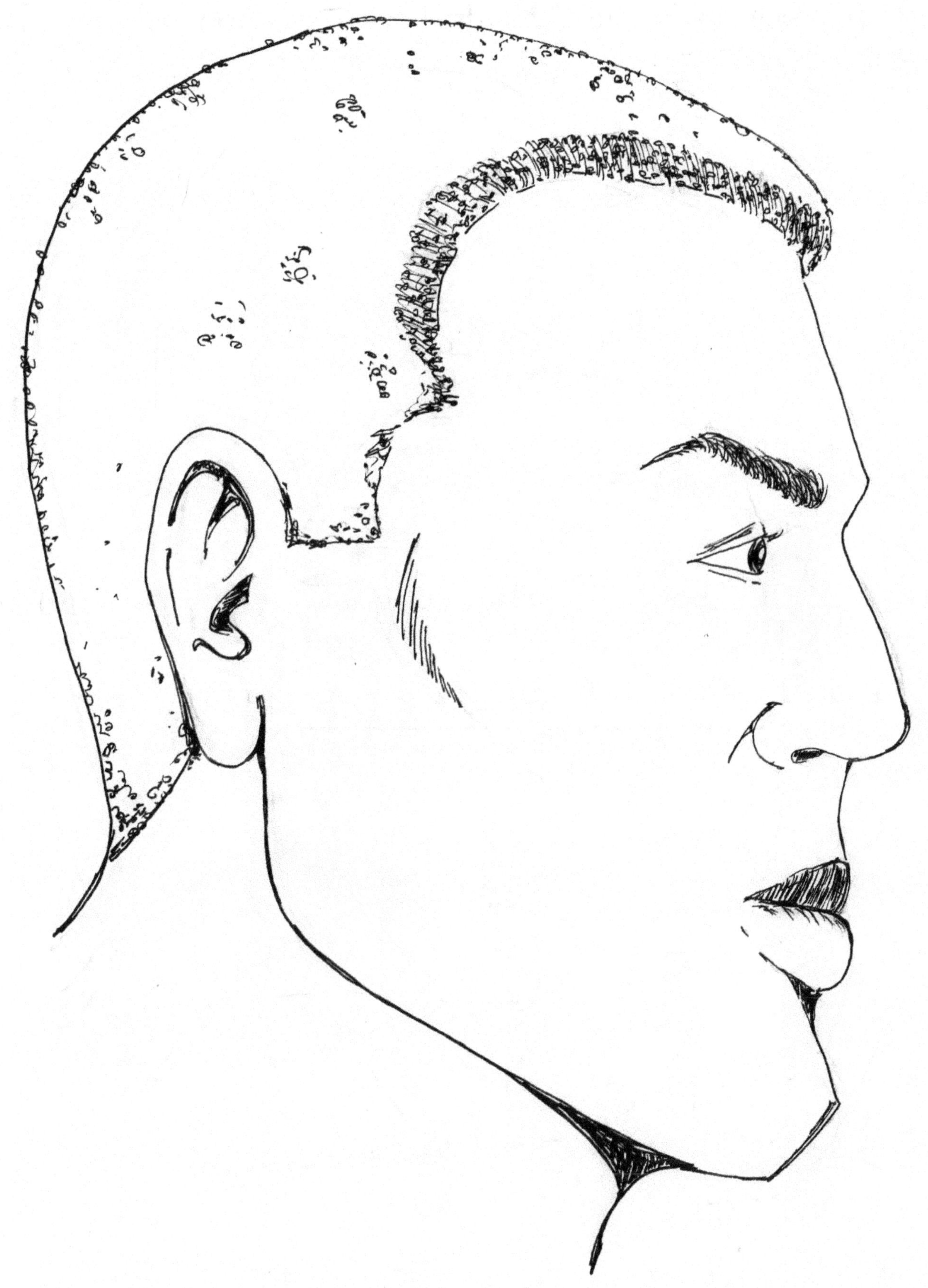

BIG HAIR LADY

Draw the shape of the head, add the neck line. Then draw the outline fo the hair then proceed with putting in the lines to position the eyes, nose and mouth.

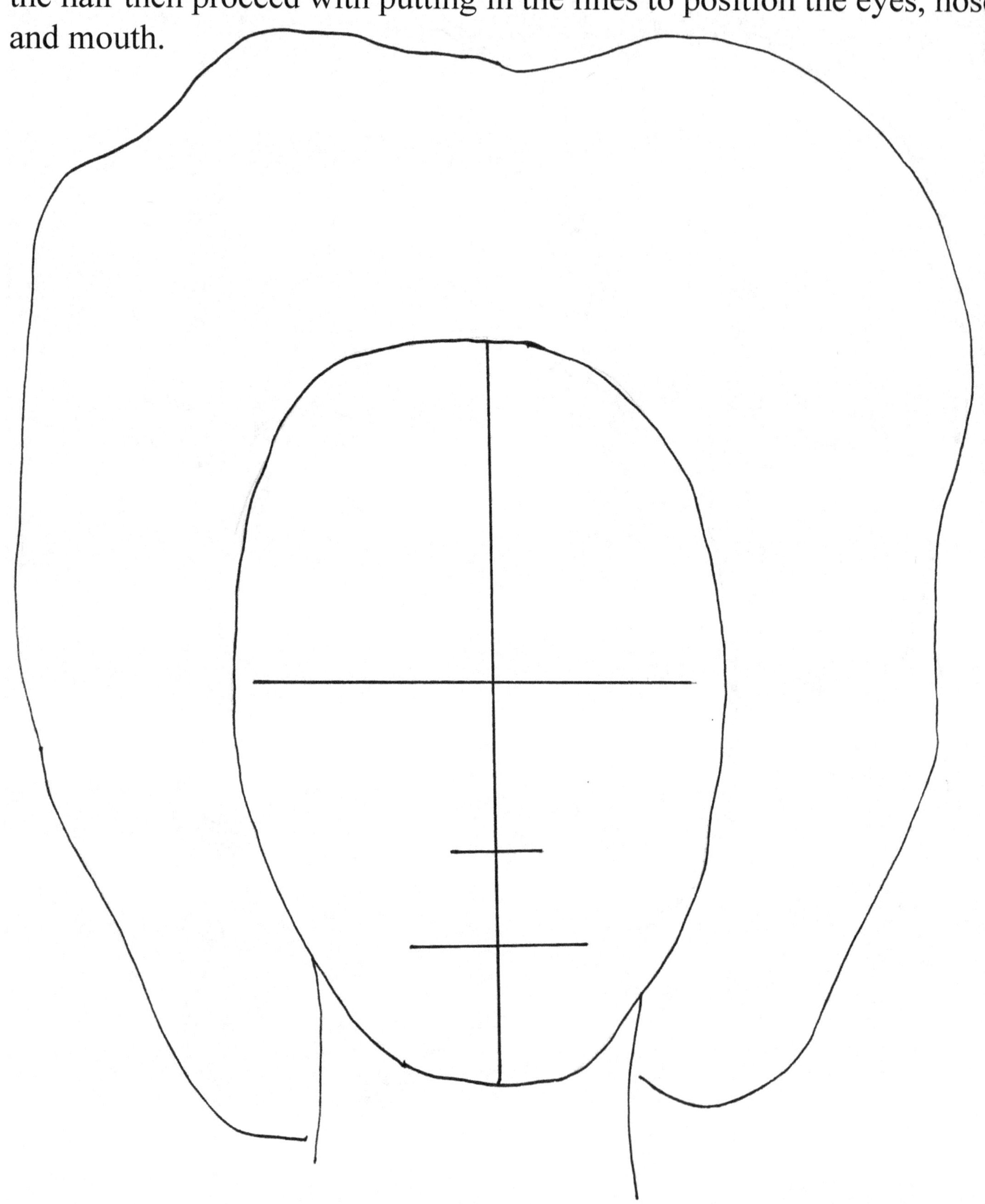

Draw in the eyes, nose, and mouth. Curve in the shape of her face.
Remember There's always more than one way to do things.

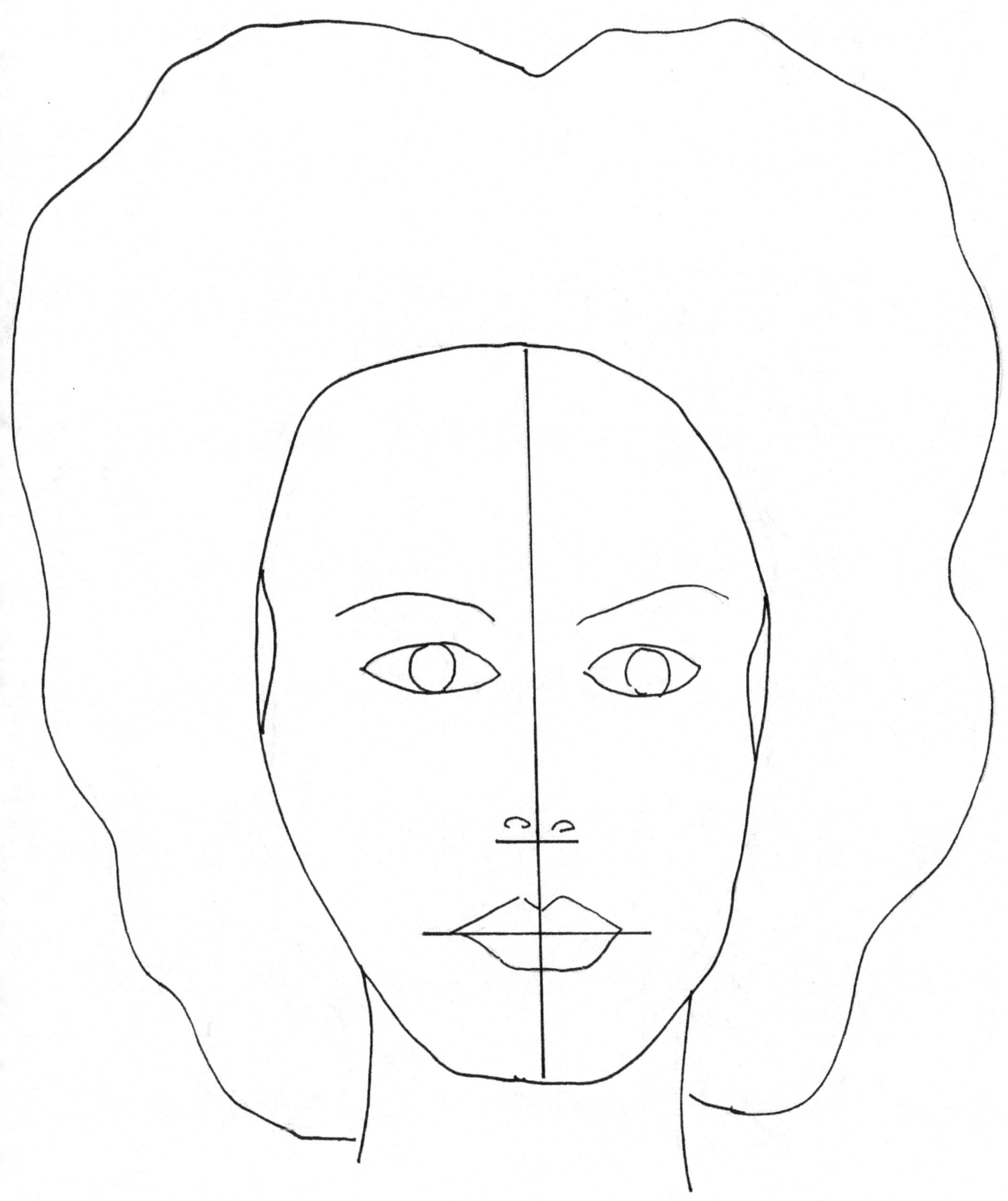

19

Draw in small curvy lines for the hair formation. Put in more details for the eyebrows, eyes, nose and mouth.

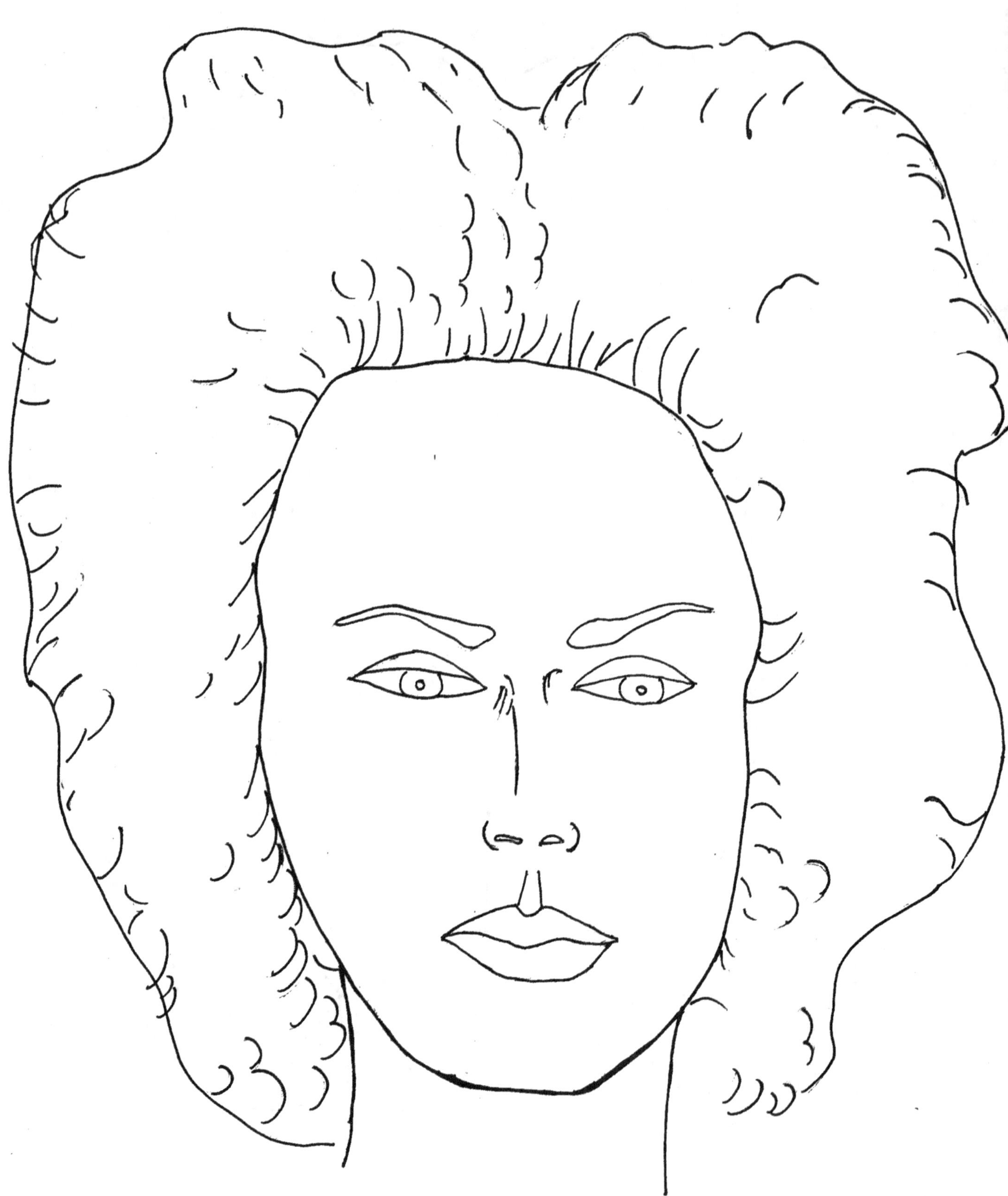

Draw in more small curvy lines in the hair and sketch in lights and darks to complete your fantastic art of work.

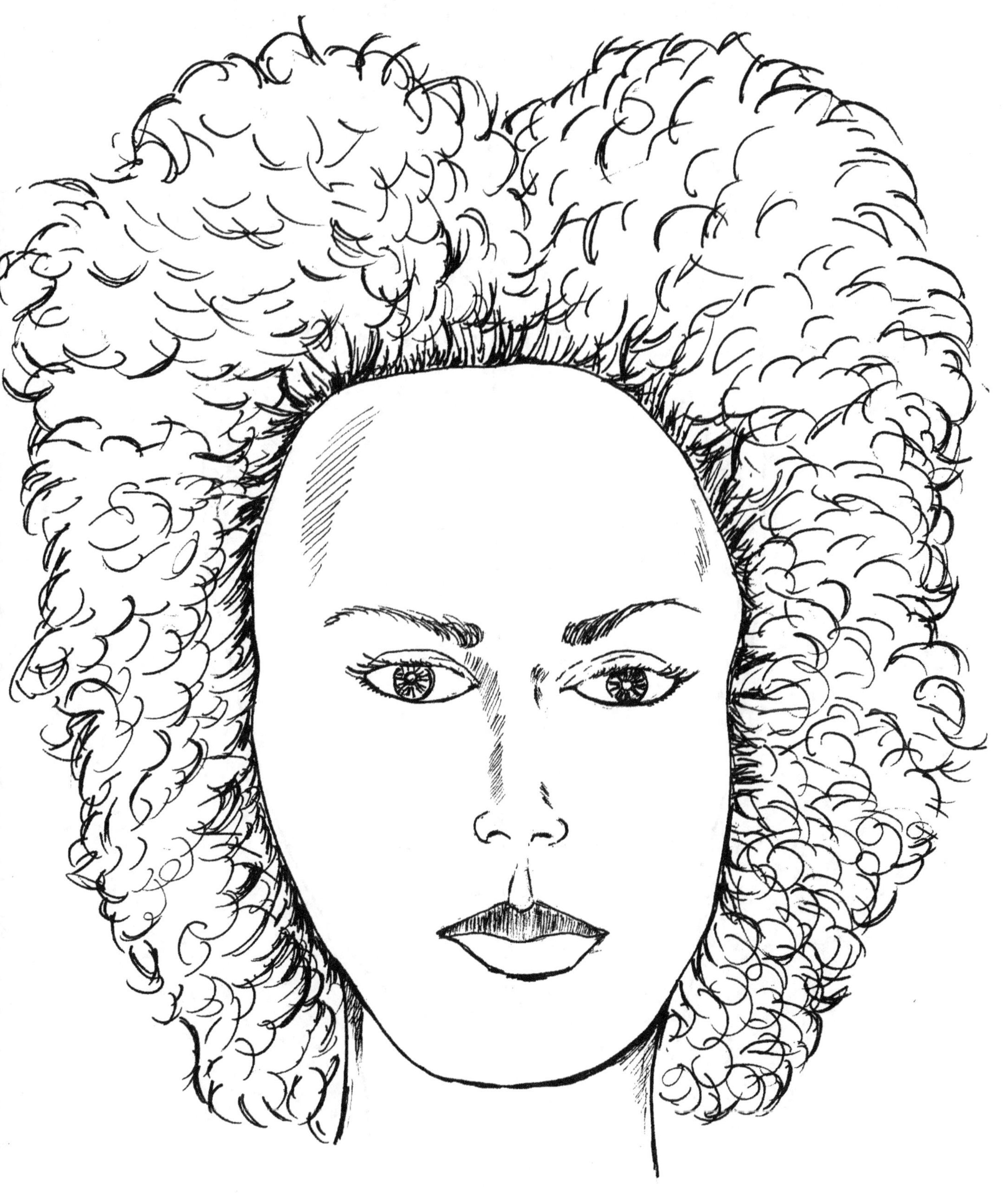

CLASSY LADY

I will give no instructions for this one. Remember a picture is worth a thousand words. Draw this Classy lady by yourself.

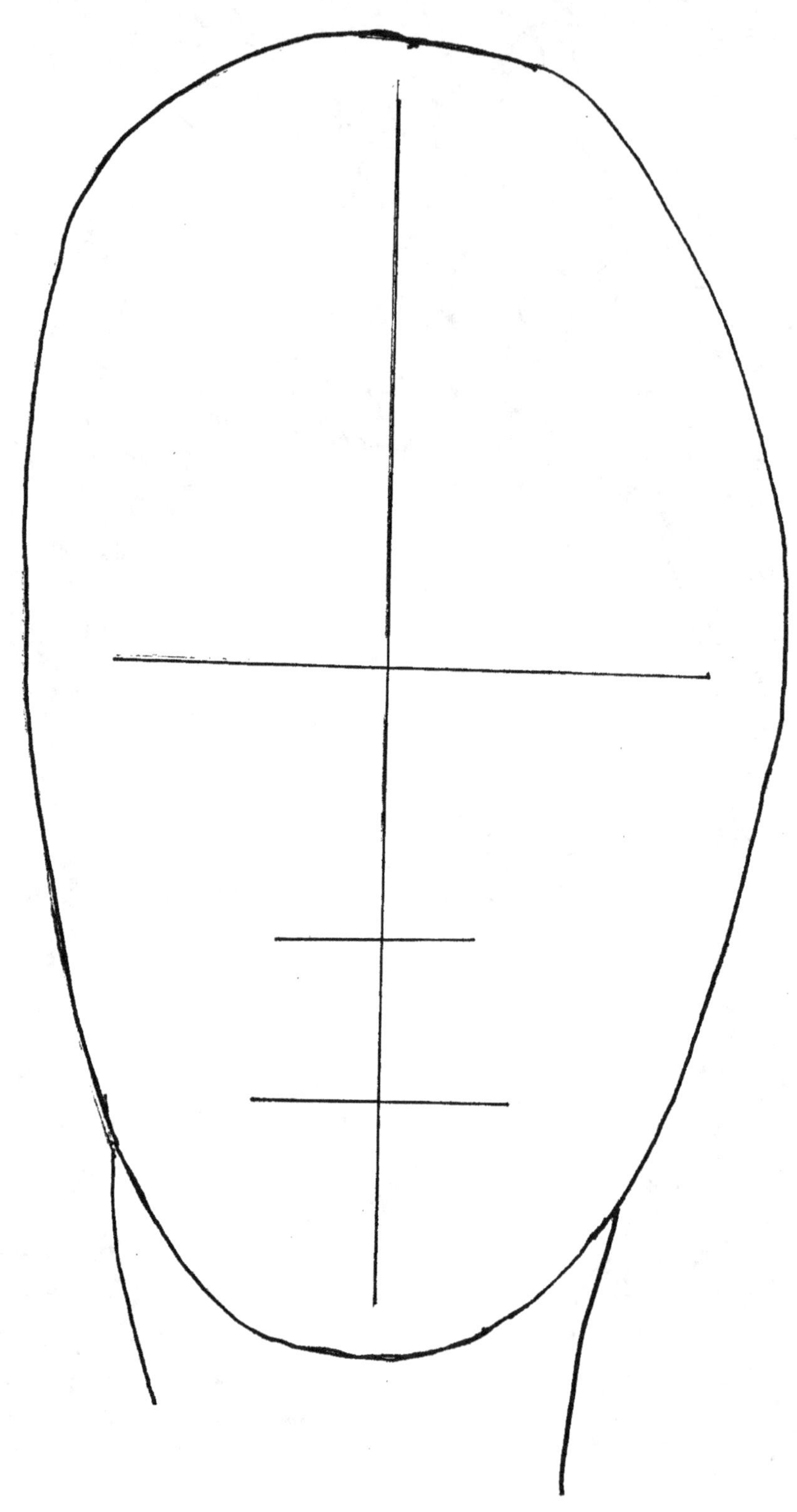

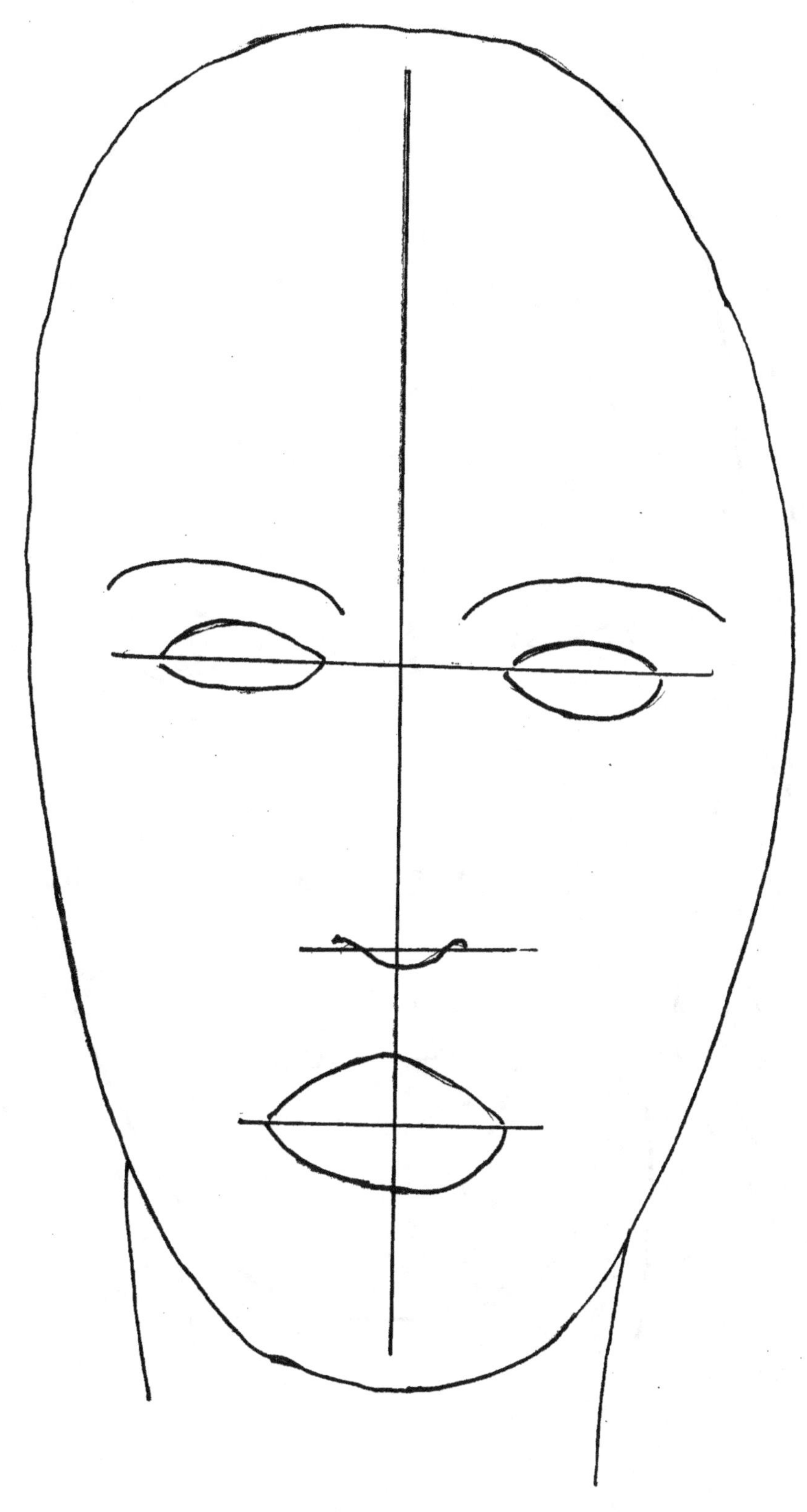

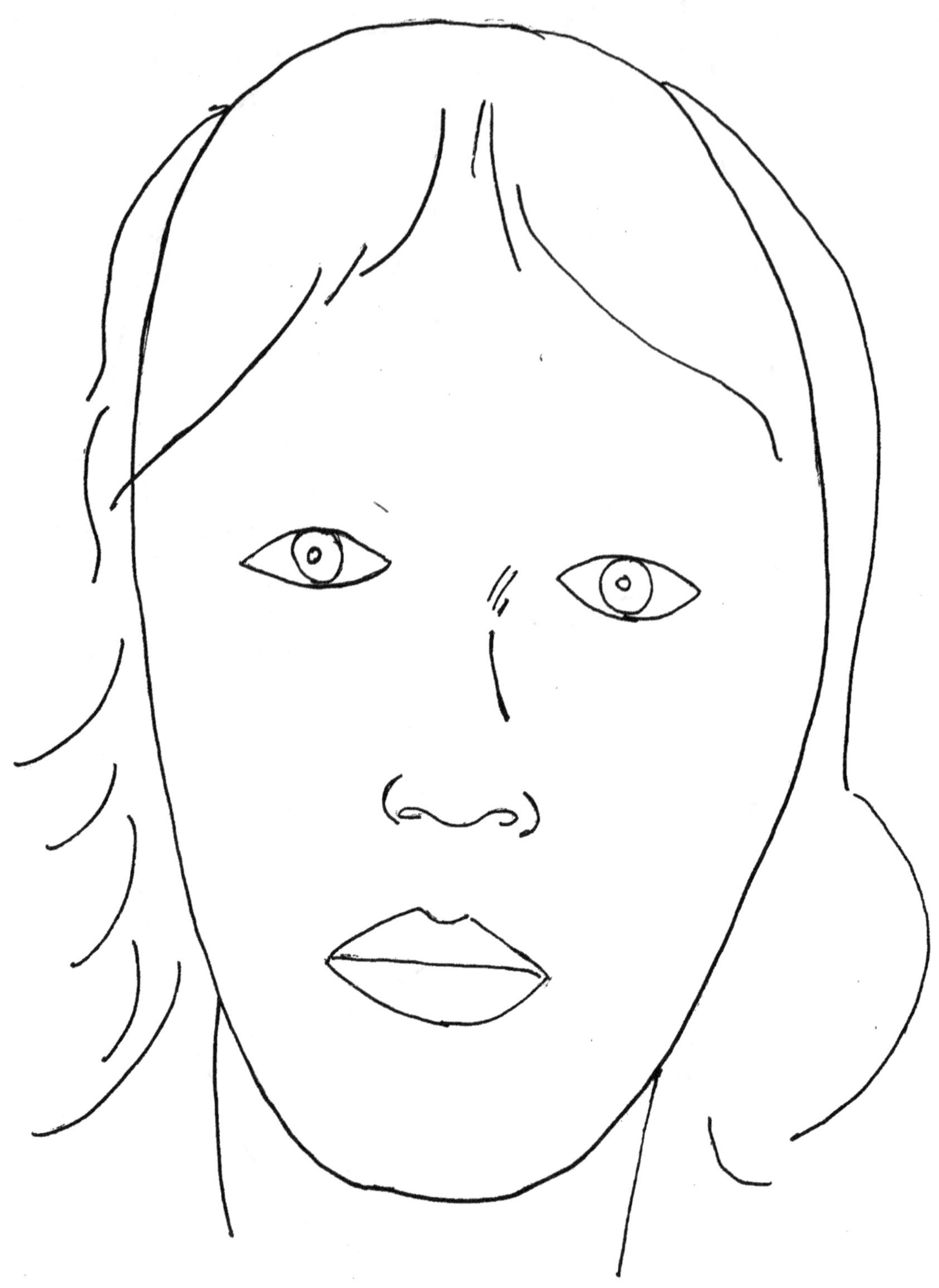

Here's the finish artwork you did on your own.

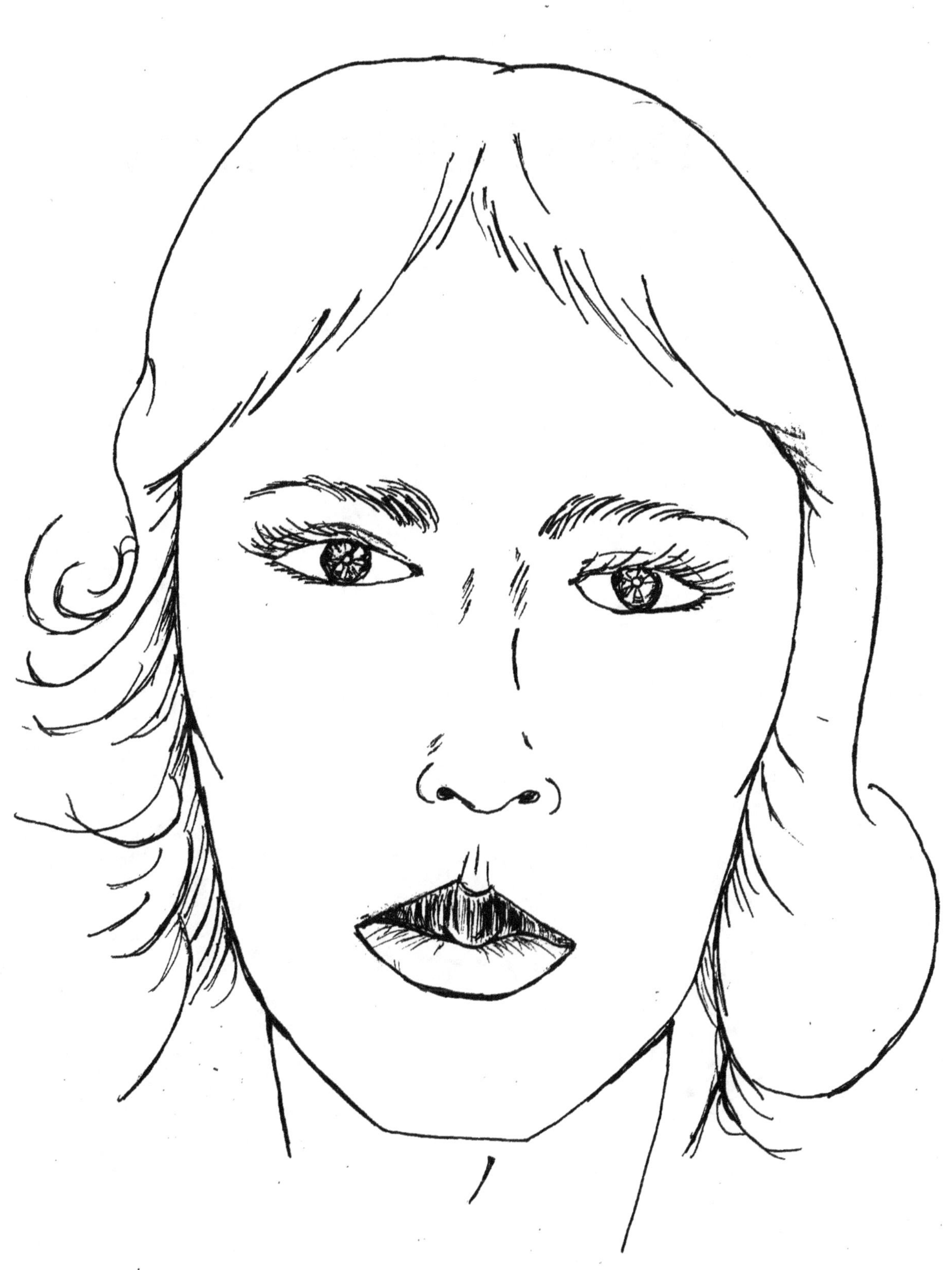

Mind Over Matter.

Draw! Draw! Draw!

HUMAN FIGURE

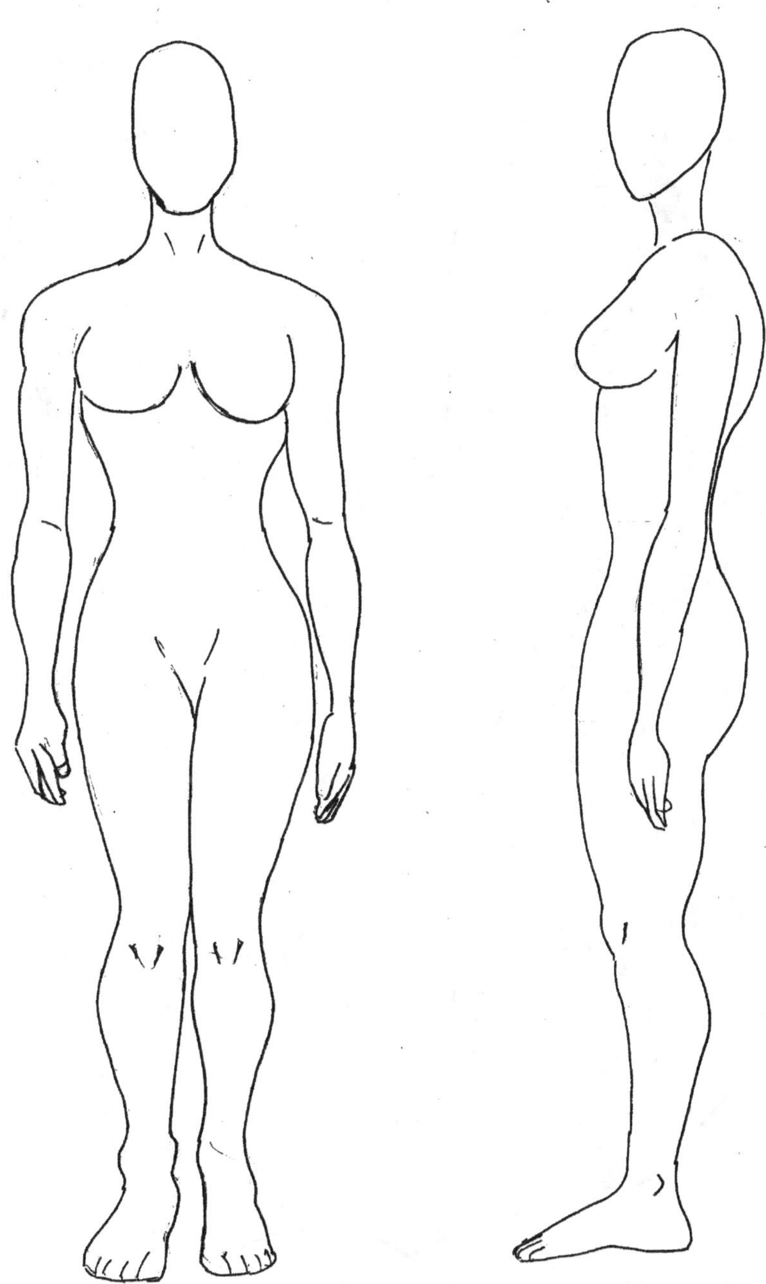

ARM STRUCTURE

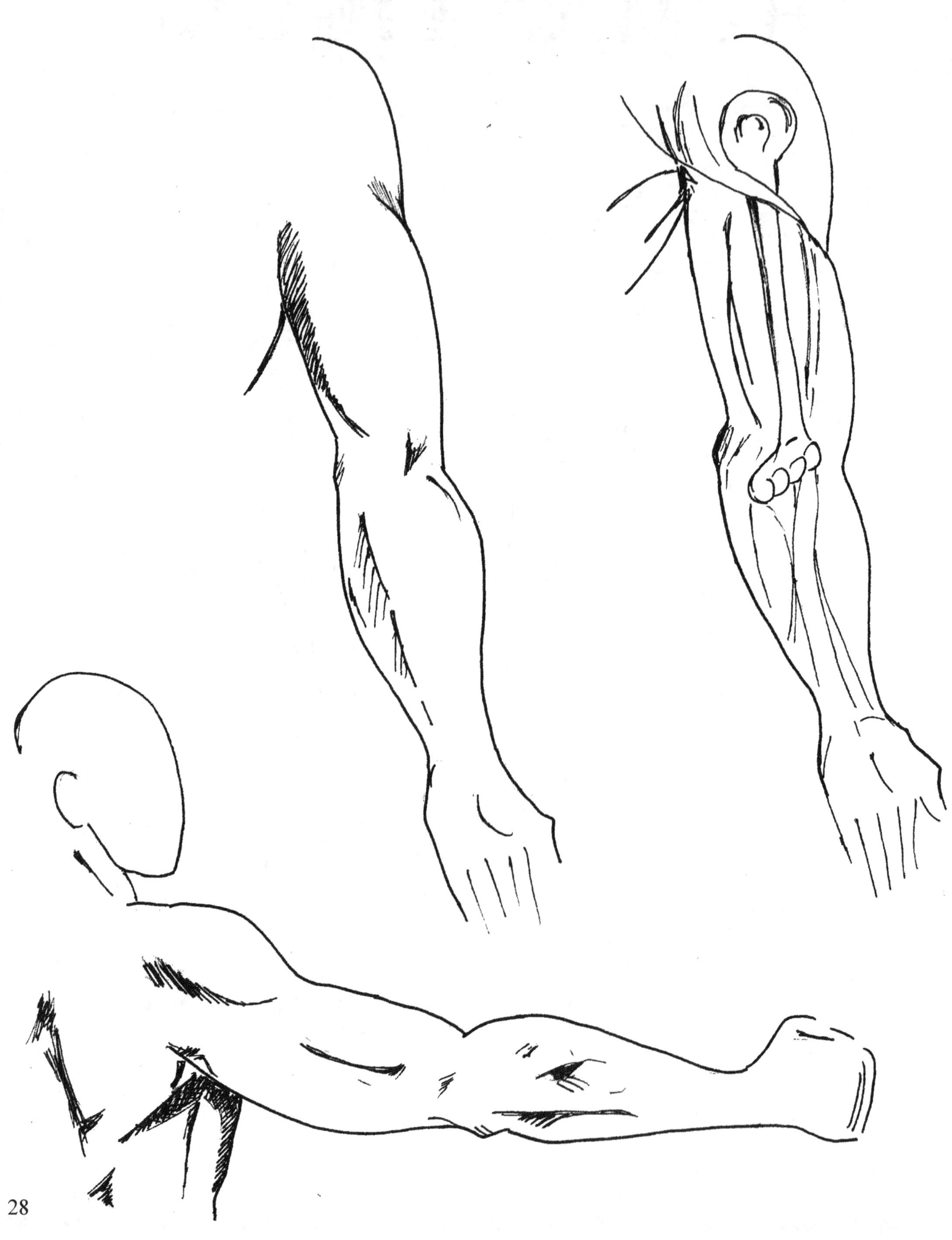

HANDS

look at your own
hand and practice
drawing it.

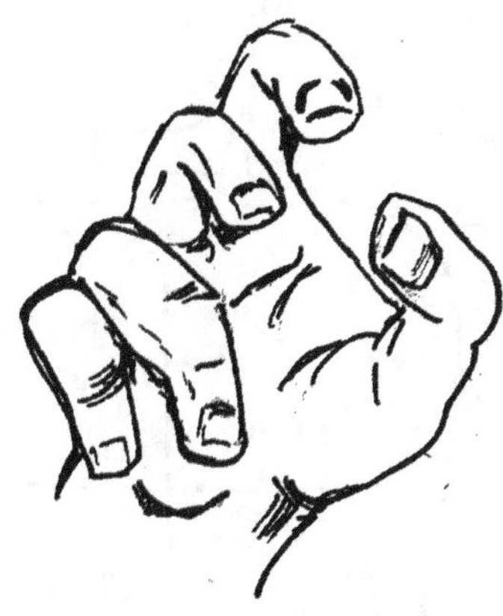

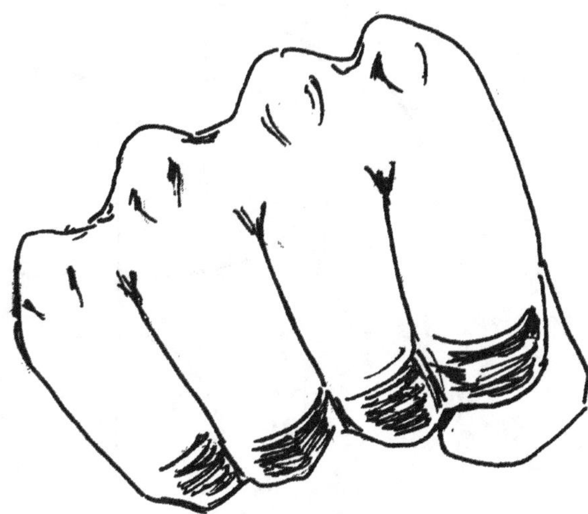

Put your hand in
different positions.

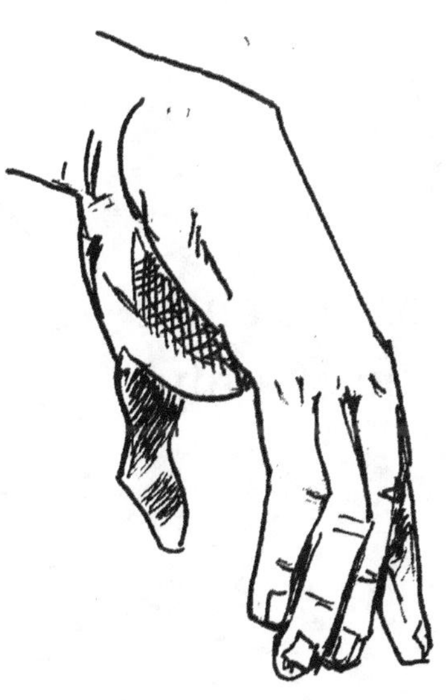

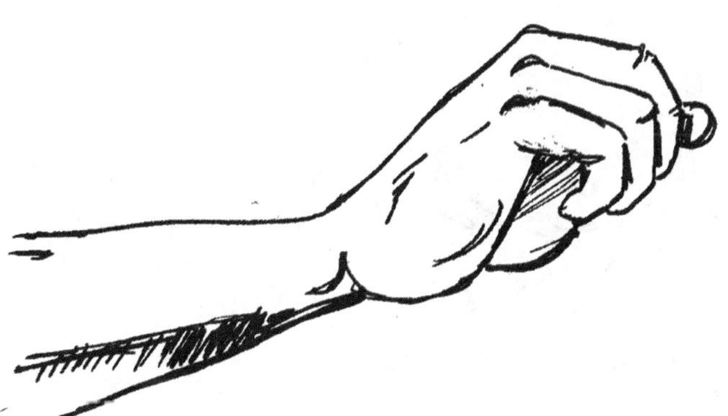

TORSO

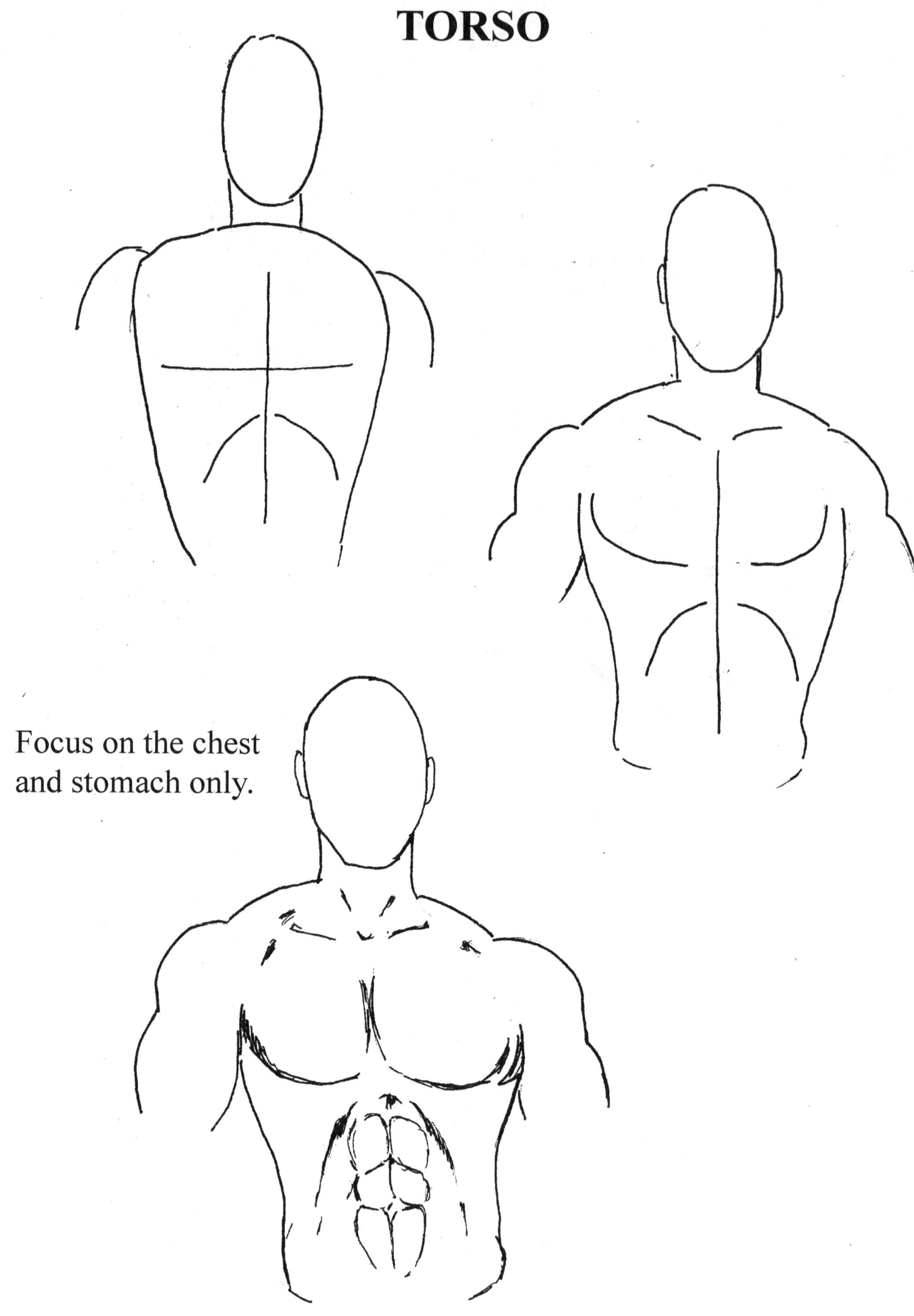

Focus on the chest
and stomach only.

FEMALE FIGURE

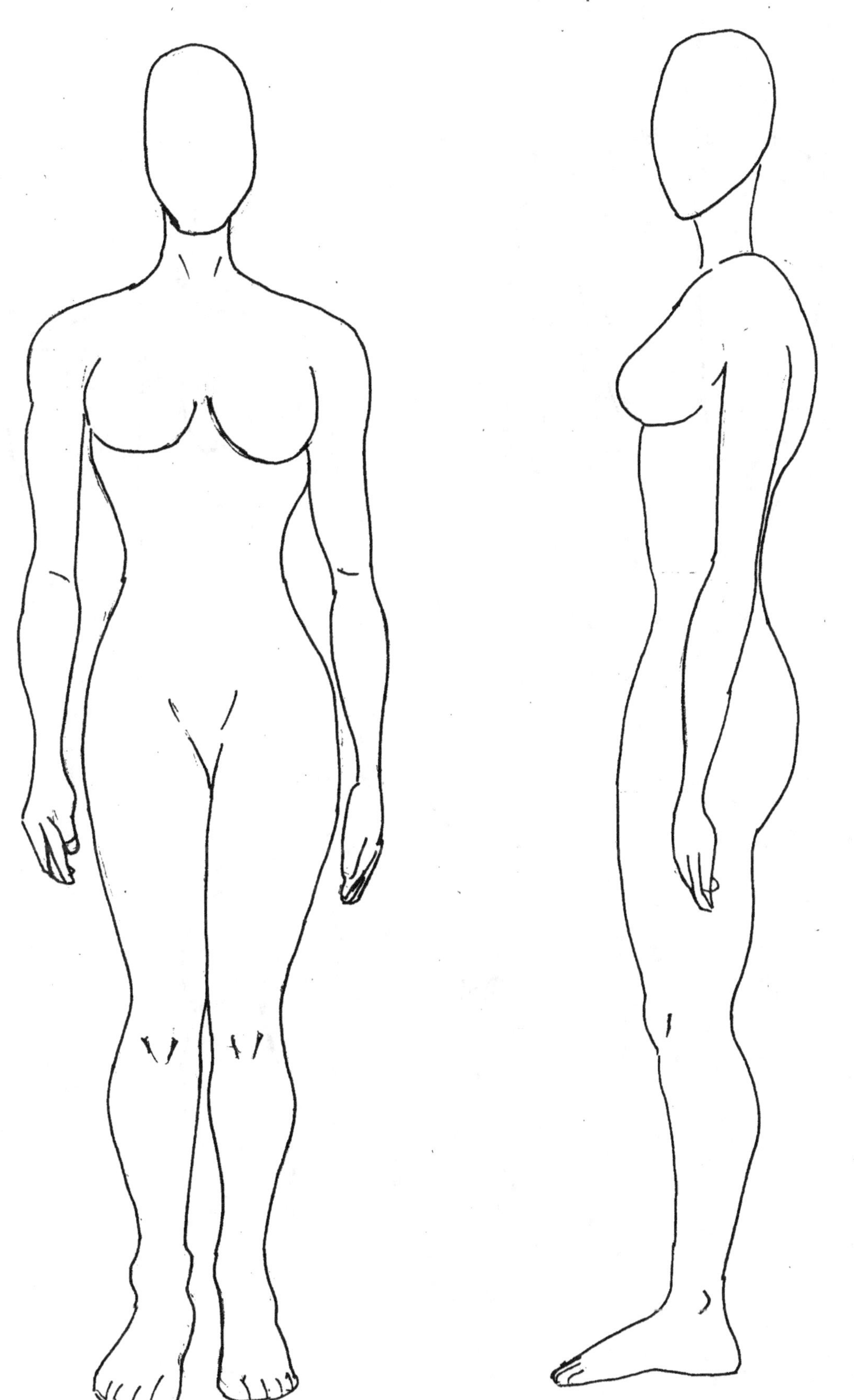

MALE BACK

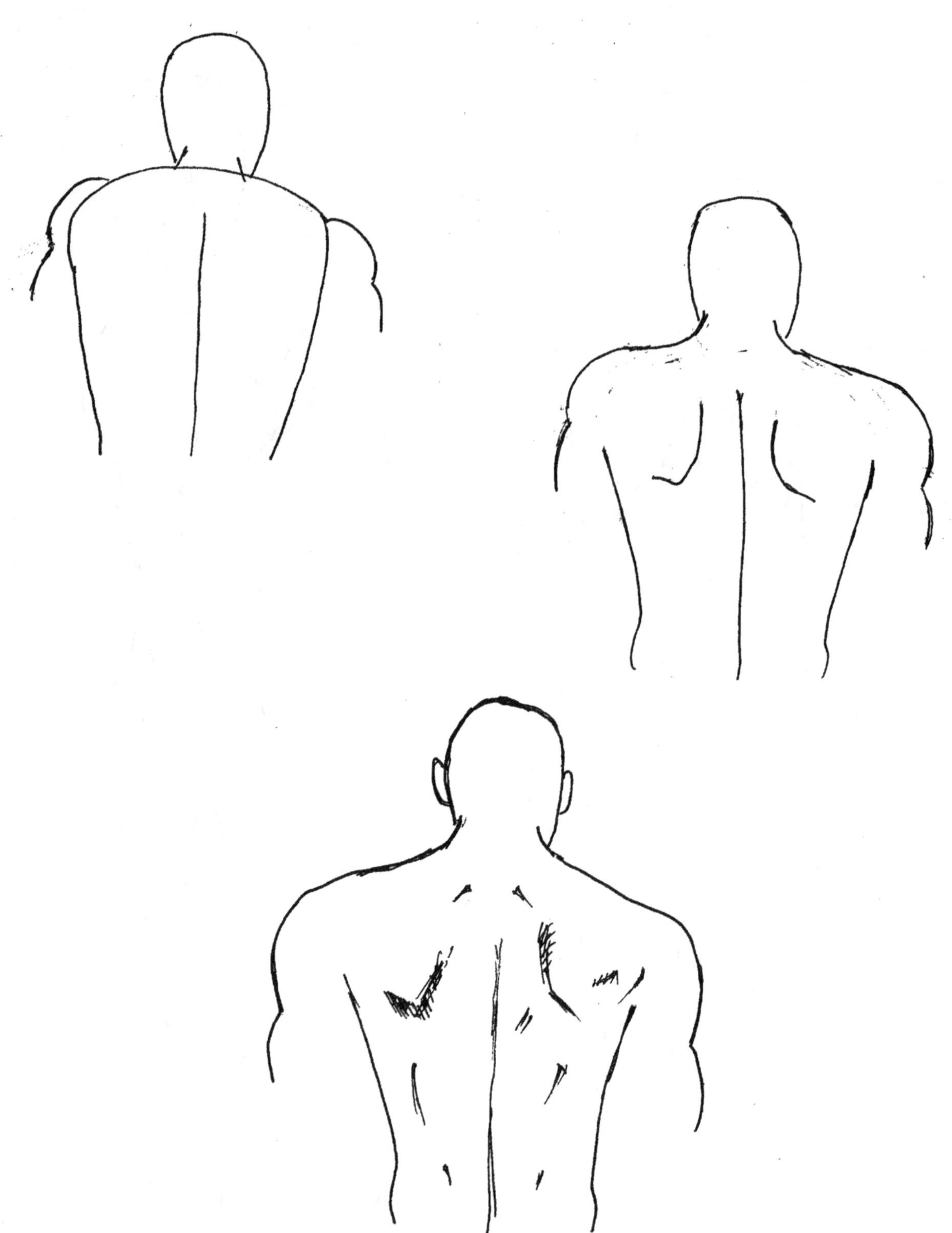

MALE LEGS

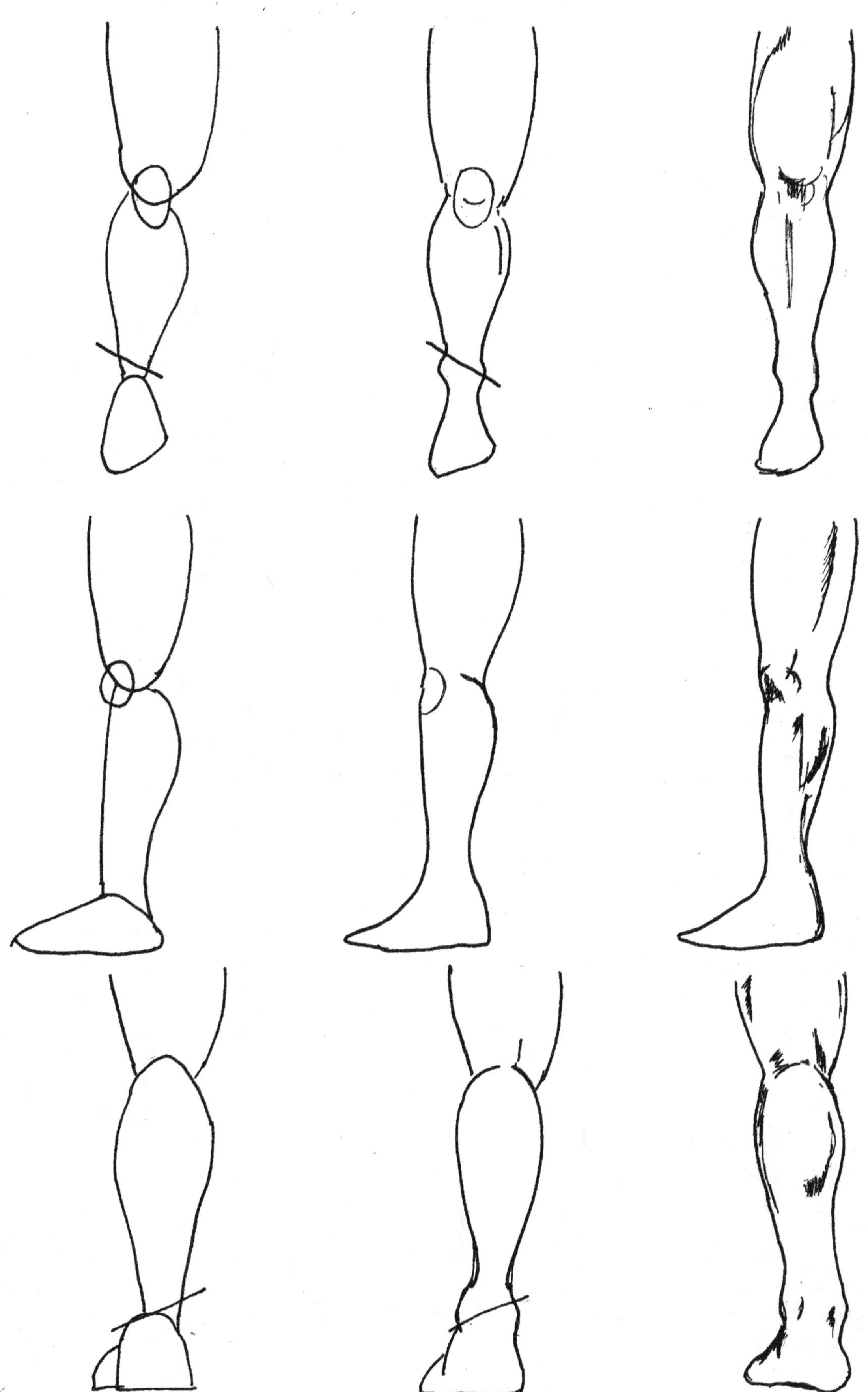

FEET

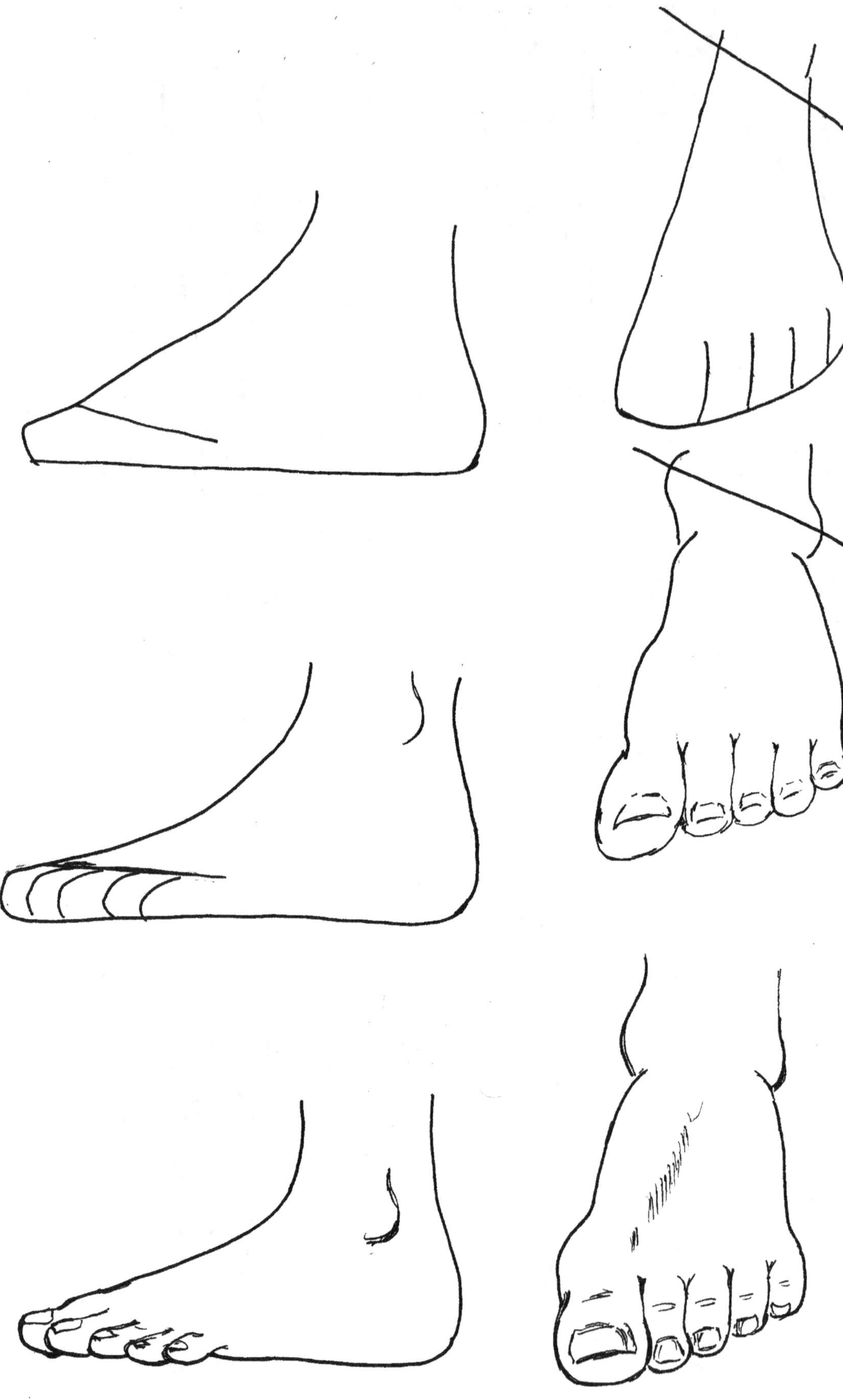

STILL LIFE

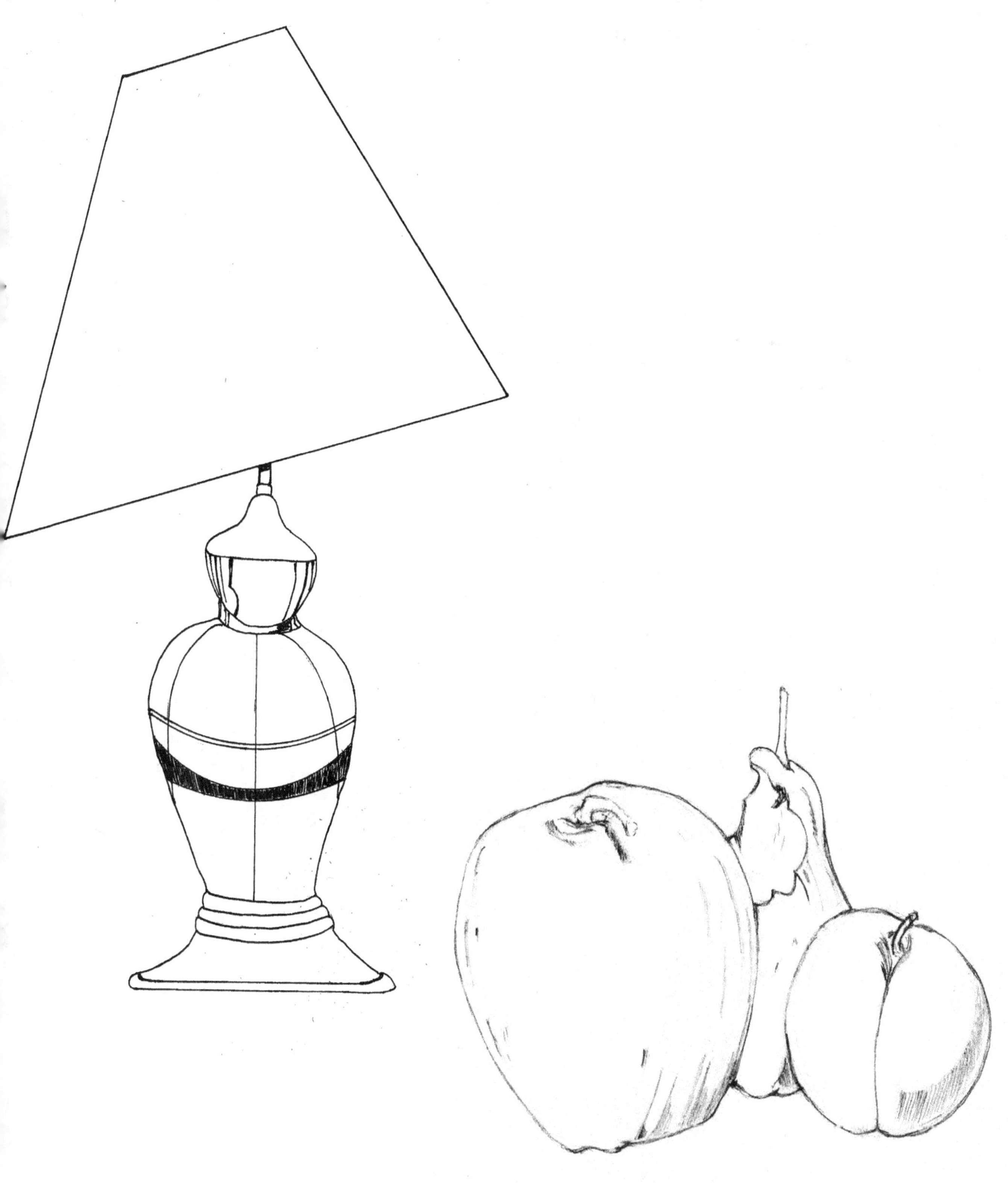

APPLE and BANANA

Draw some guidelines to get the shape of
the apple and banana.

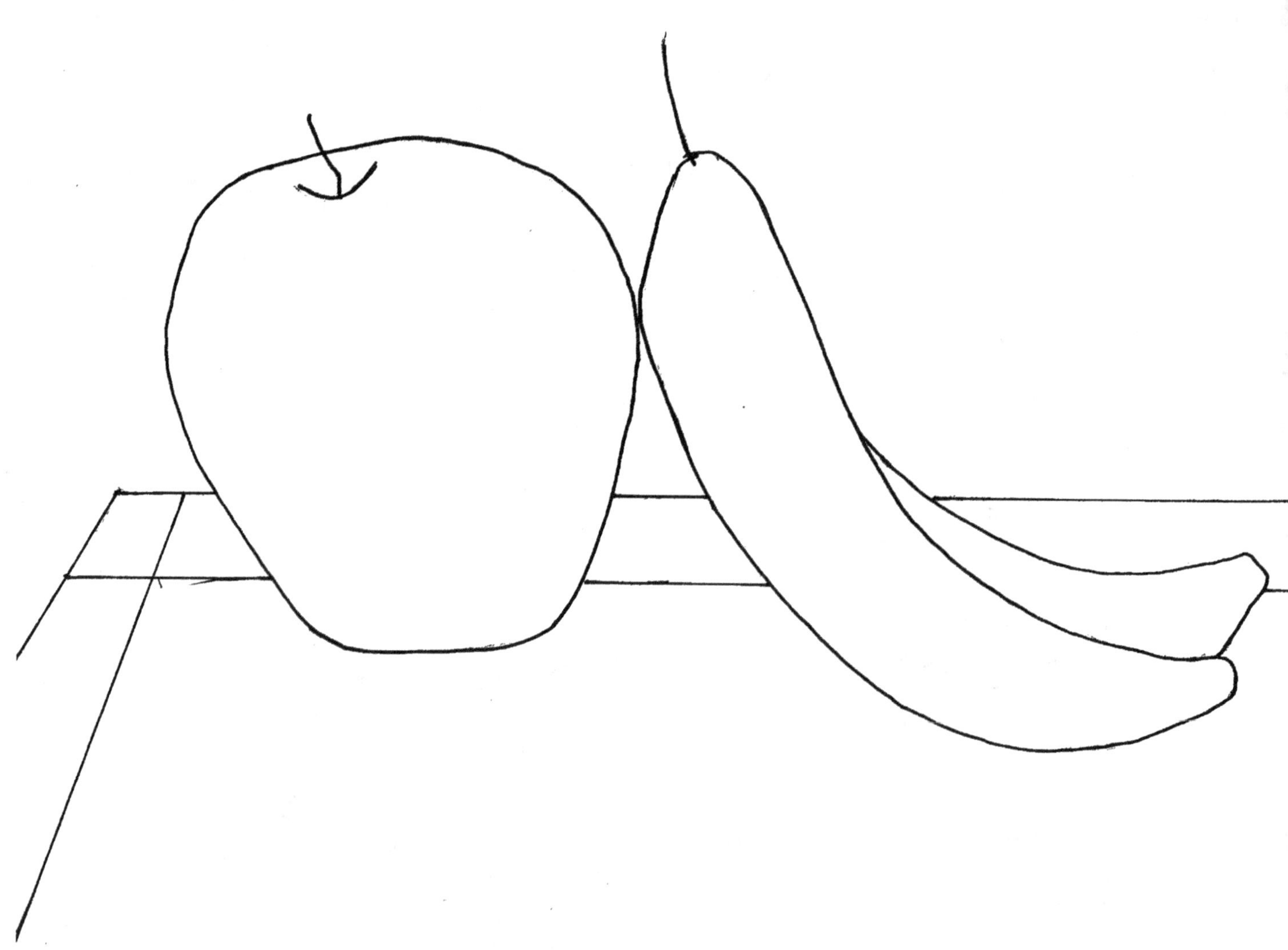

Add some more basic lines to define the shape of the
apple and banana.

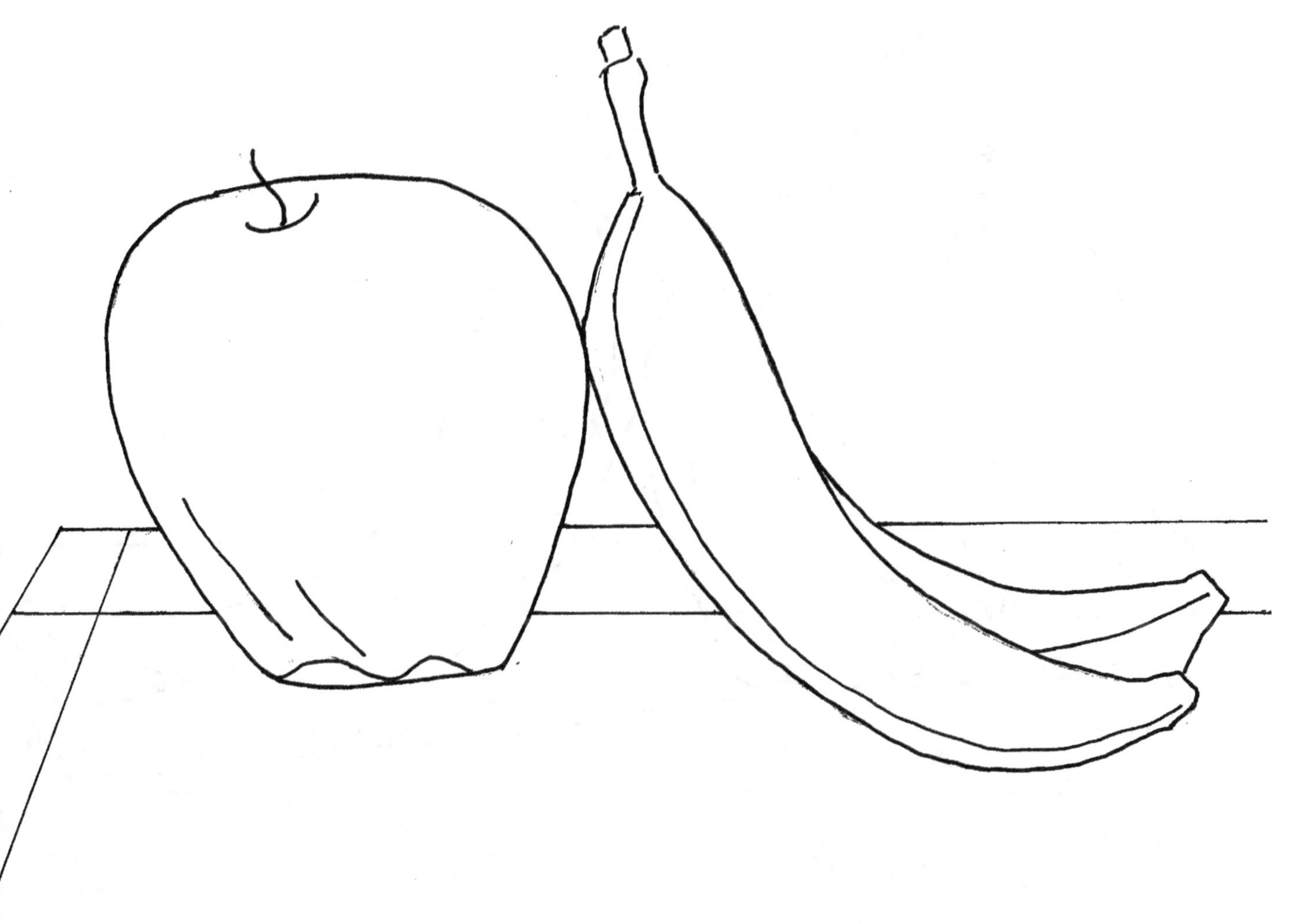

Now, let's erase the below the apple and throw
in the shadow of both the apple and banana
with your marker.

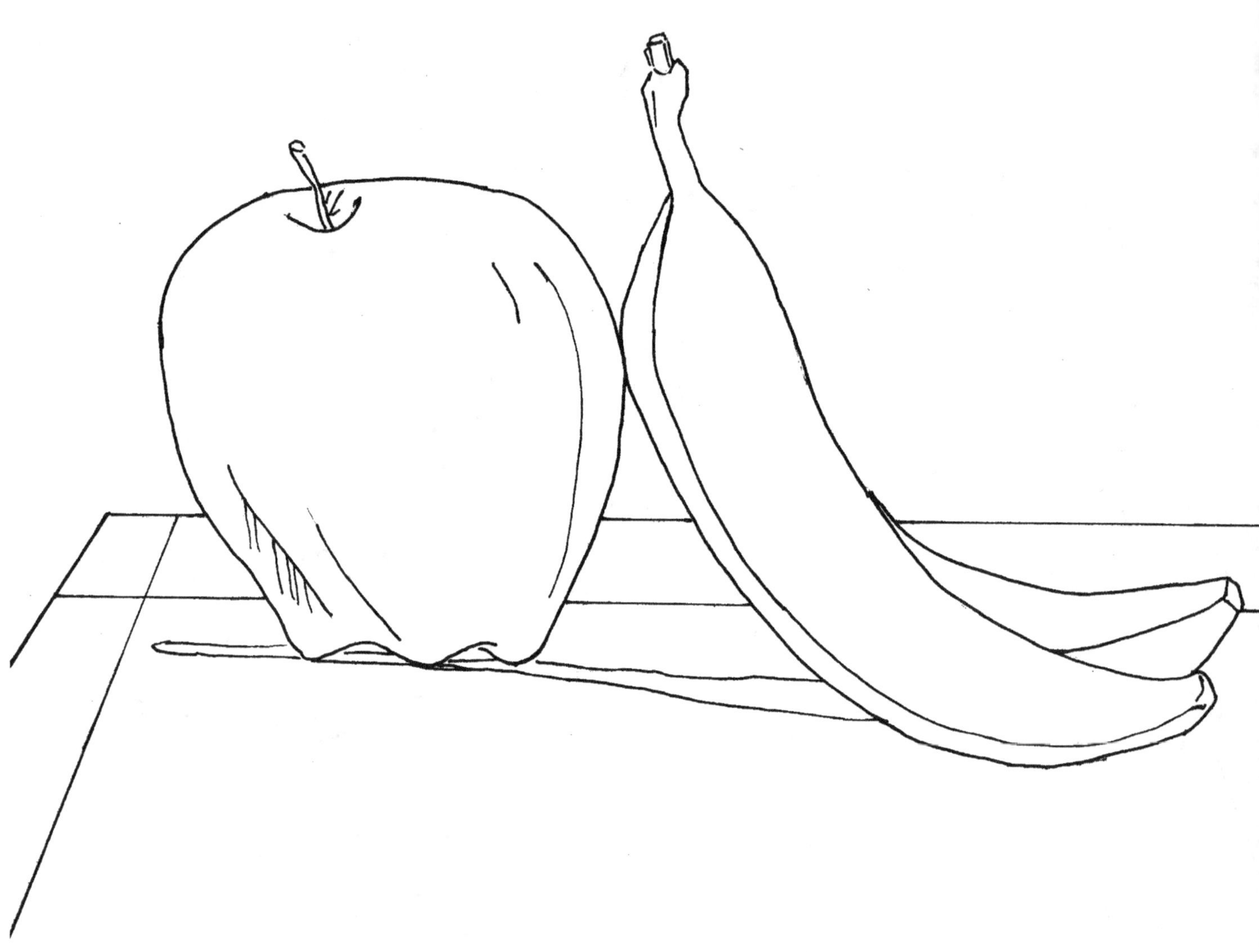

Shade in the rest the drawing to get your finish
ink artwork.

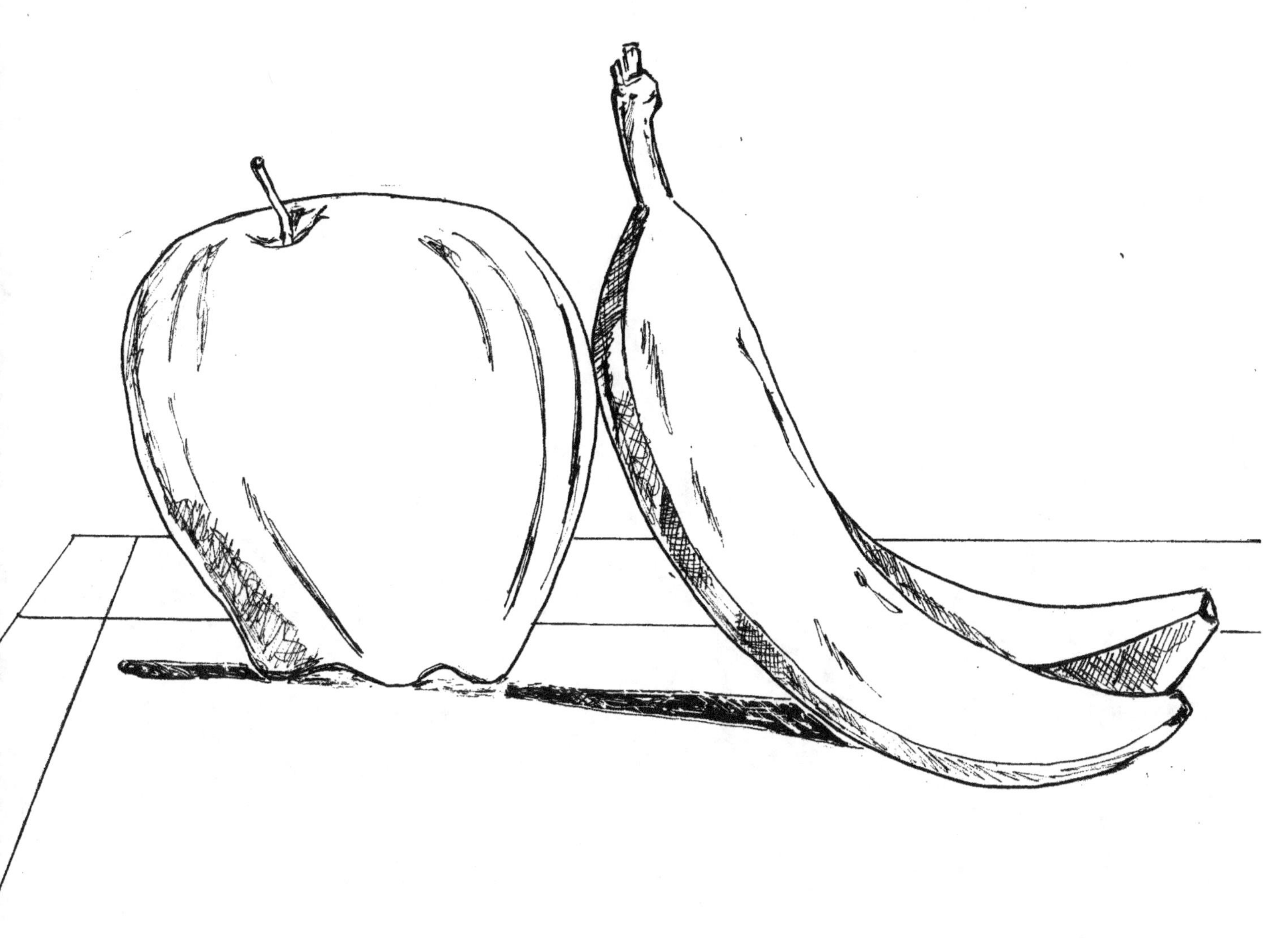

APPLE, PEAR, and PLUM

Since I like fruit, here's another basic fruit drawing. Let's start with the apple which you're familiar with from the previous drawing. Add two oval shapes for the pear and a round shape for the plum.

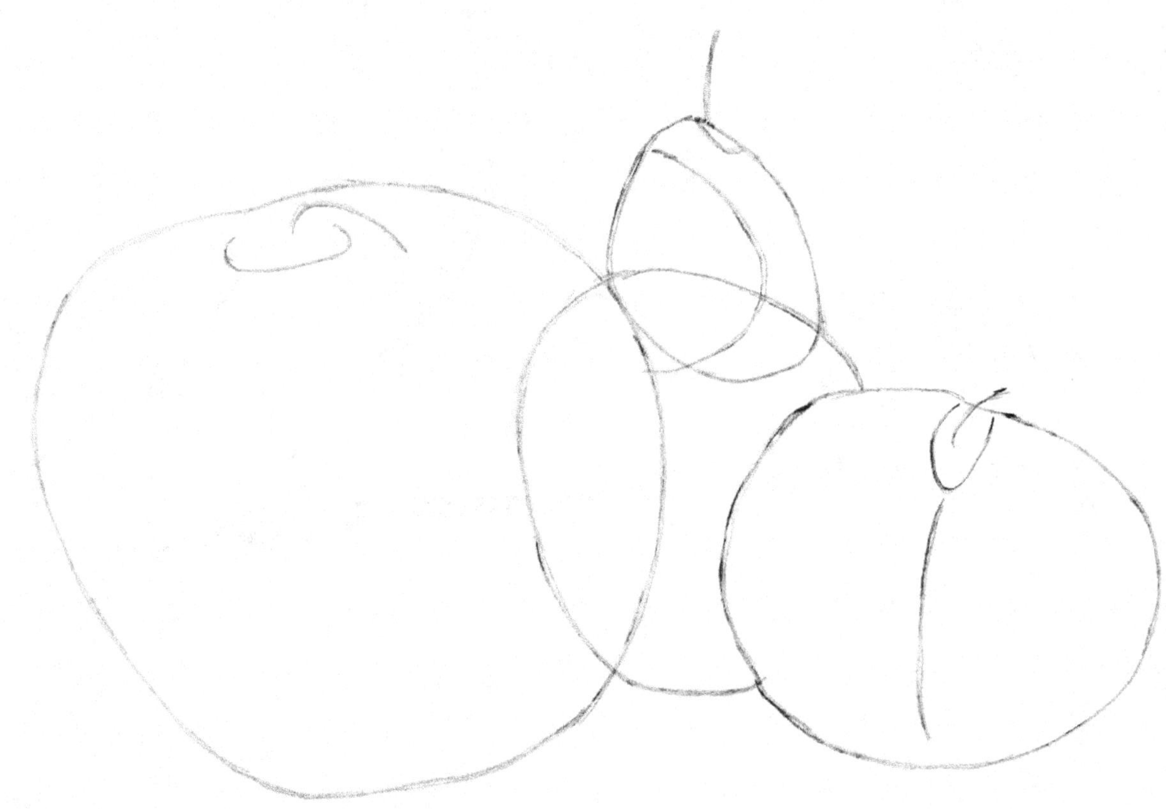

Draw in the area of the pear where I've taken a big bite out of it. Add some basic detail lines to form the texture of these delicious fruits.

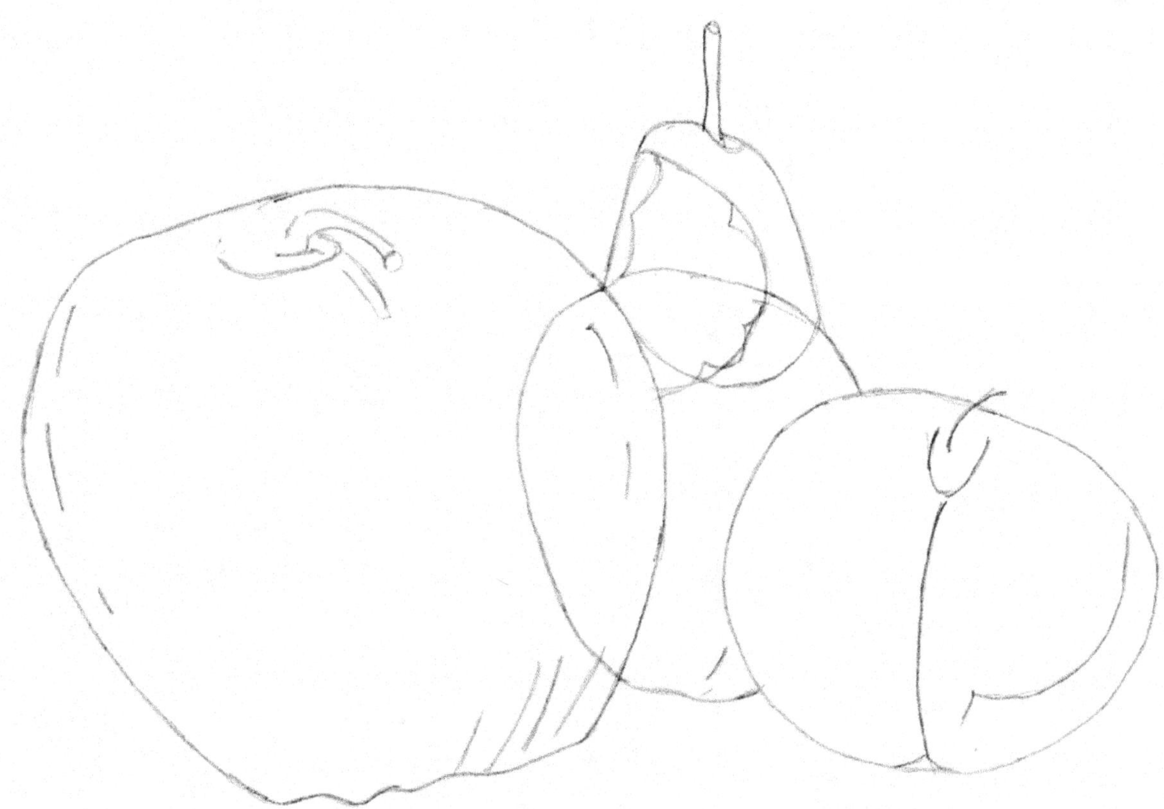

Erase all of the guidelines to come up with your almost finish pencil picture.

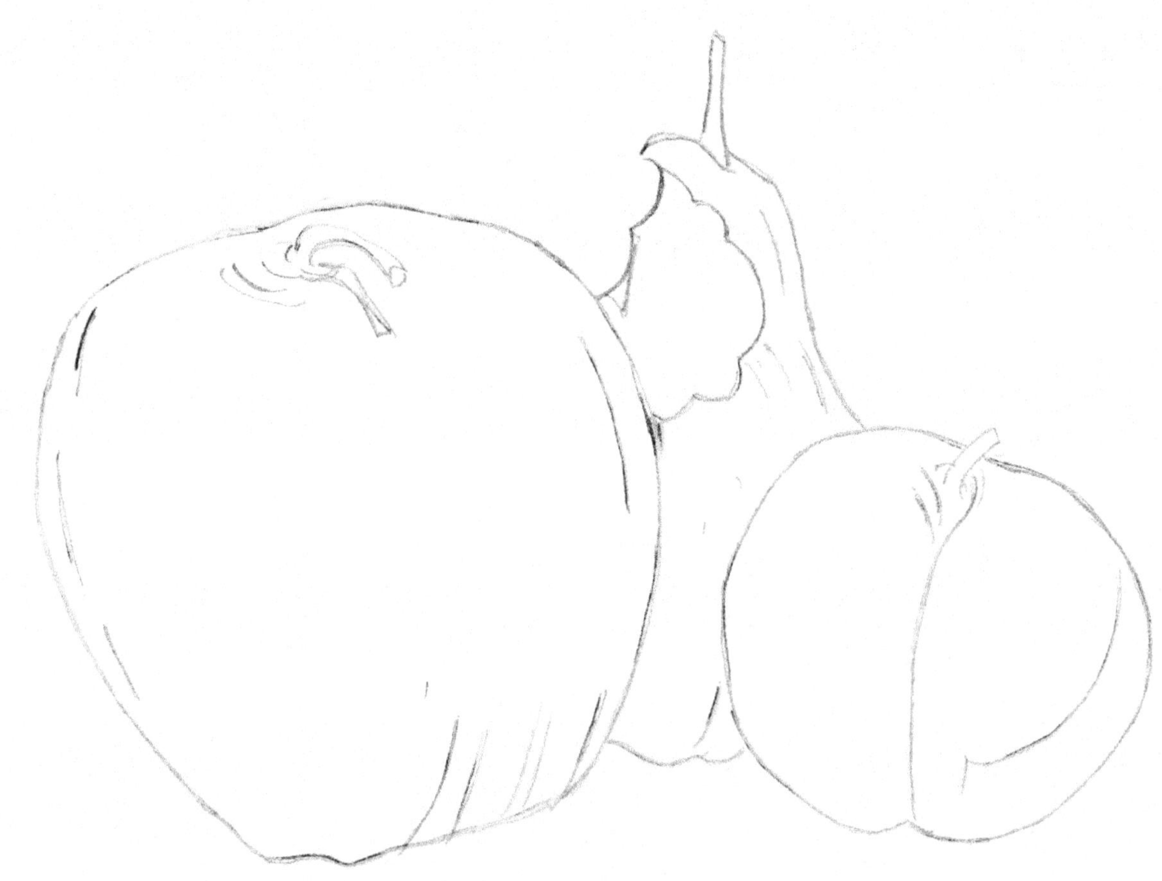

Here's your finished masterpiece after you
have penciled in all of the lights and darks of
your apple, pear, plum to create texture for
completed picture.

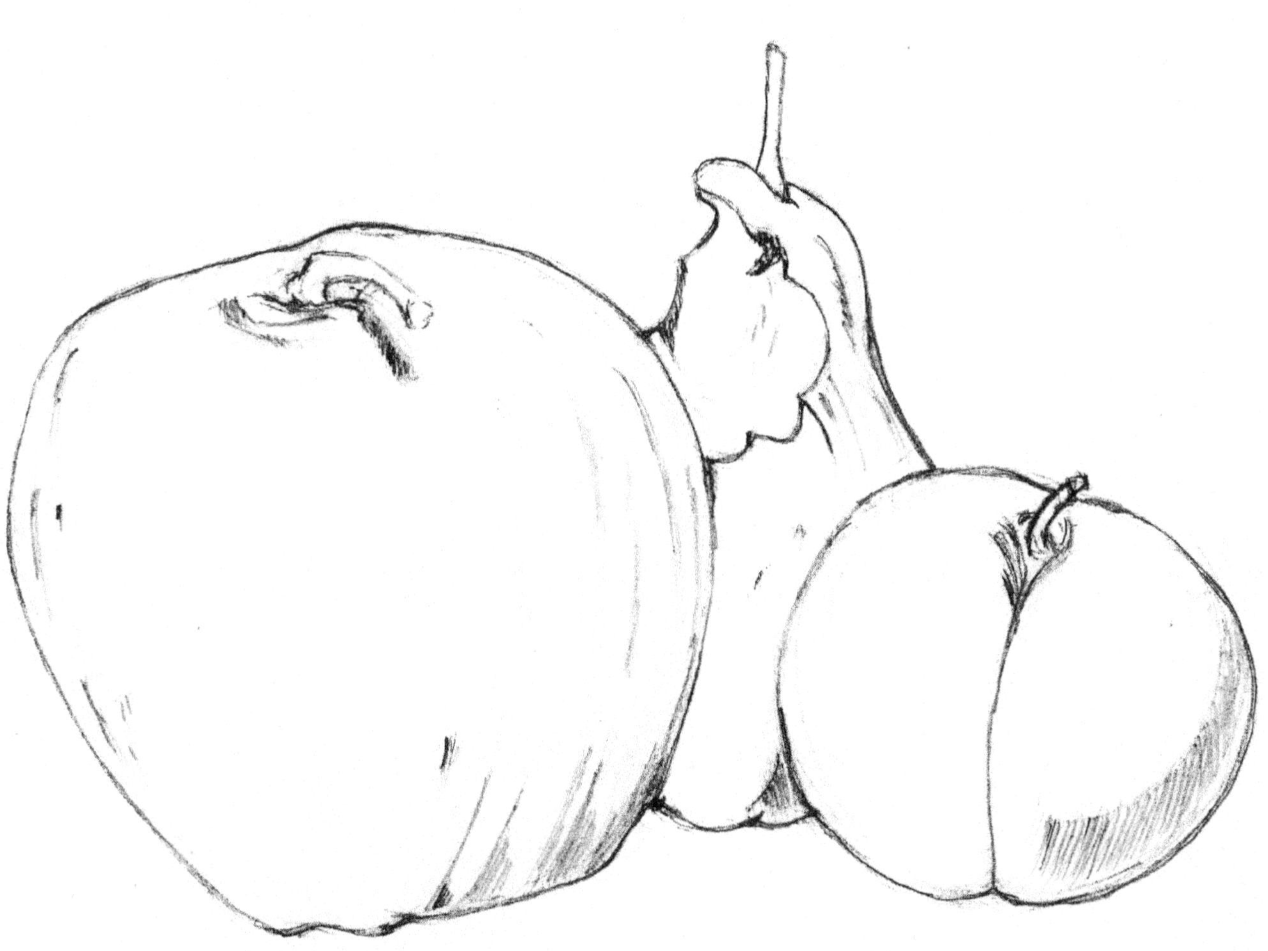

APPLE, BANANA, ORANGE, and PEAR

Hey, you're progressing! You've went from drawing two different fruits to three fruits, now four different fruits. You'll be drawing the previous fruits with the addition of an orange. Yeah, I didn't strutter, so let's draw the basic lines to form all these fruits from another mother.

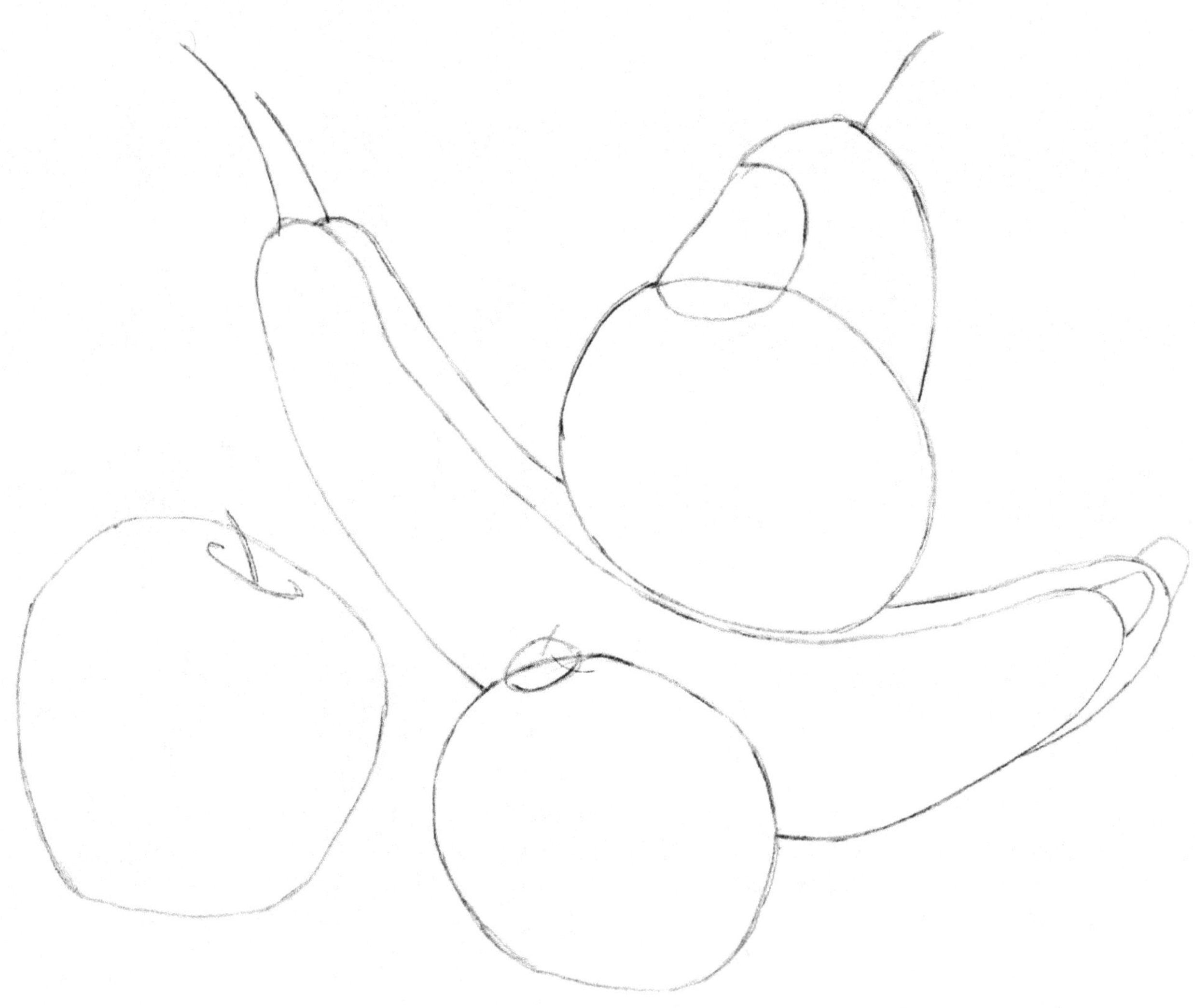

Let's draw in structure guidelines and circles
for the fruits. Choose any fruit you want to start
with first.

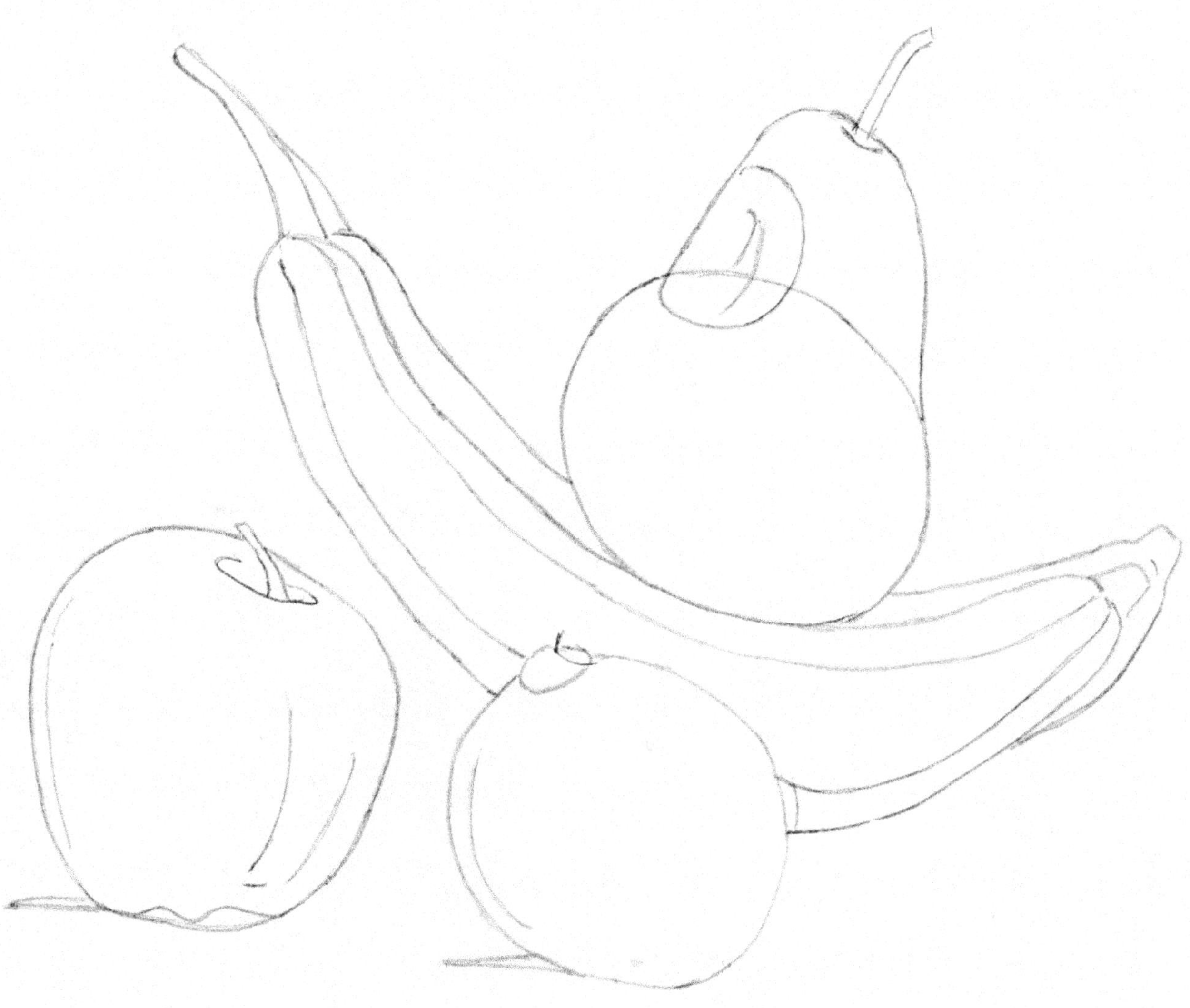

I forgot to add, this is a pencil drawing.
Erase all guidelines and circles to better
define your drawing, adding some shading.

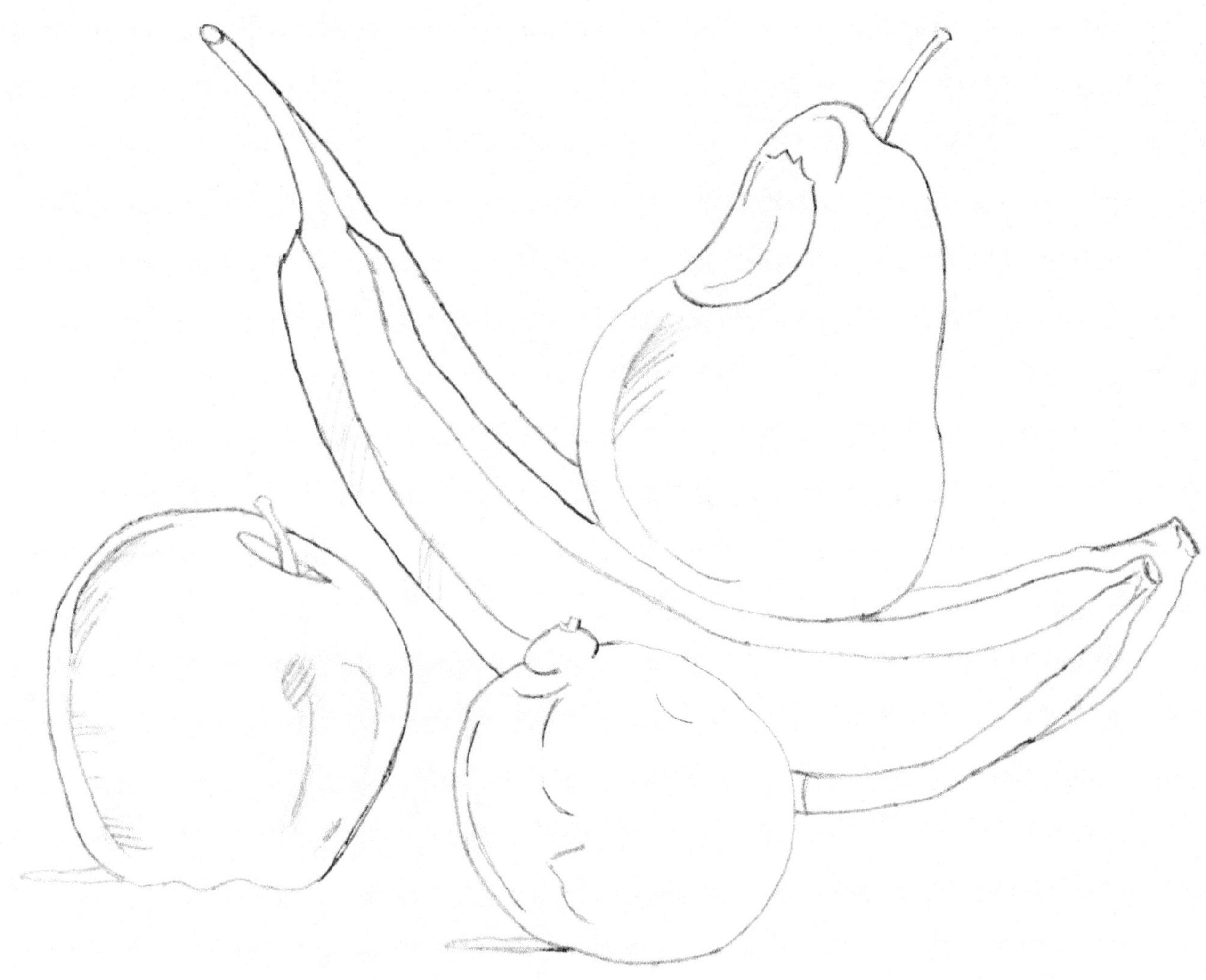

After penciling in the fades and shades
with no blunder. Here you have your
four fruit artwork of wonder.

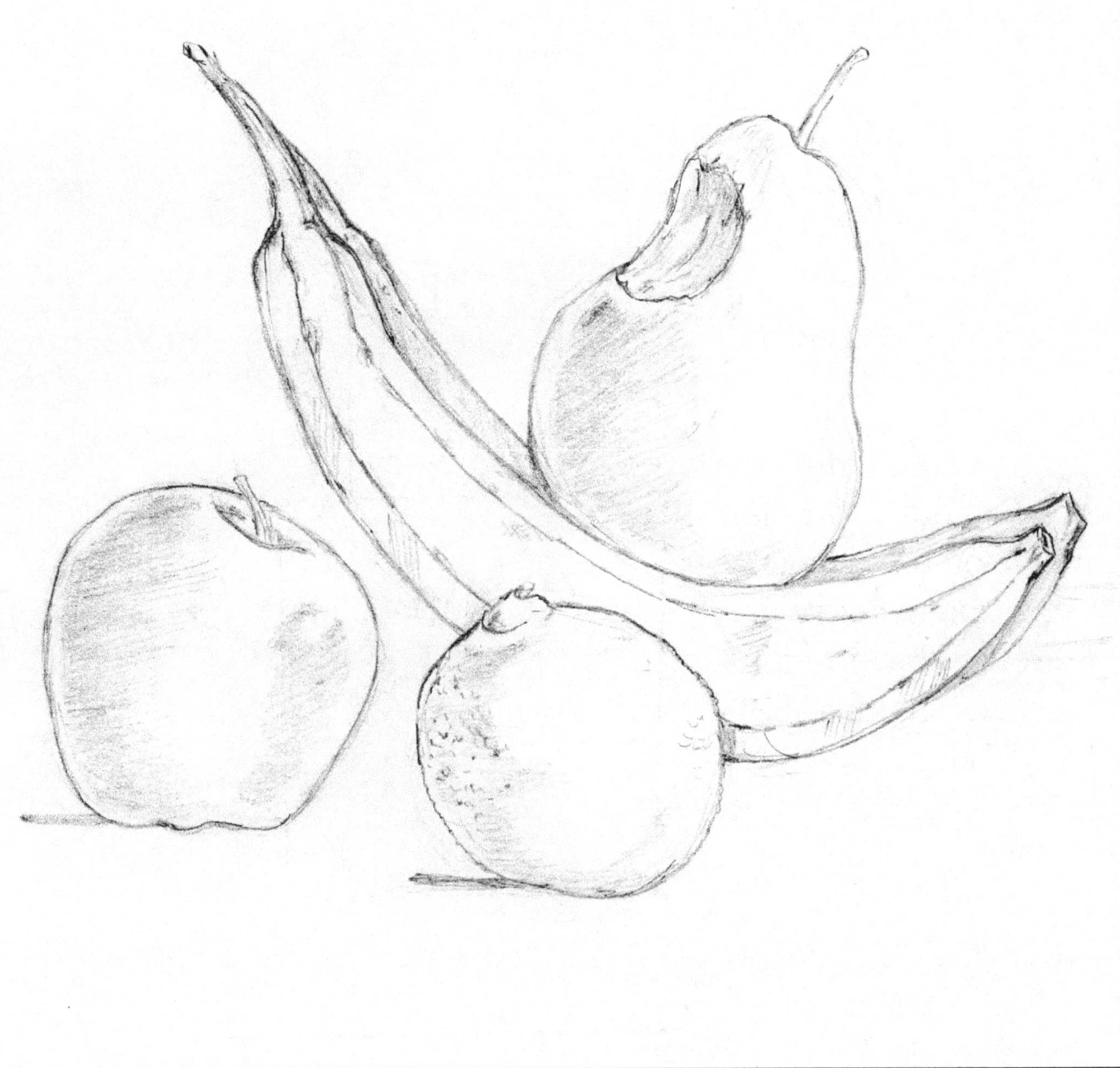

LAMP

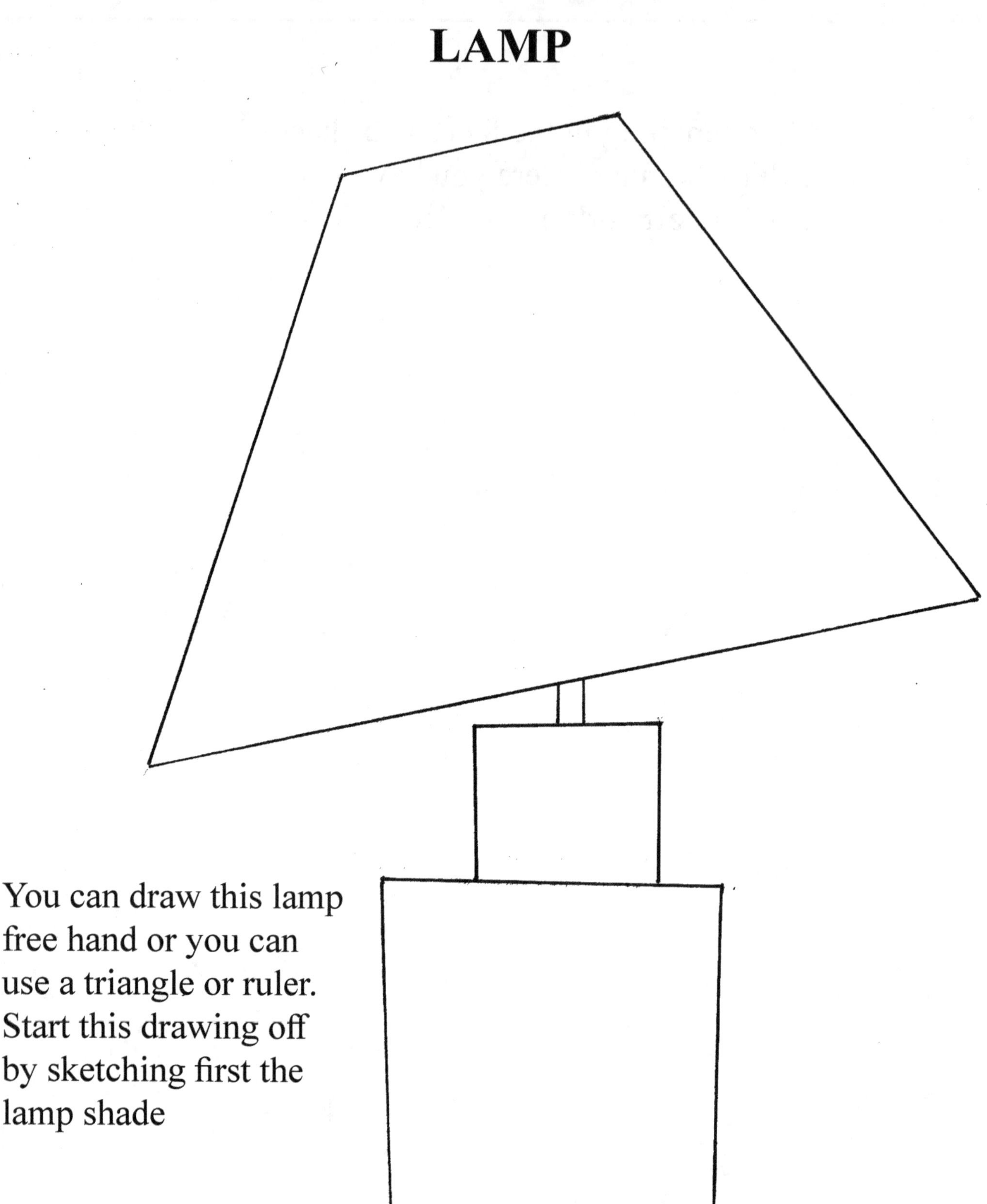

You can draw this lamp
free hand or you can
use a triangle or ruler.
Start this drawing off
by sketching first the
lamp shade

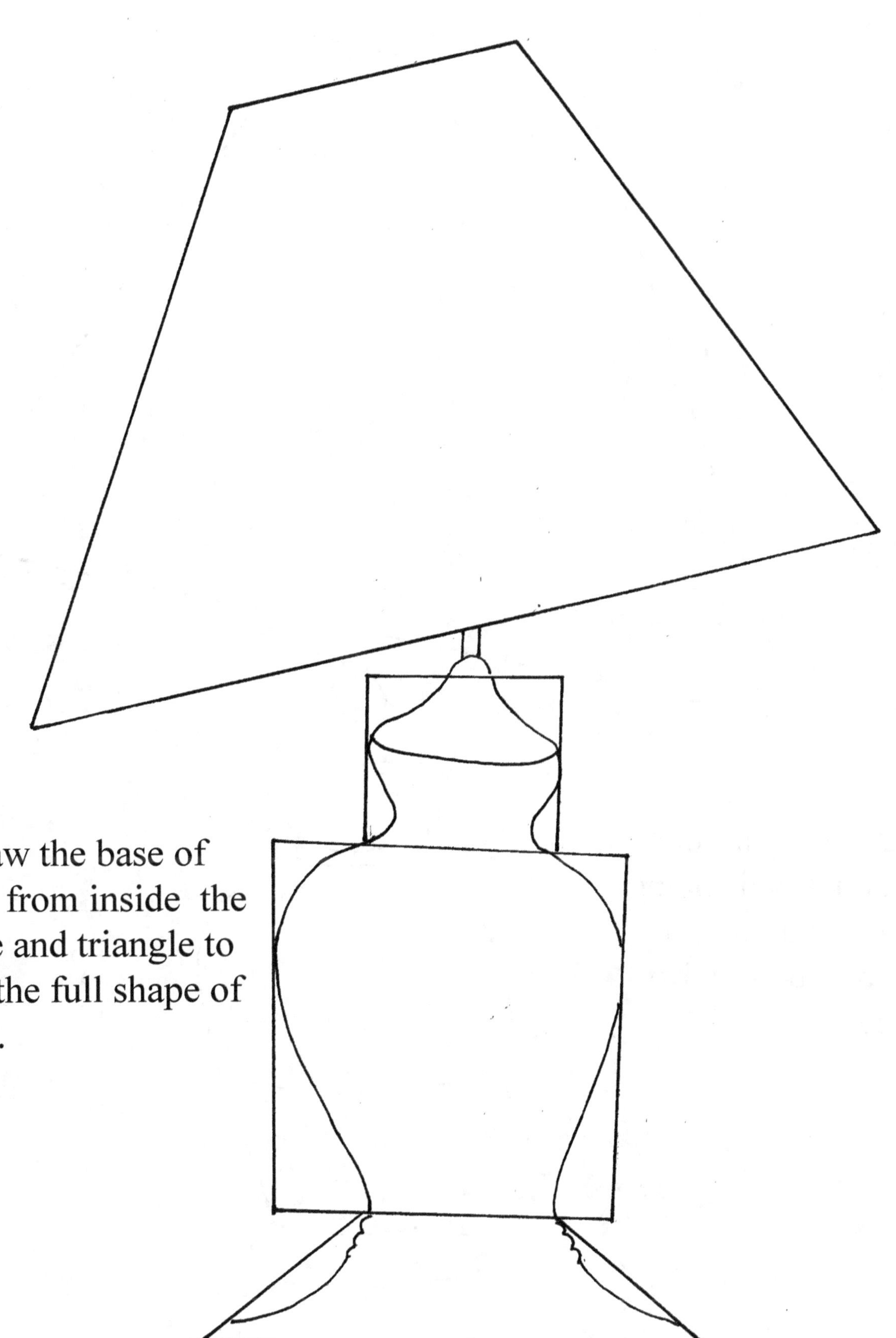

Now, draw the base of the lamp from inside the rectangle and triangle to develop the full shape of the lamp.

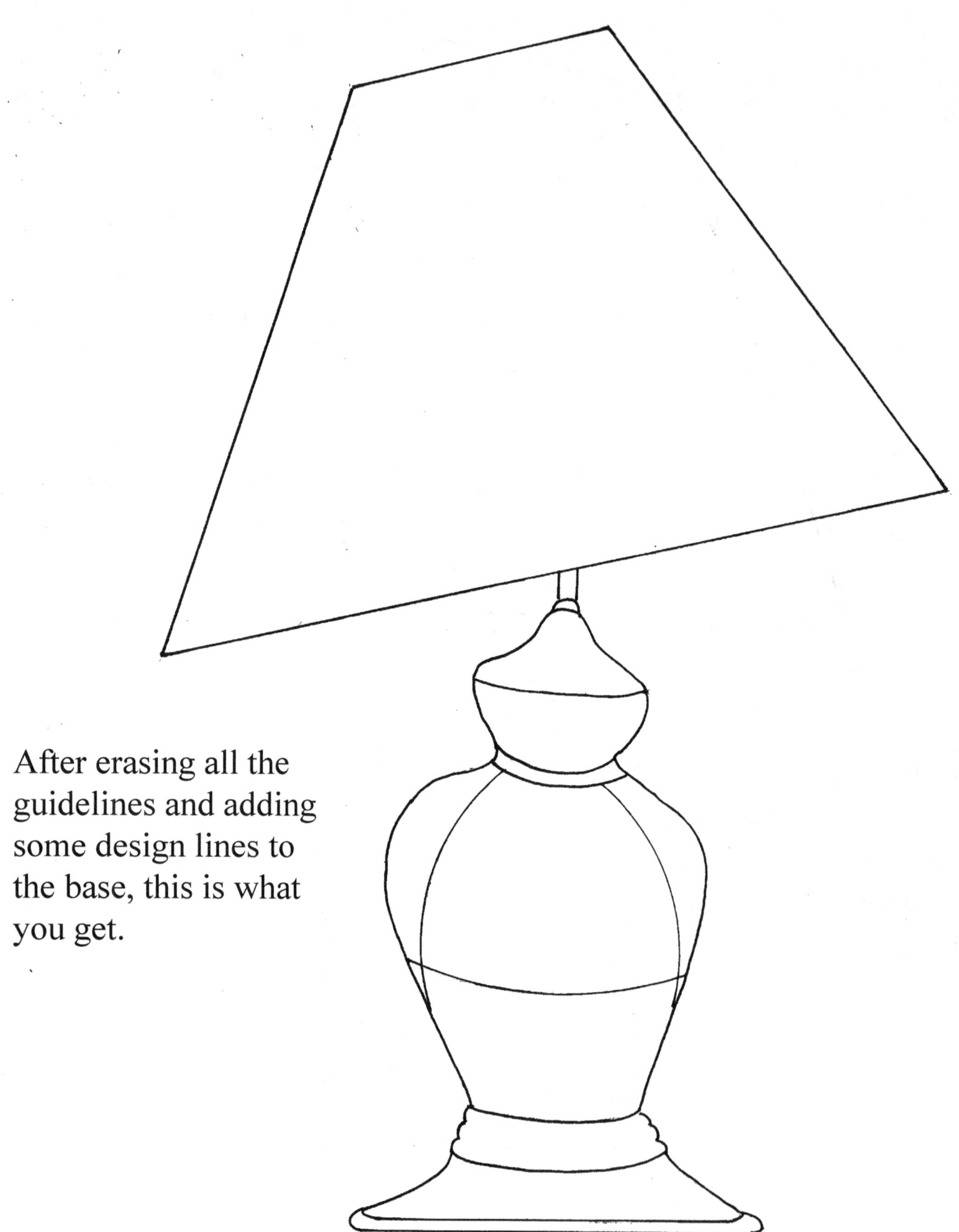

After erasing all the
guidelines and adding
some design lines to
the base, this is what
you get.

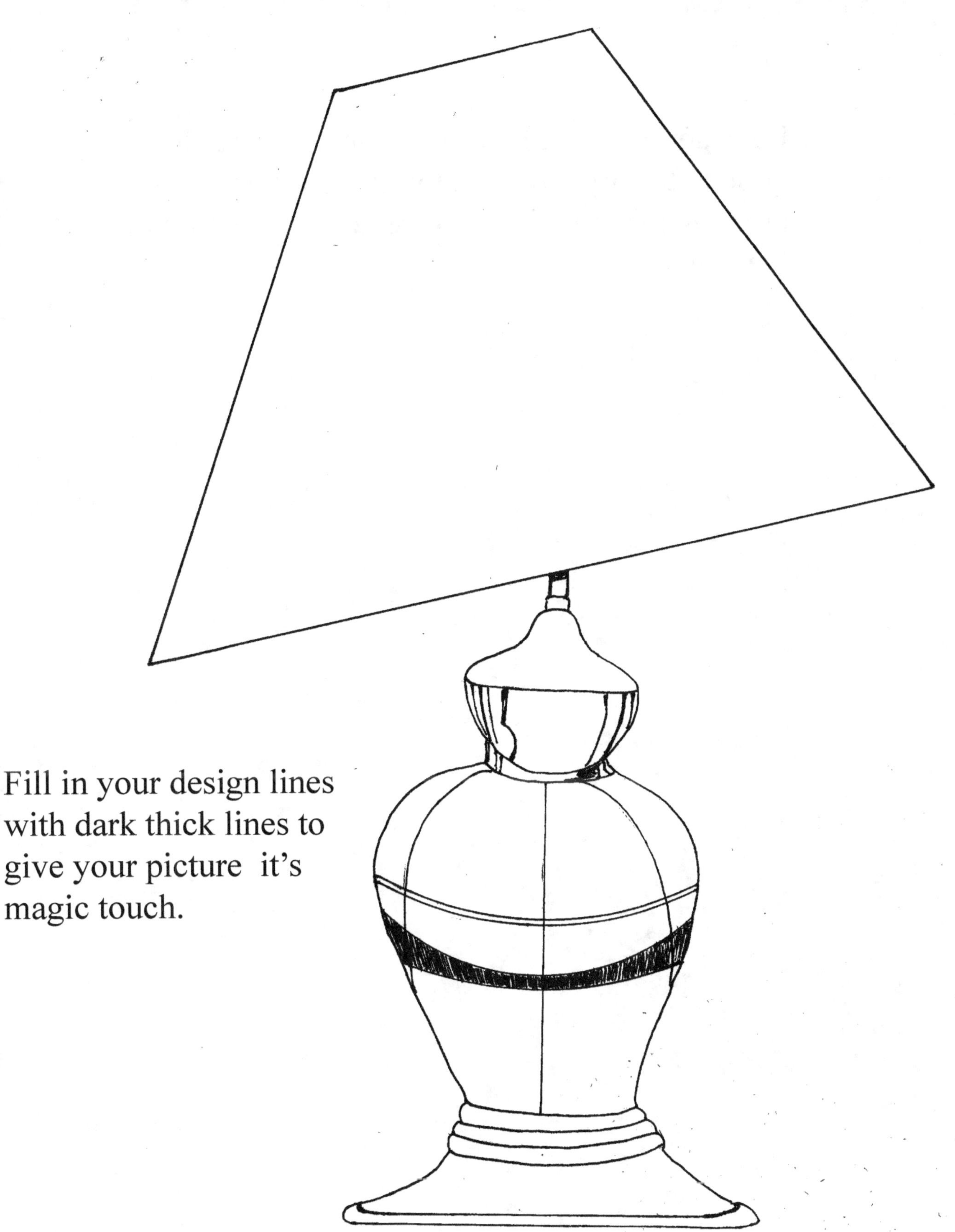

Fill in your design lines
with dark thick lines to
give your picture it's
magic touch.

BANANA, ORANGE, GRAPES, and APPLE

Let's get back to the fruits again. You should be good at this by now. Start with your pencil by drawing the guidelines to create the structure of the fruits.

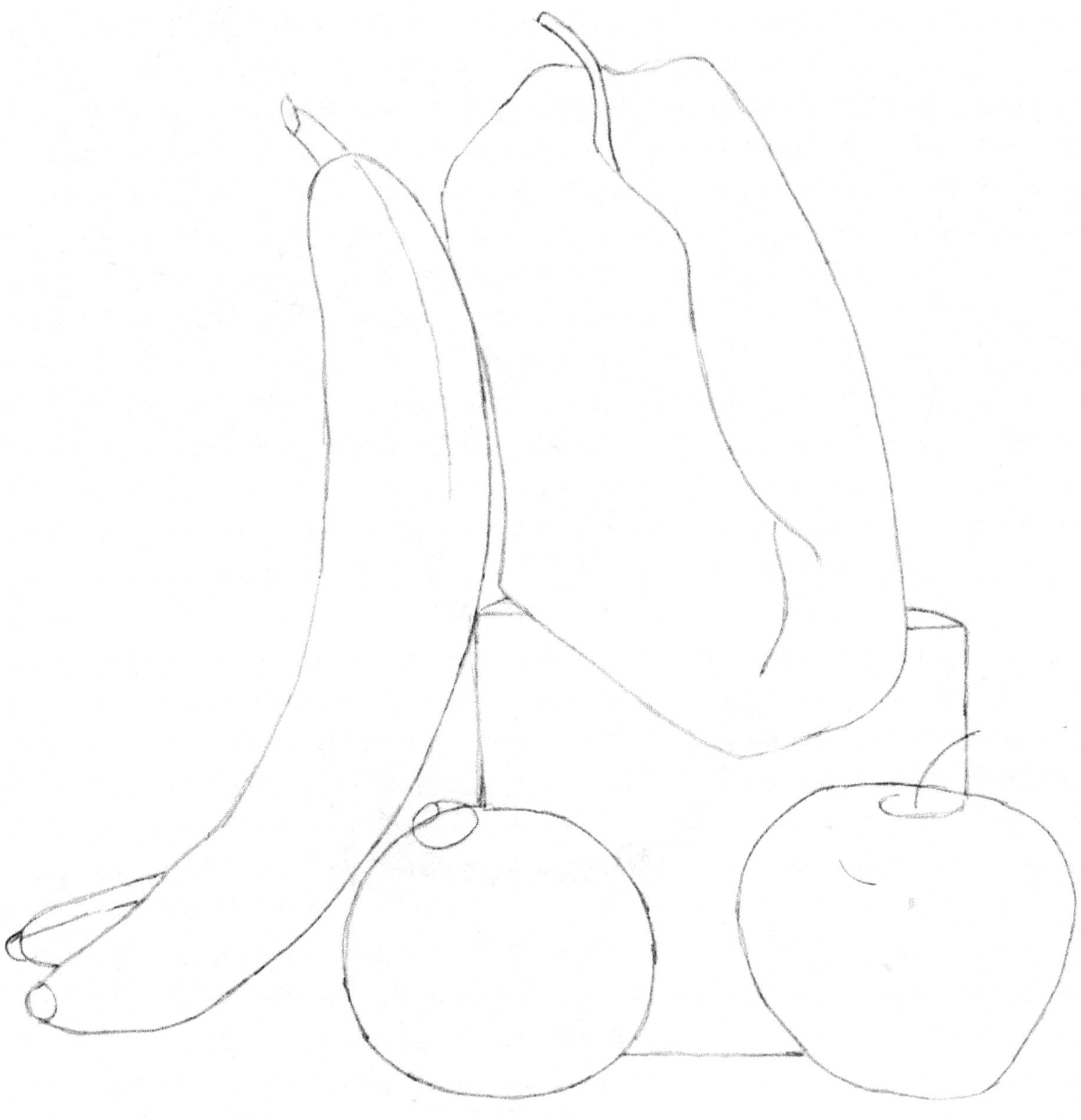

Let's put in more details with your pencil.
Make little circles for your grapes within
the guidelines.

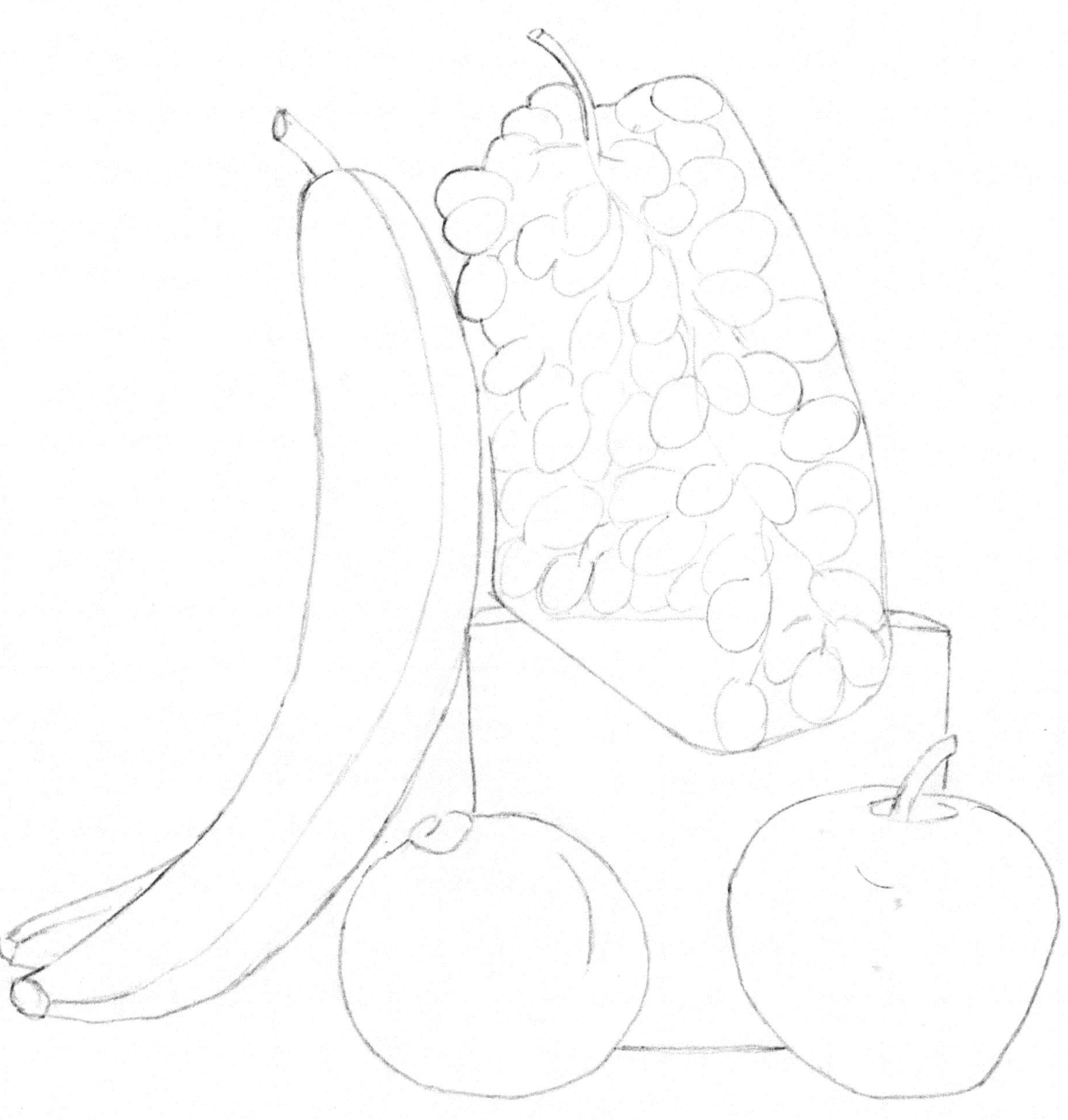

Now that you have a solid drawing, erase
the guidelines from the grapes, then add
more grapes.

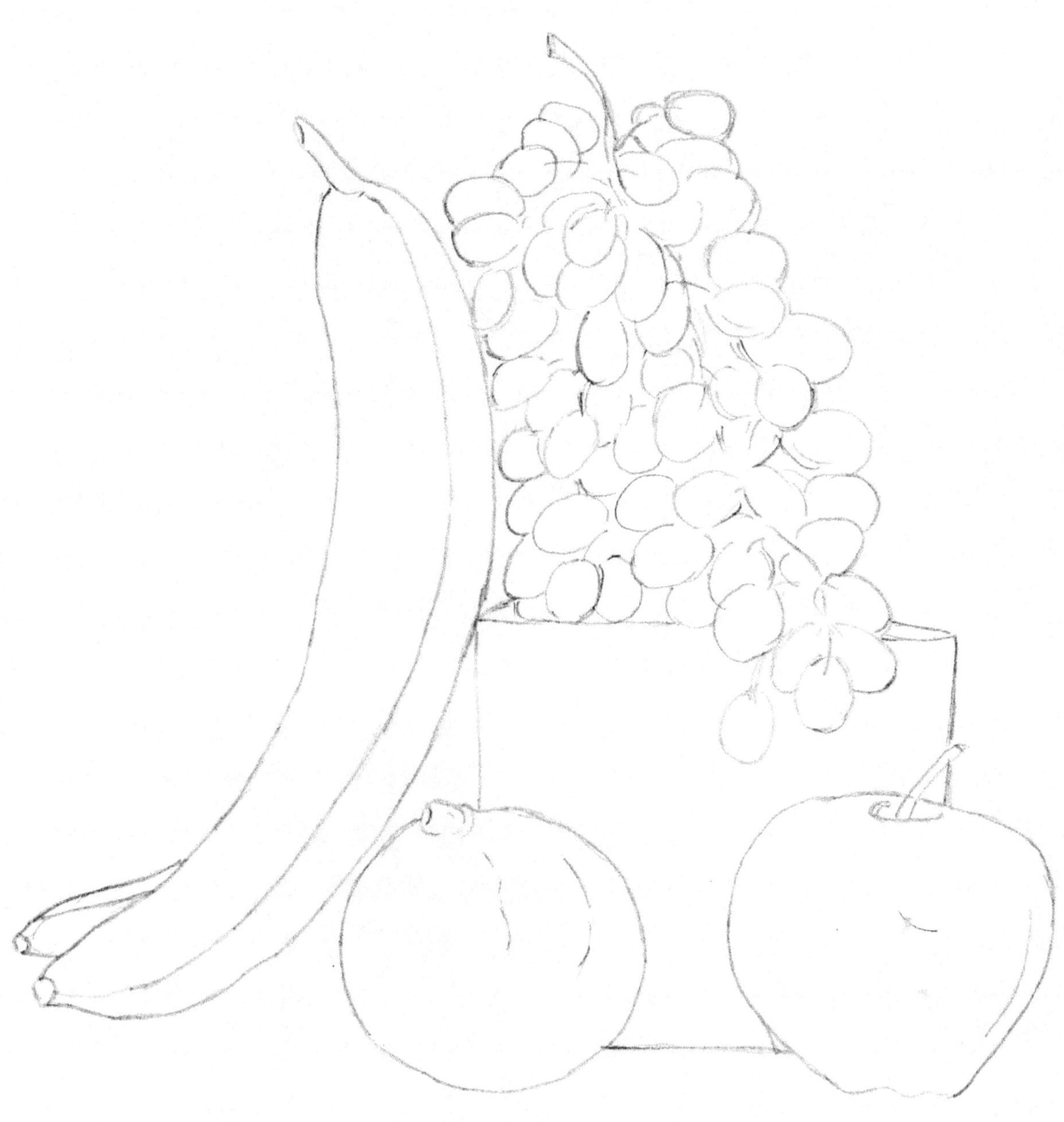

With your pencil, sketch and shade in more
details in your drawing to make it a complete
work of art.

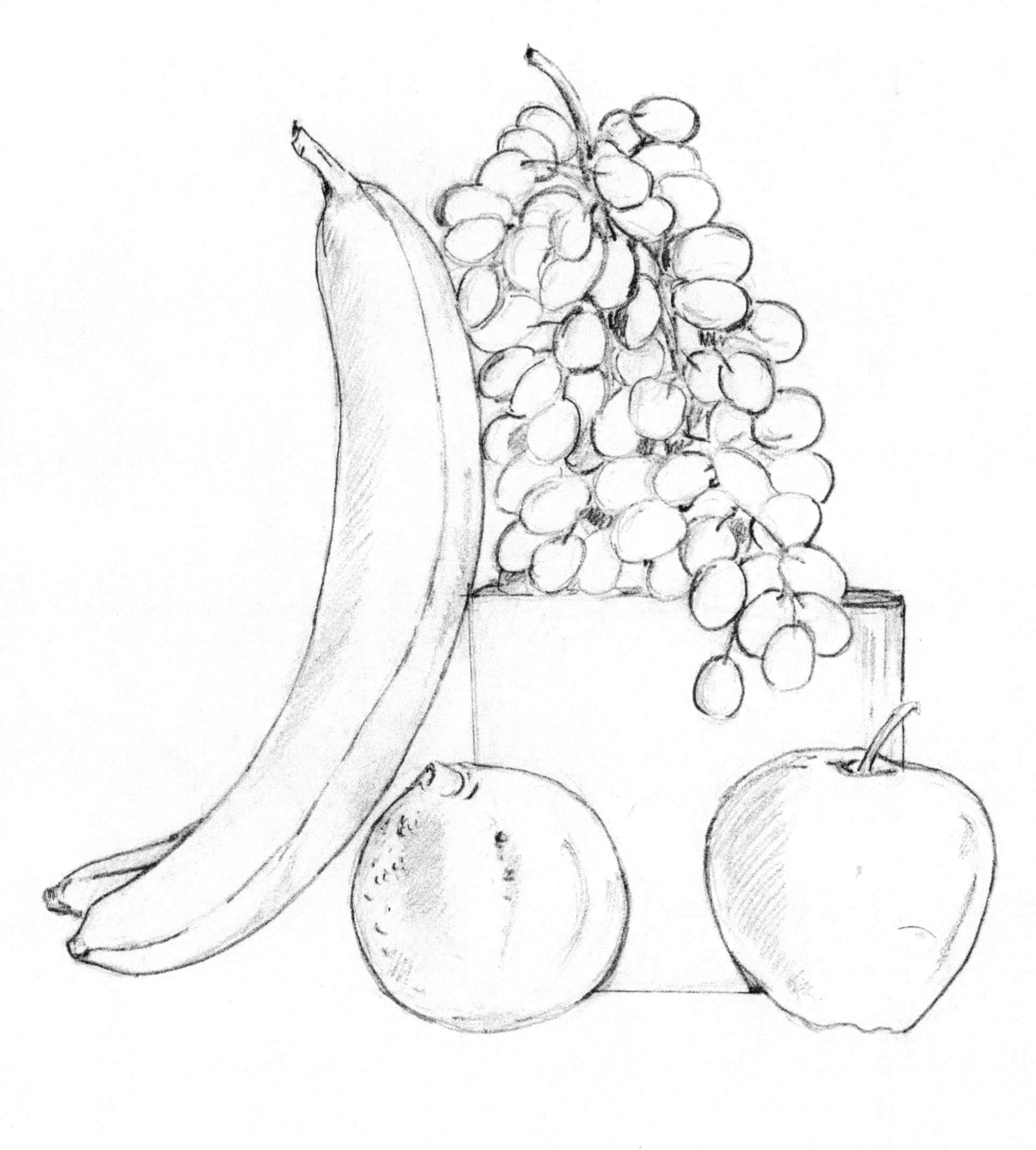

The Perspective of Life.
When you are walking your
path, always learning and
always growing.

BASIC PERSPECTIVE

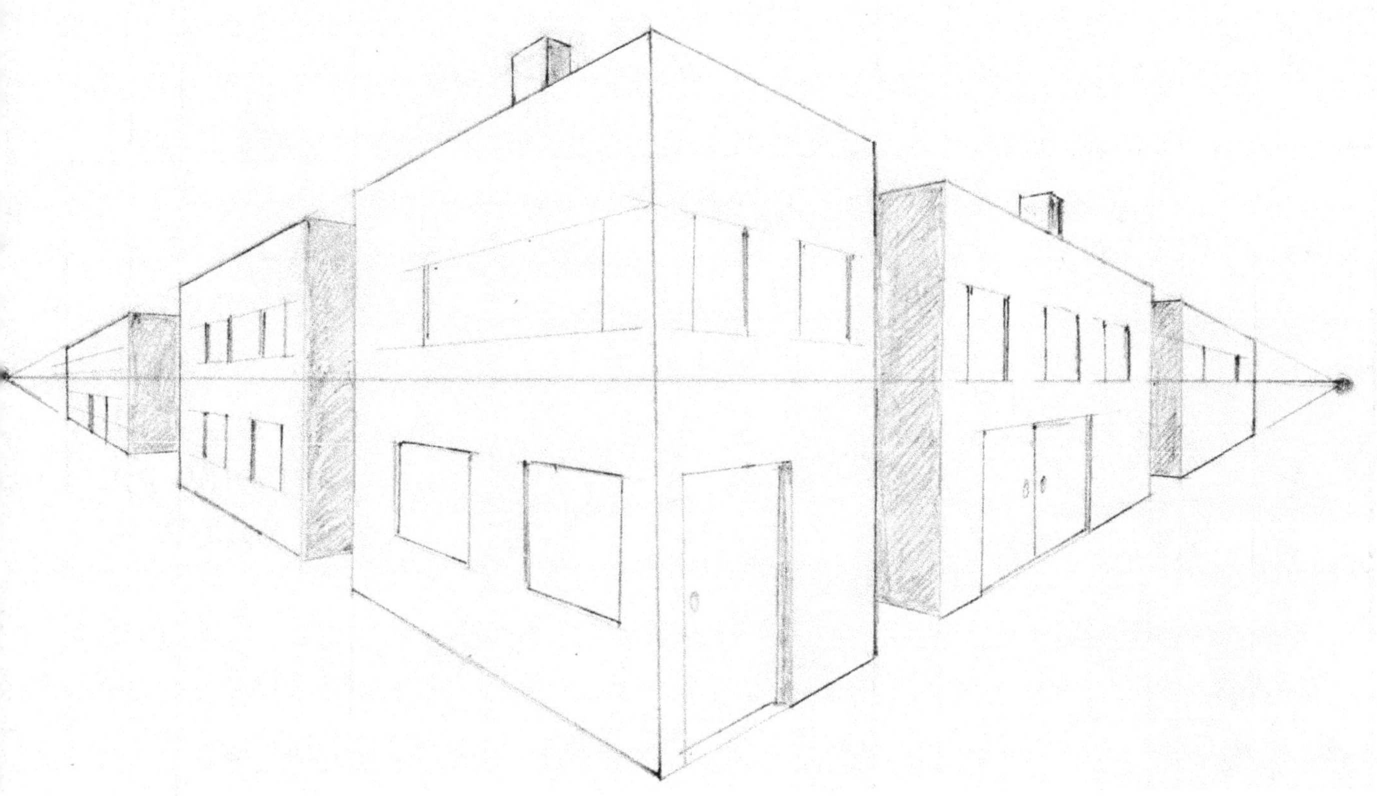

ONE POINT PERSPECTIVE

Is a drawing containing only one vanishing point on the horizon line. The horizon line is the dark line in the middle below.

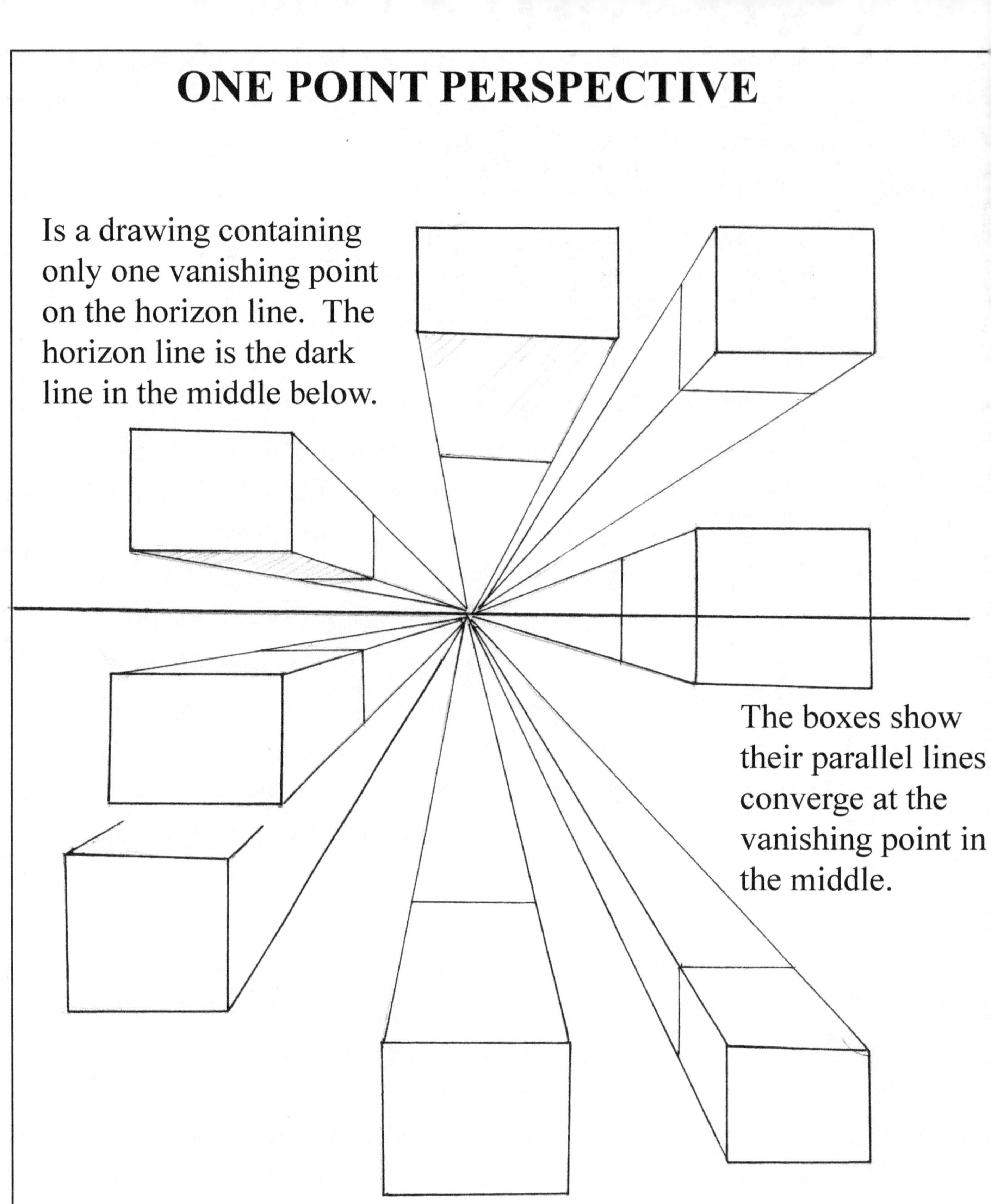

The boxes show their parallel lines converge at the vanishing point in the middle.

TWO POINT PERSPECTIVE

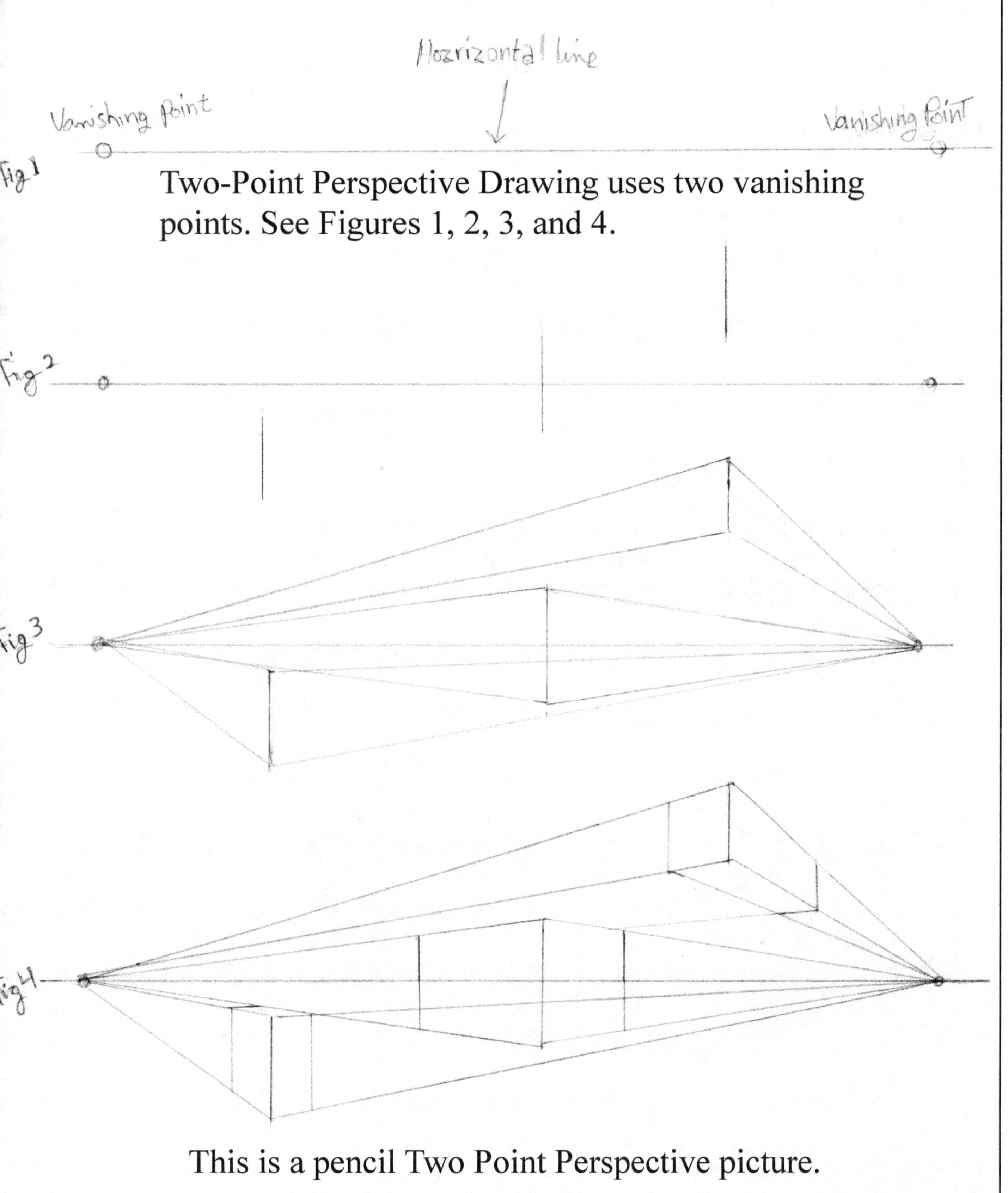

Two-Point Perspective Drawing uses two vanishing points. See Figures 1, 2, 3, and 4.

This is a pencil Two Point Perspective picture.

TWO POINT PERSPECTIVE BUILDINGS

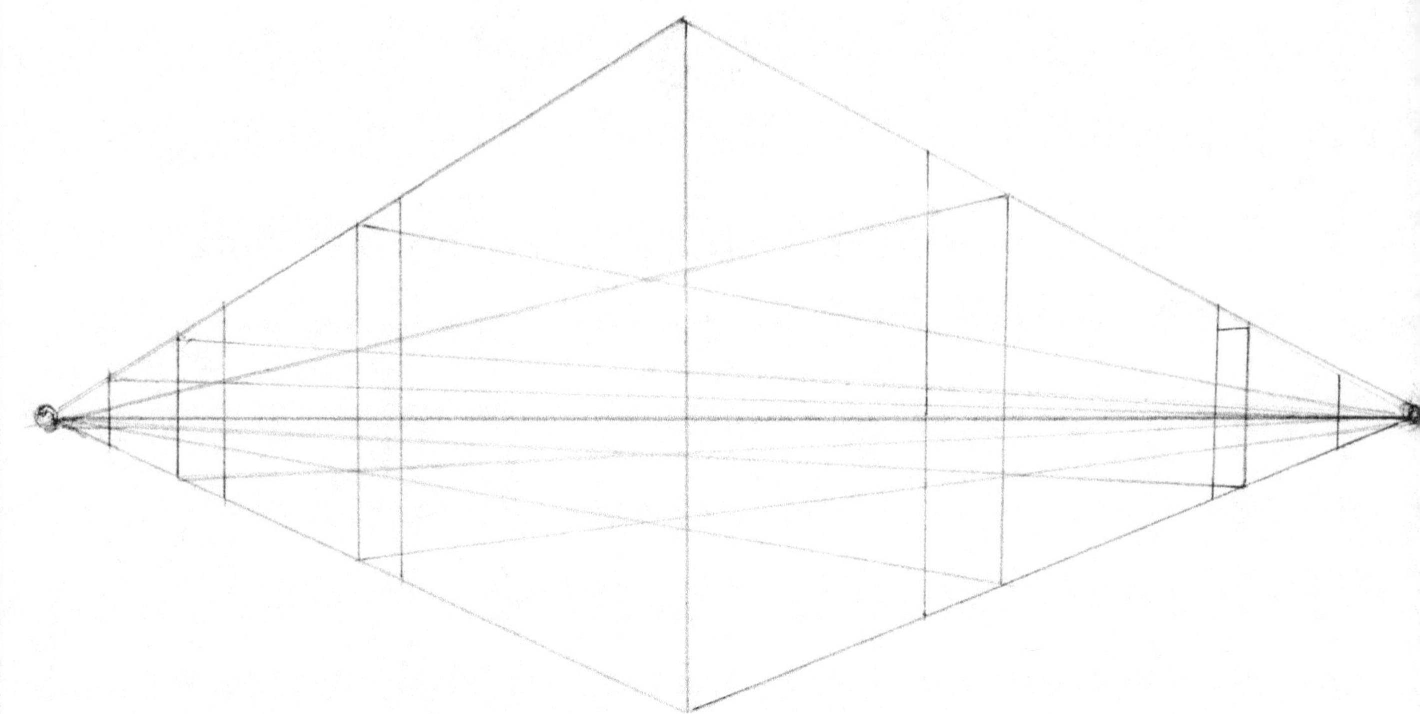

Pencil drawing of buildings with two vanishing points at the end of the horizon line.

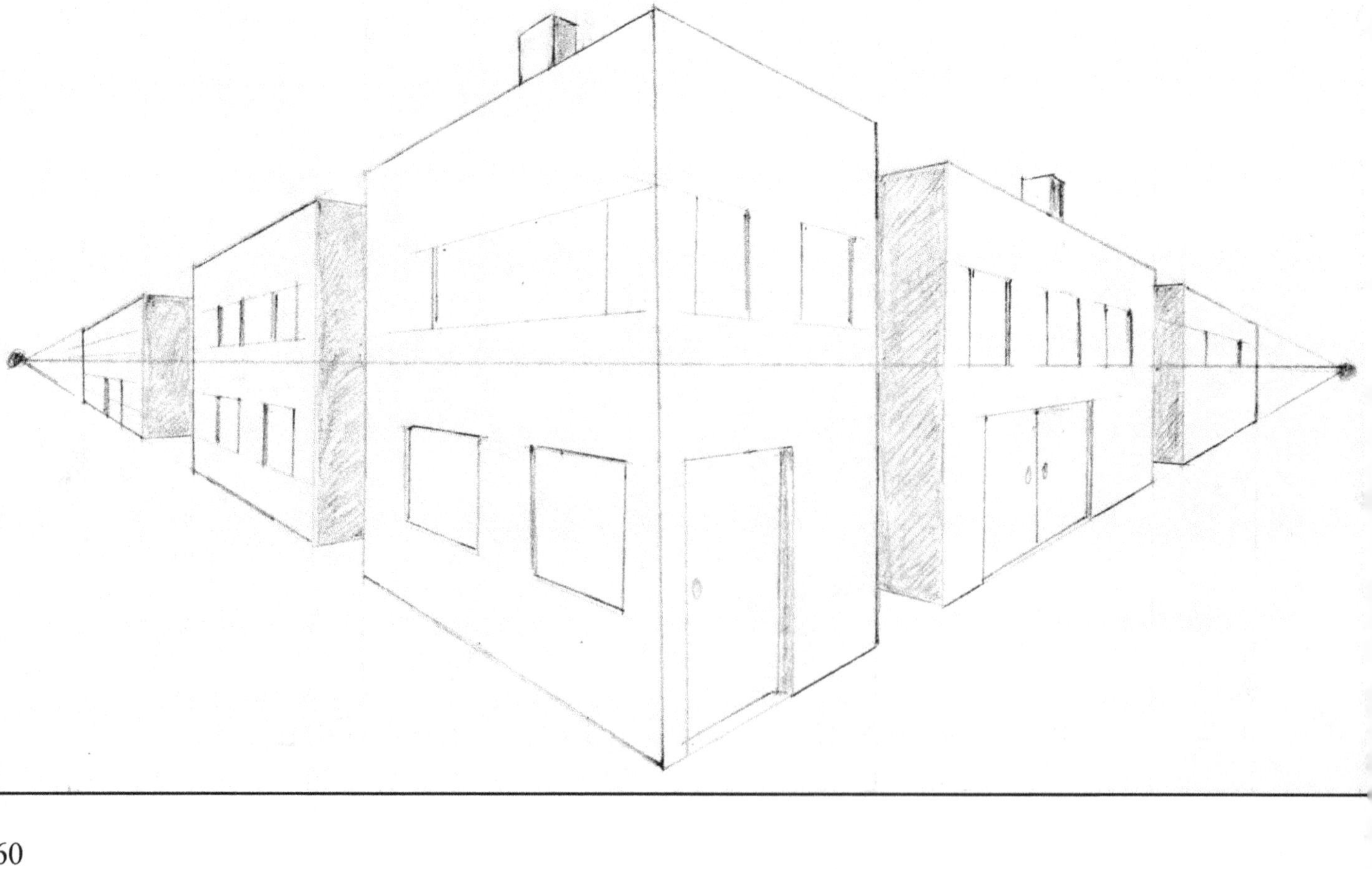

DRAWING REPTILES

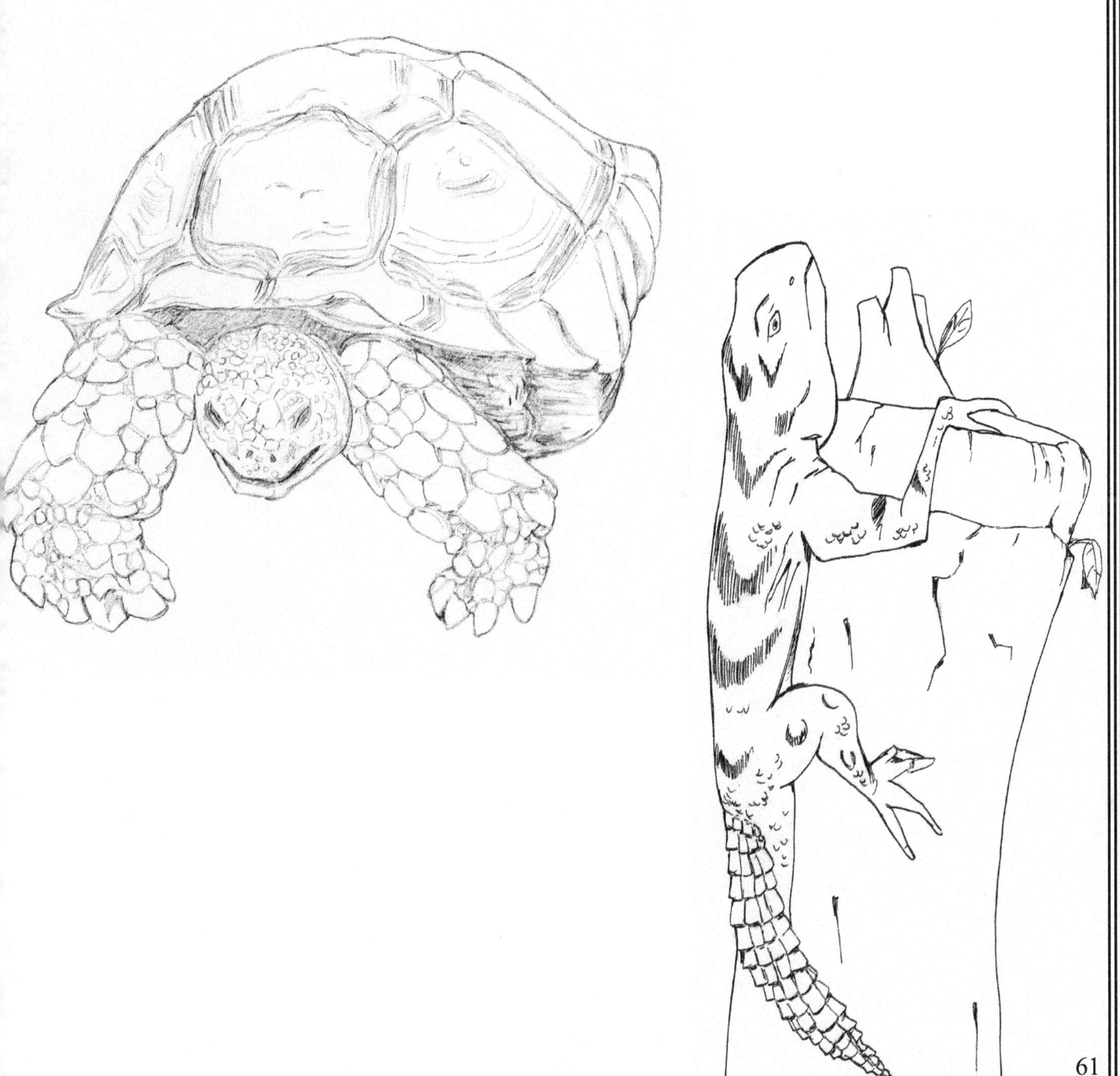

TURTLE

Start outlining the head of the turtle with his eyes, nose and mouth, then follow that with sketching the shell, draw on the legs and feet last.

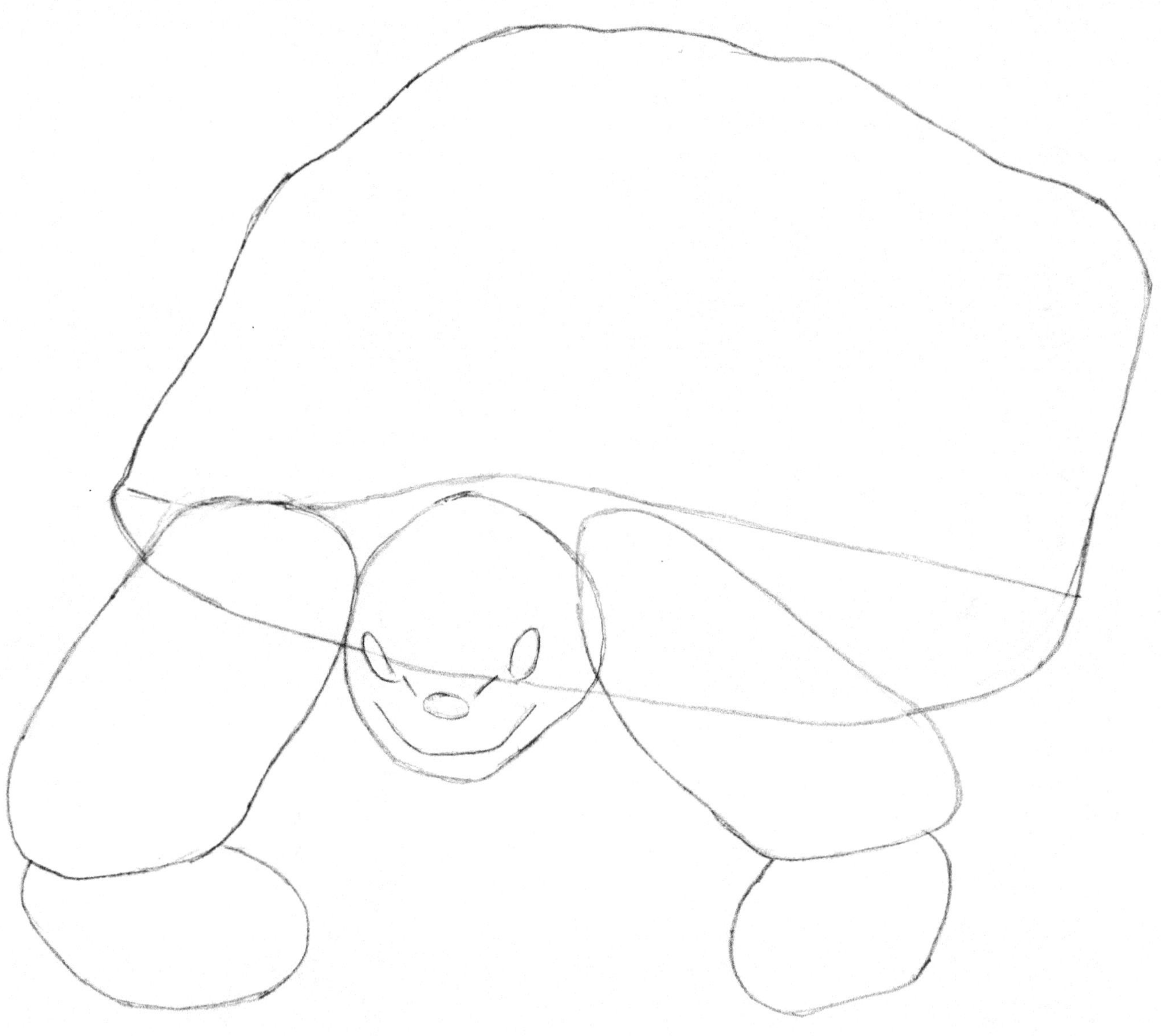

With your pencil, now it's time to start drawing on the formation structure of the shell, legs, feet, and head.

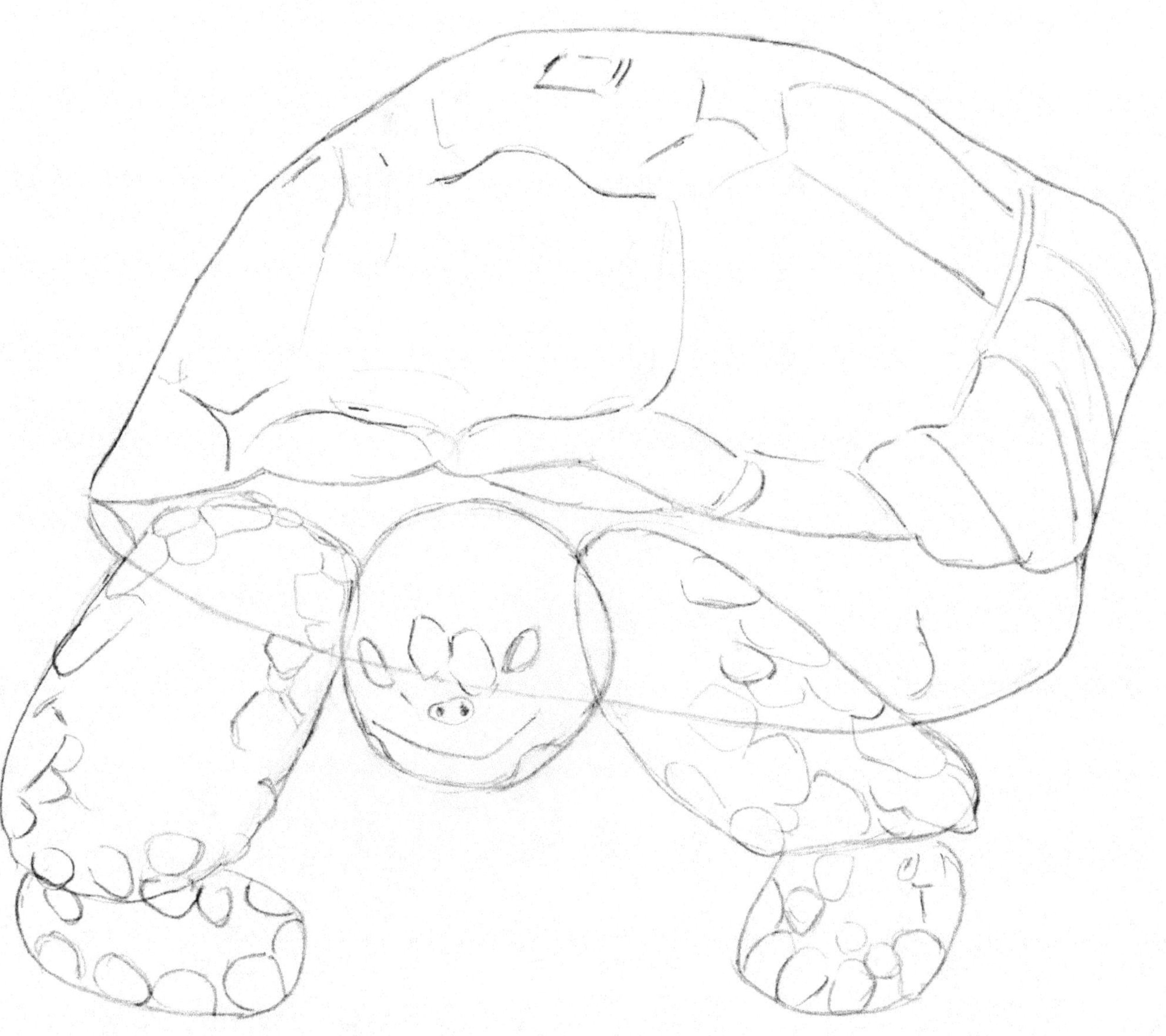

Continue to create more detail in your artwork
by drawing on some rectangle, triangle, polygon
shapes. You're almost done.

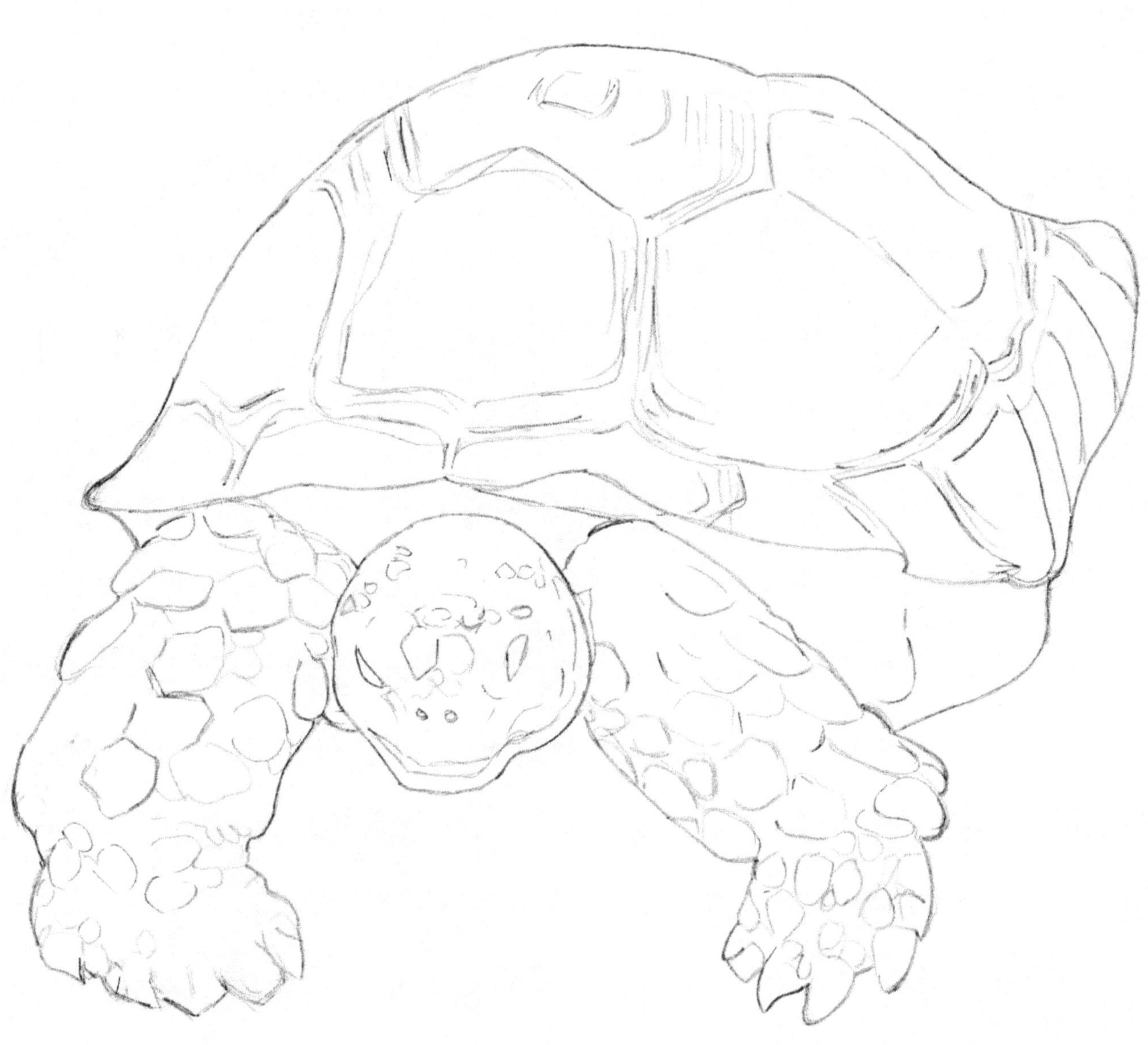

This is your artwork, after you have finished adding more detail and shading with your pencil to the turtle's shell, head, legs and feet. This turtle was in a race, but he was moving at a slow pace. Guess who he faced?

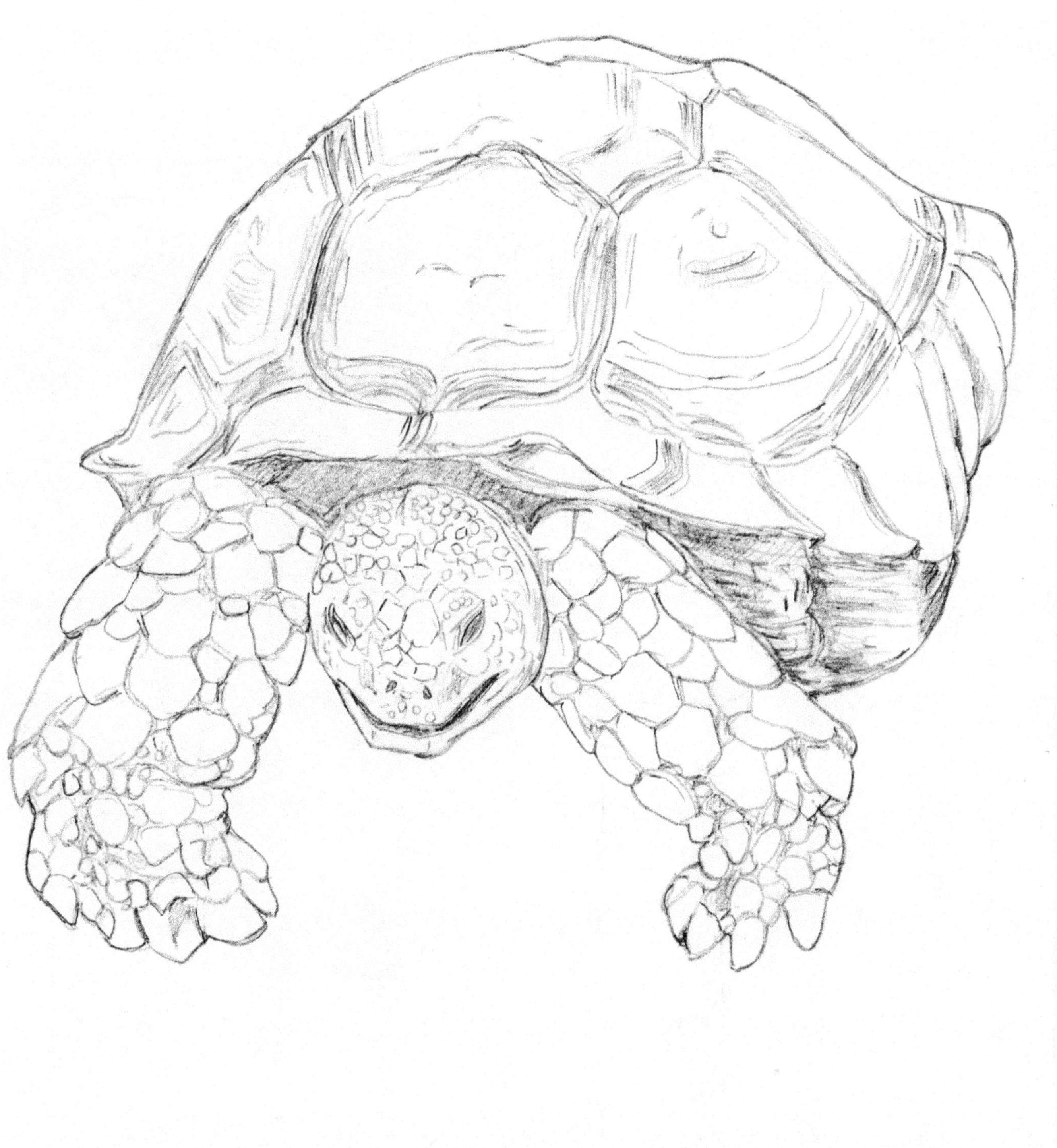

LIZARD

No instructions
on this one, let's
see how you do on
your own...

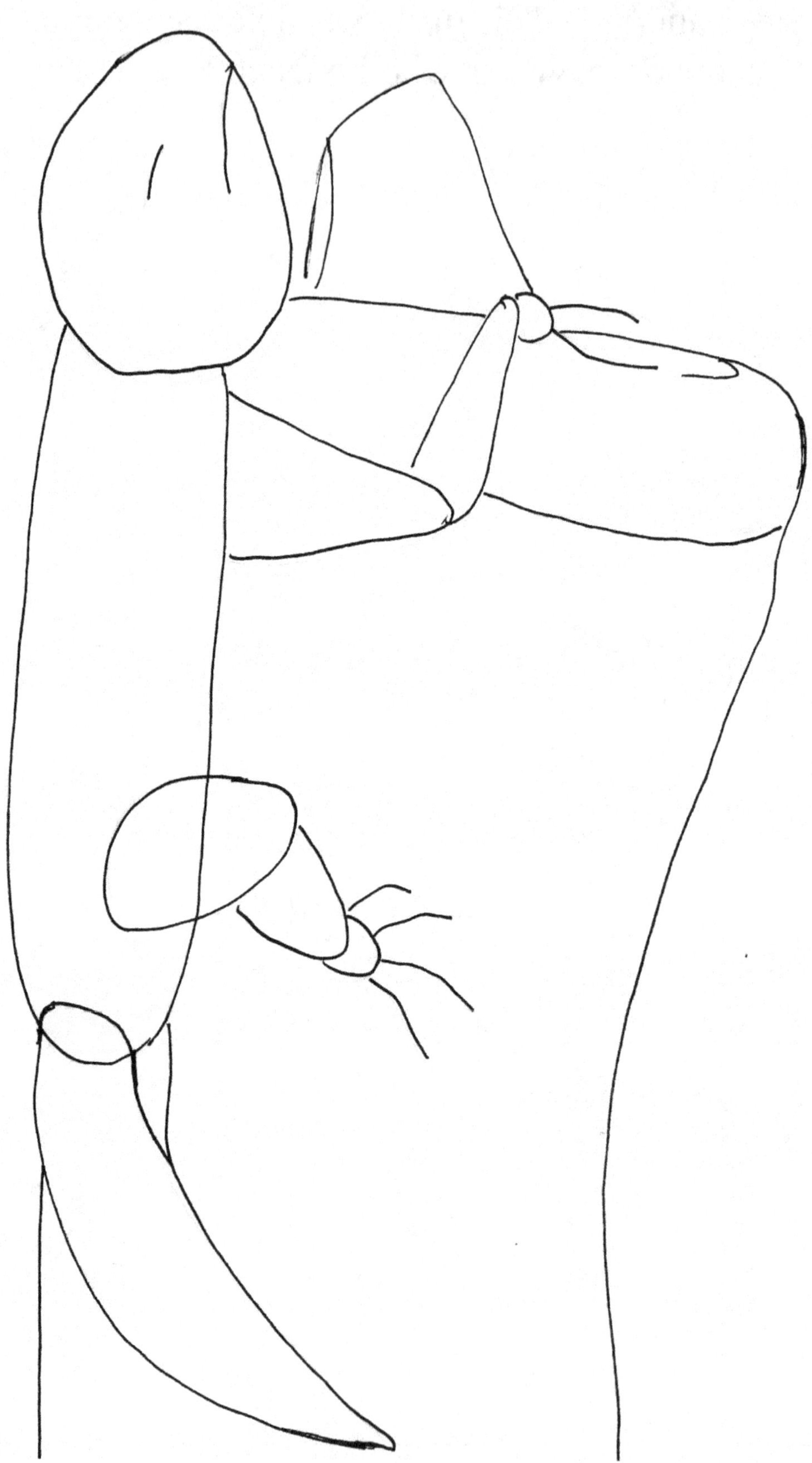

...Remember, a
picture is worth
a thousand words!!

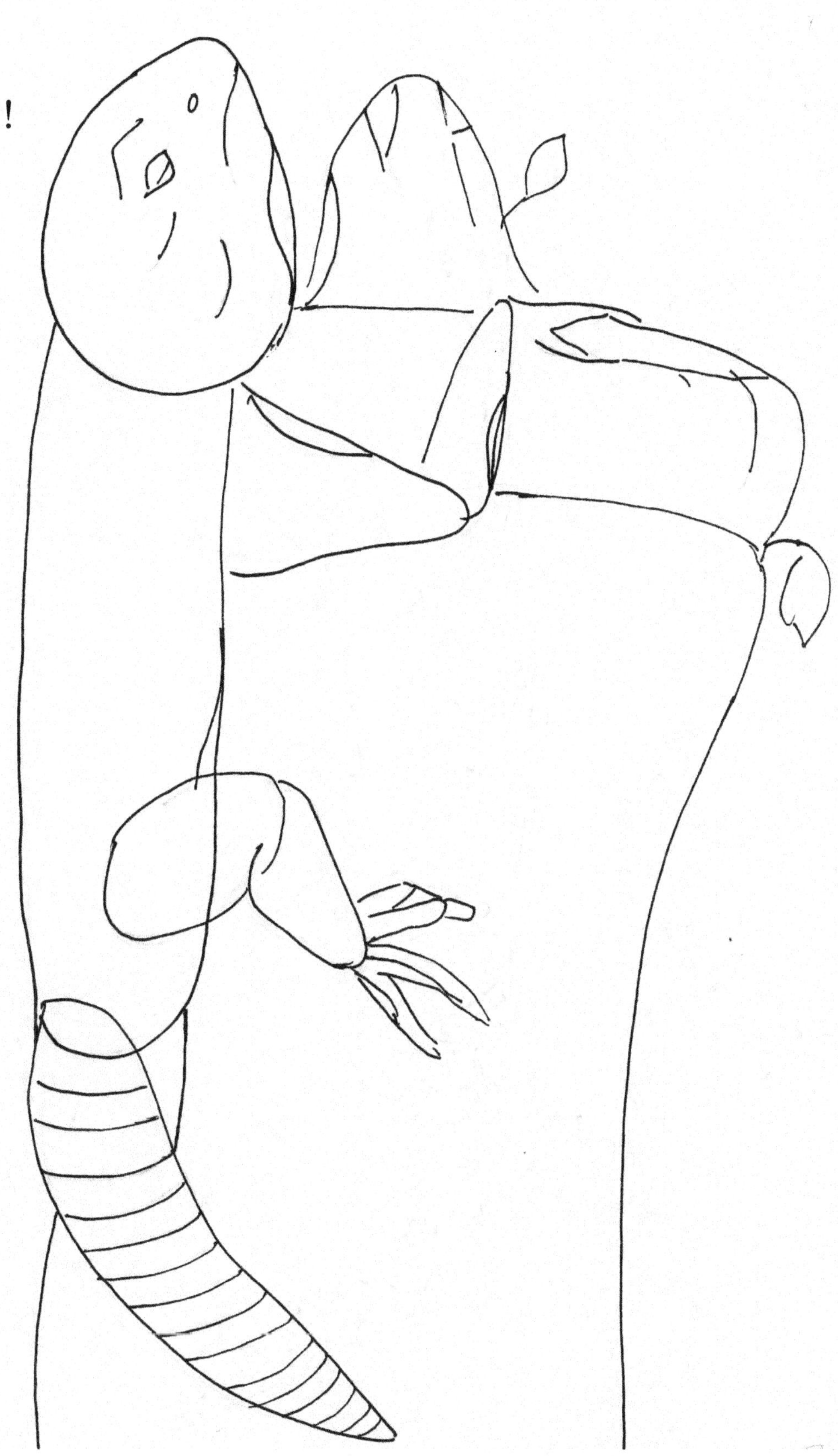

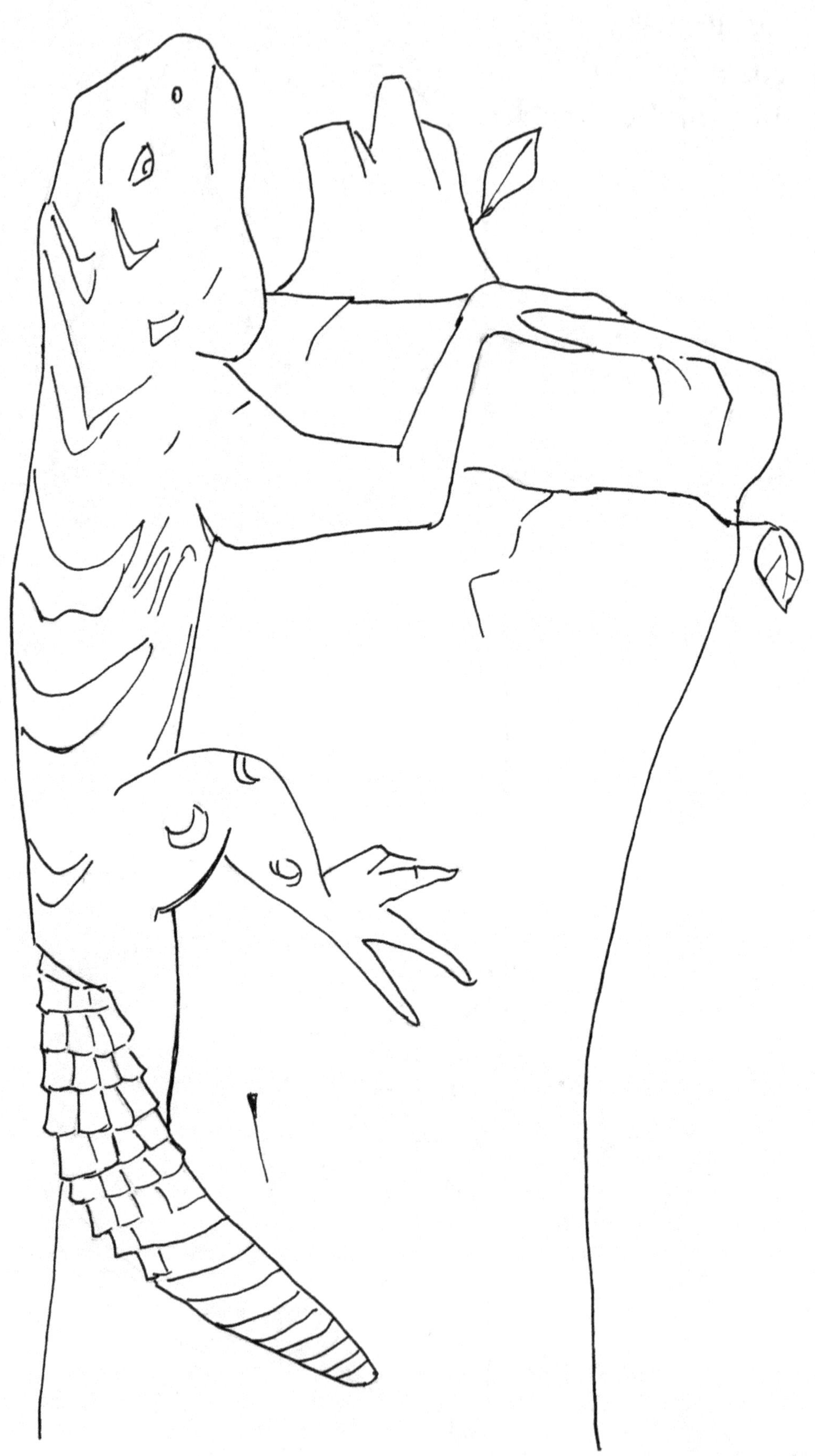

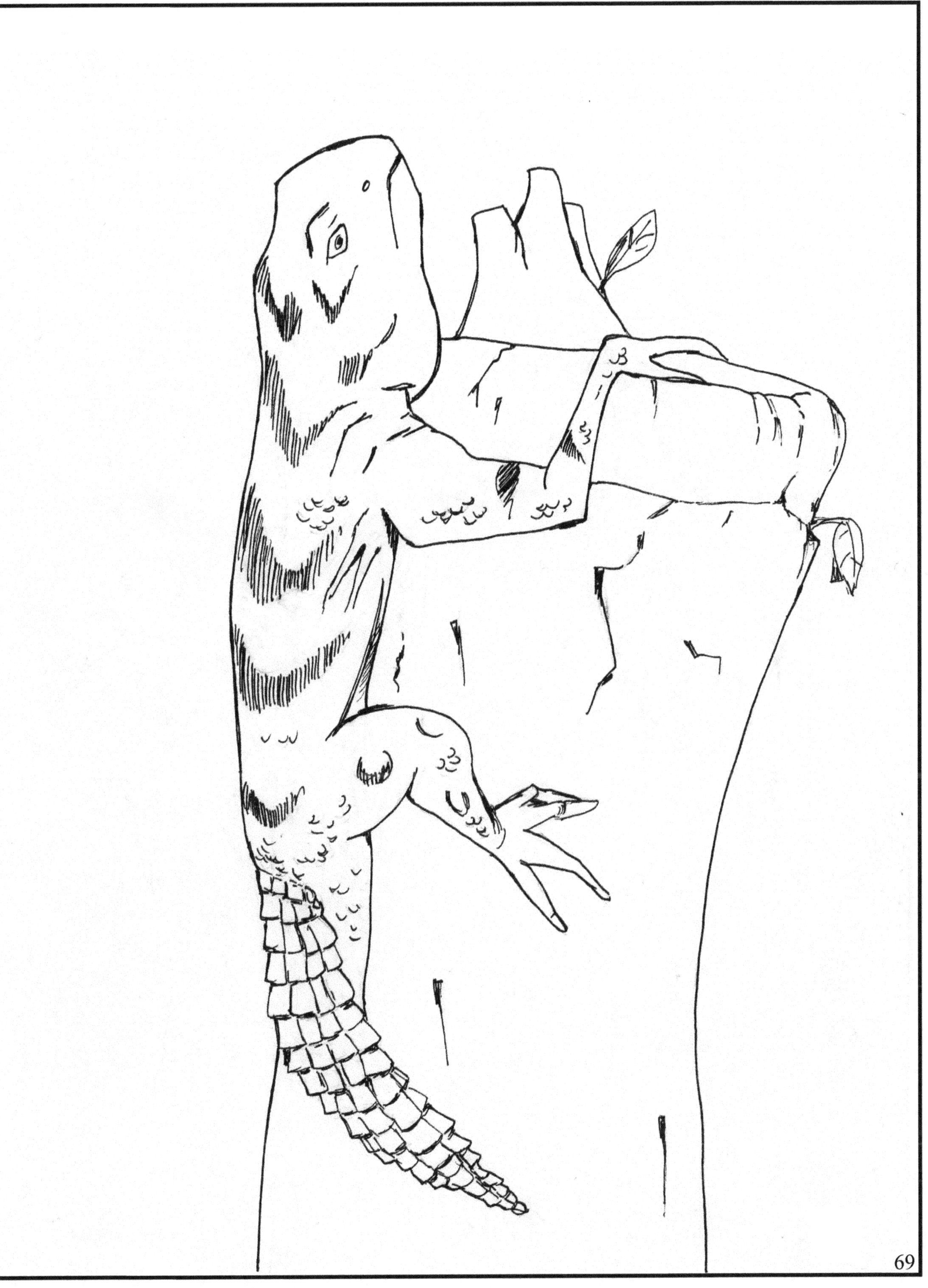

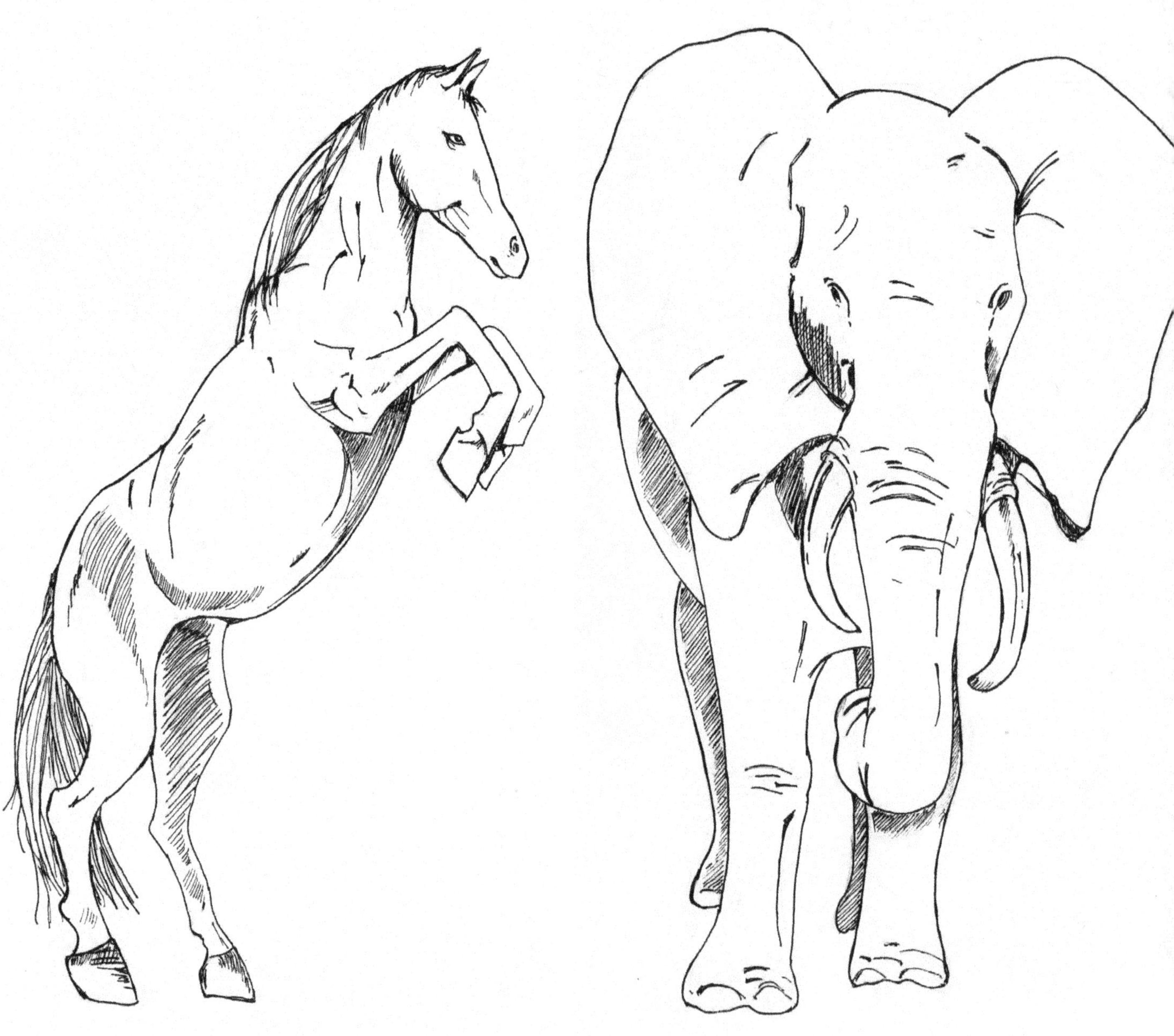

DRAWING MAMMALS

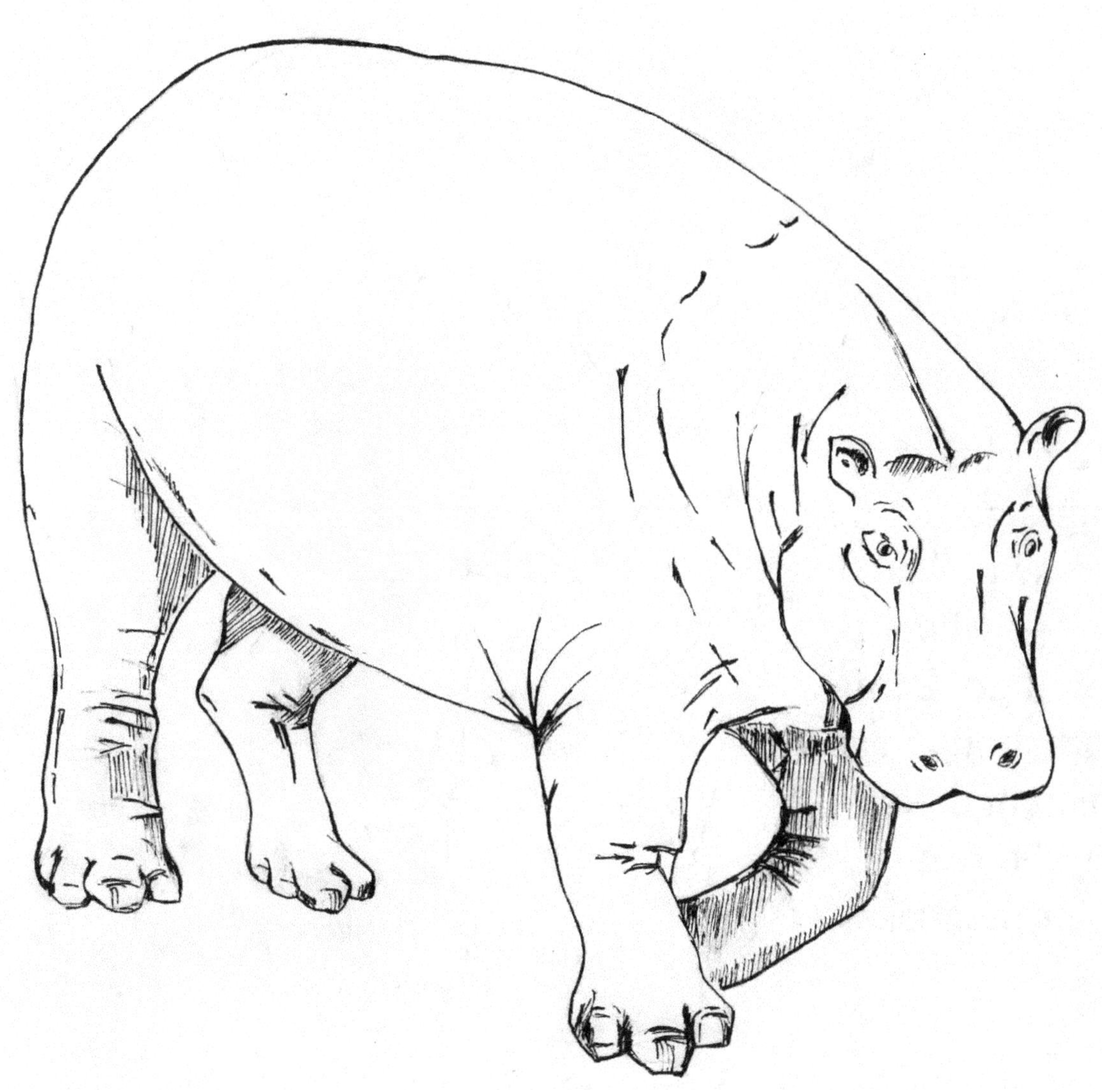

ELEPHANT

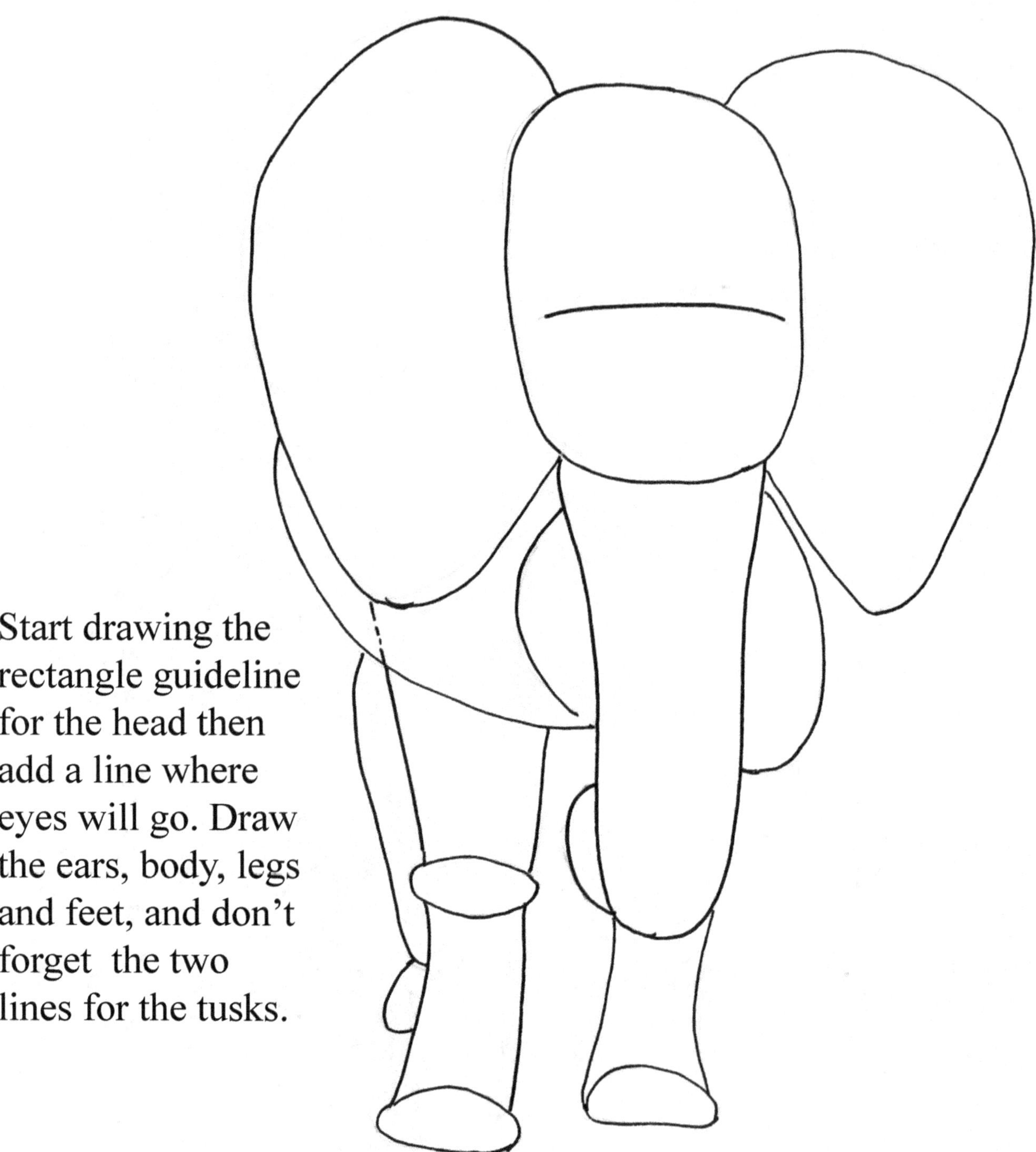

Start drawing the rectangle guideline for the head then add a line where eyes will go. Draw the ears, body, legs and feet, and don't forget the two lines for the tusks.

Draw and shape in more detail formation
of all of the elephant's body parts. Like
the ears, eyes and tusk.

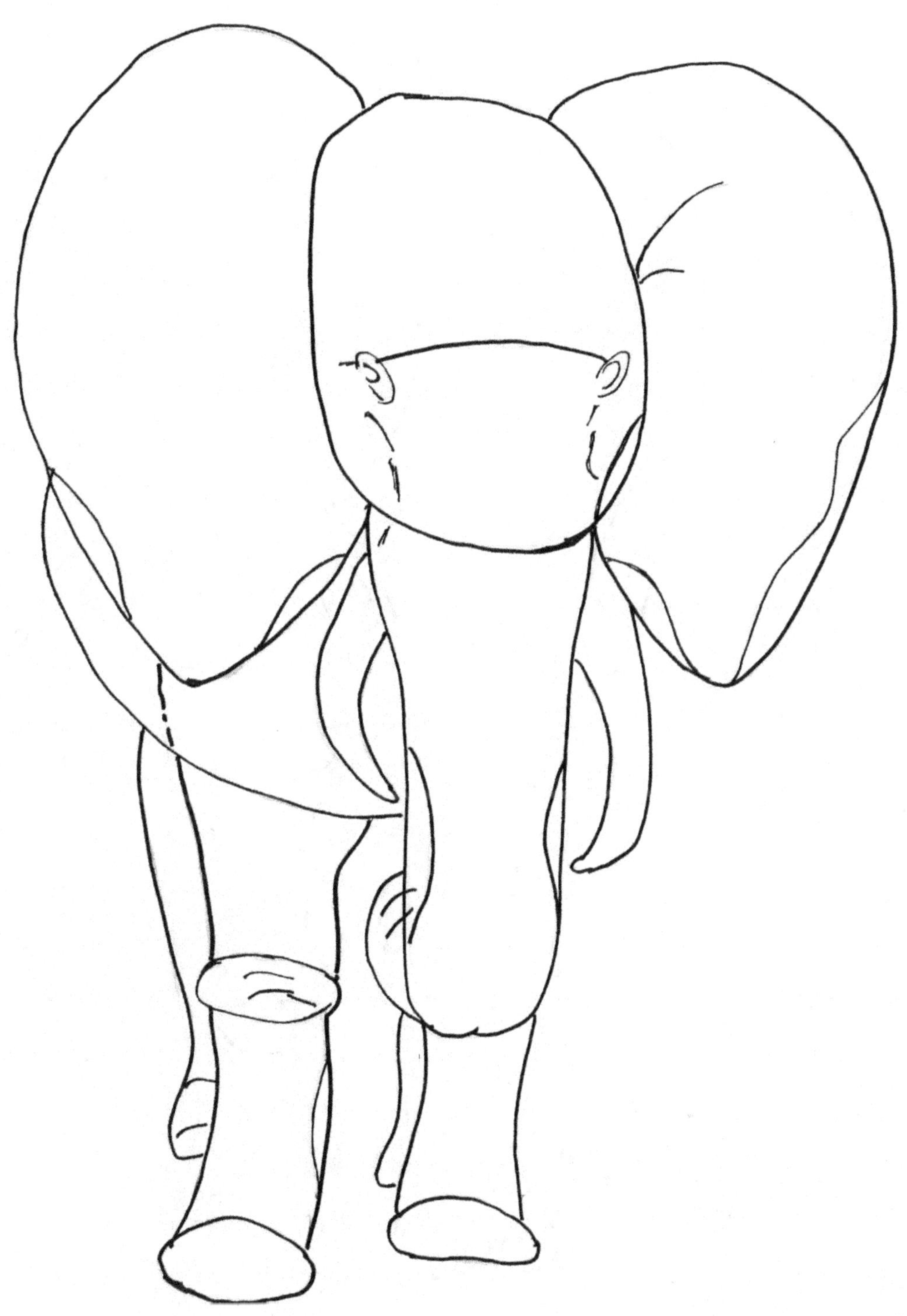

Erase all guidelines and refine
specific details in your artwork.

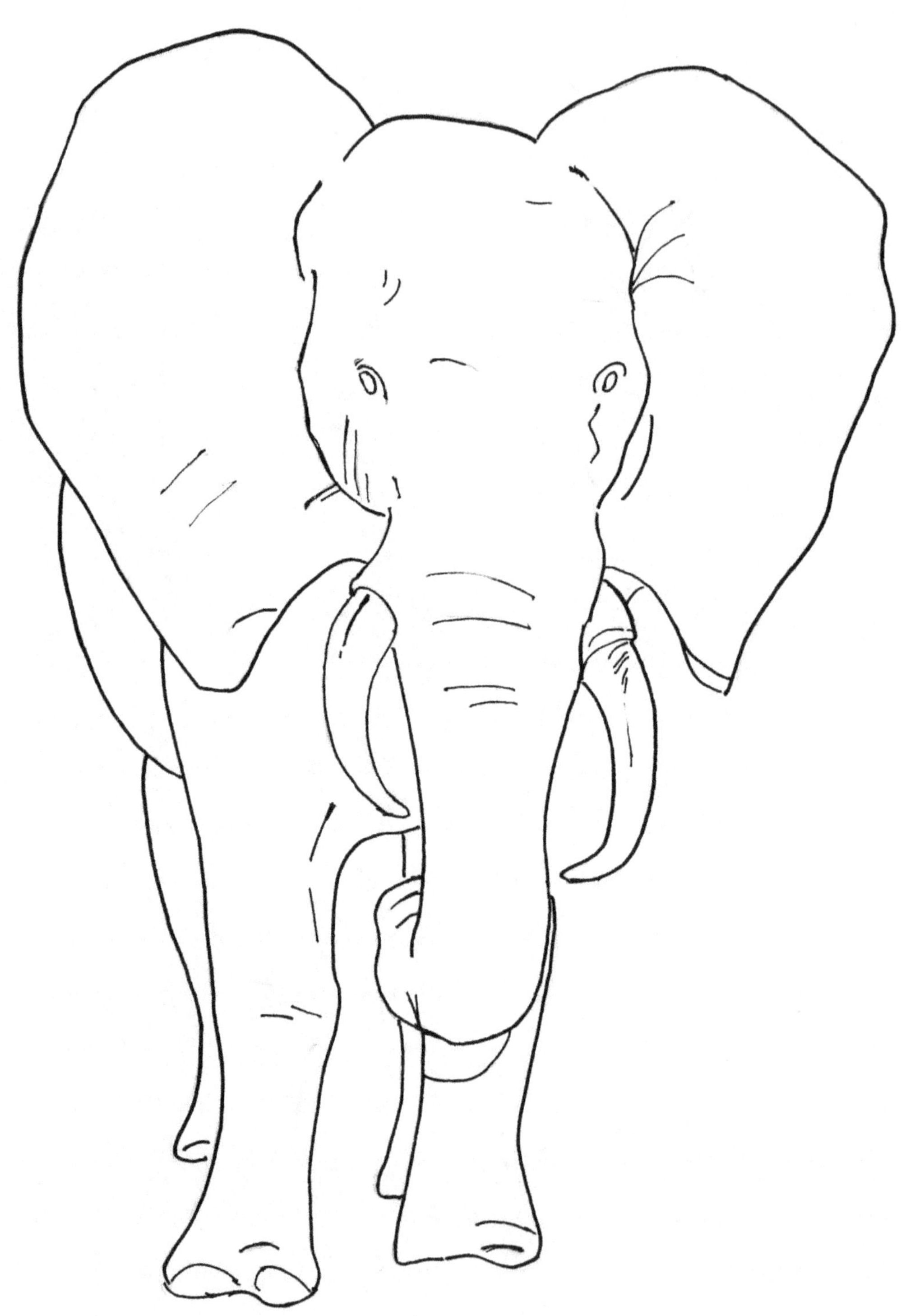

Use your marker or ink pen to draw small edgy
lines to create a 3-D look to your artwork. His
ears are big and he may be sly, but just remember
this elephant can't fly.

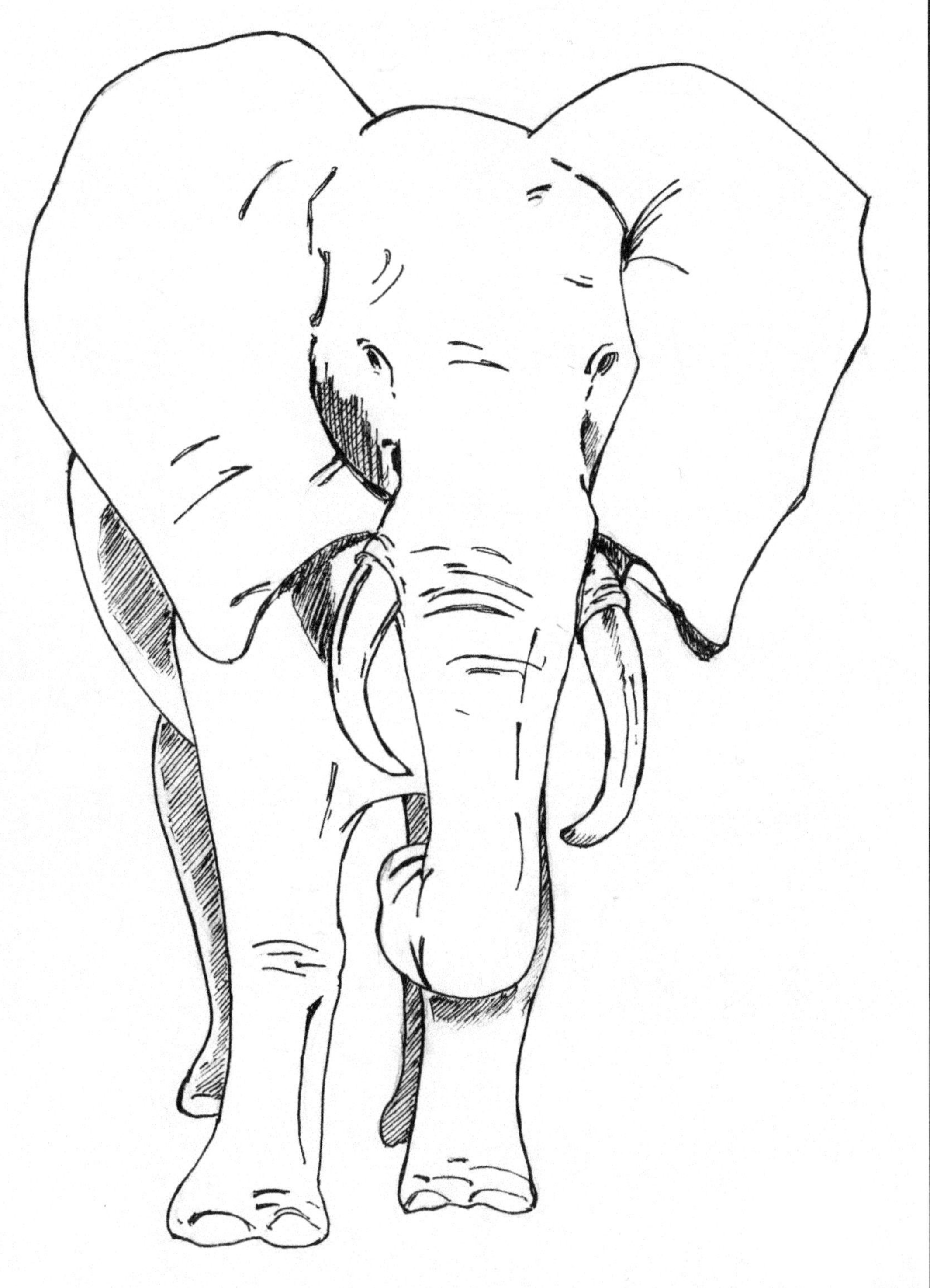

HIPPOPOTAMUS

You can first start drawing the guidelines for the head, neck and oval shape of the body. Then proceed with the legs and feet.

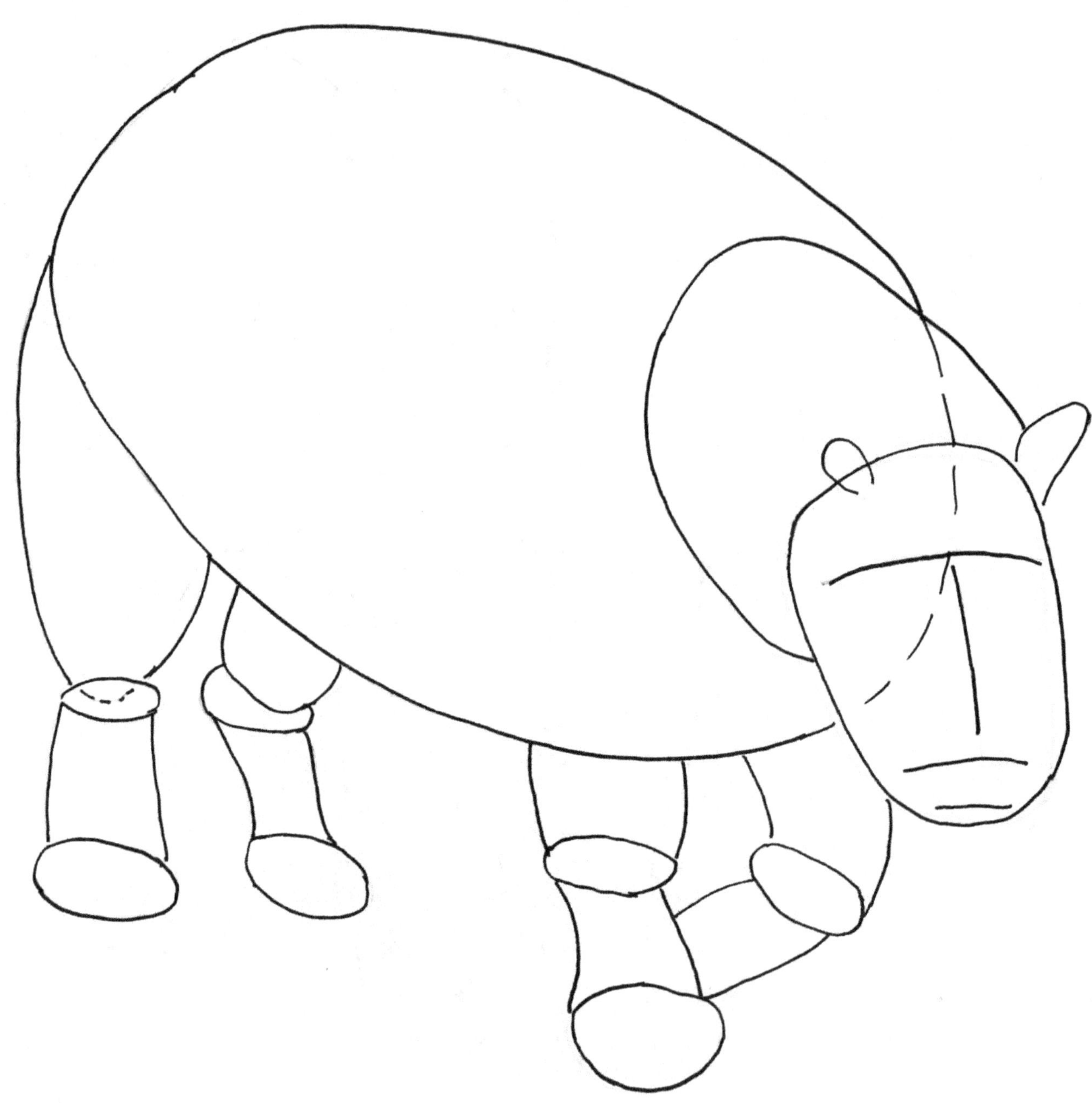

Let's begin shaping the head, face, ears
neck and feet of the Hippo. To create
formality and structure.

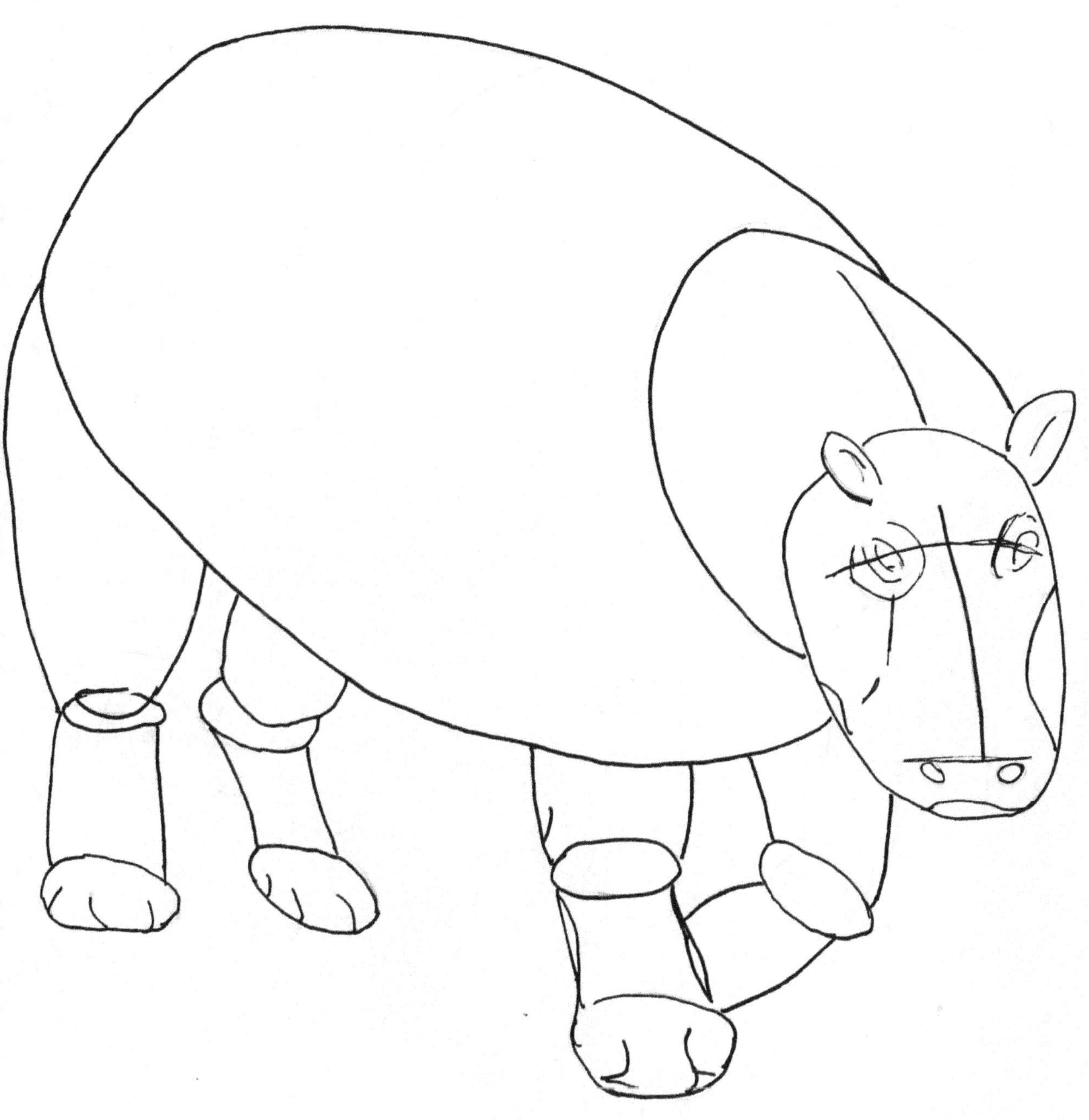

Erase all guidelines. Sketch in small
lines to add more details to the hippo.

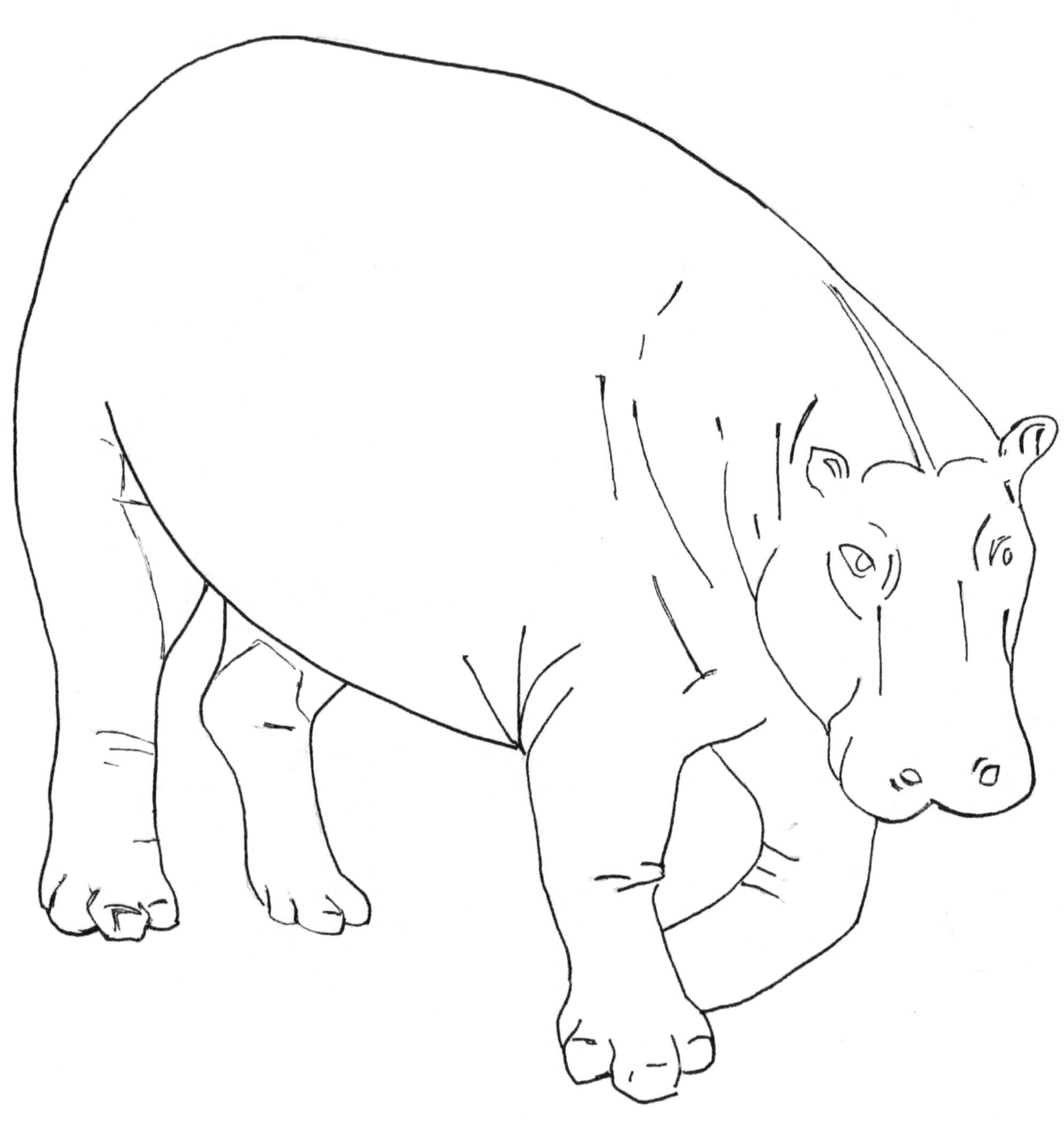

Sketch and shade in more small lines to
create dark and light areas to make for a
dynamic art piece!!

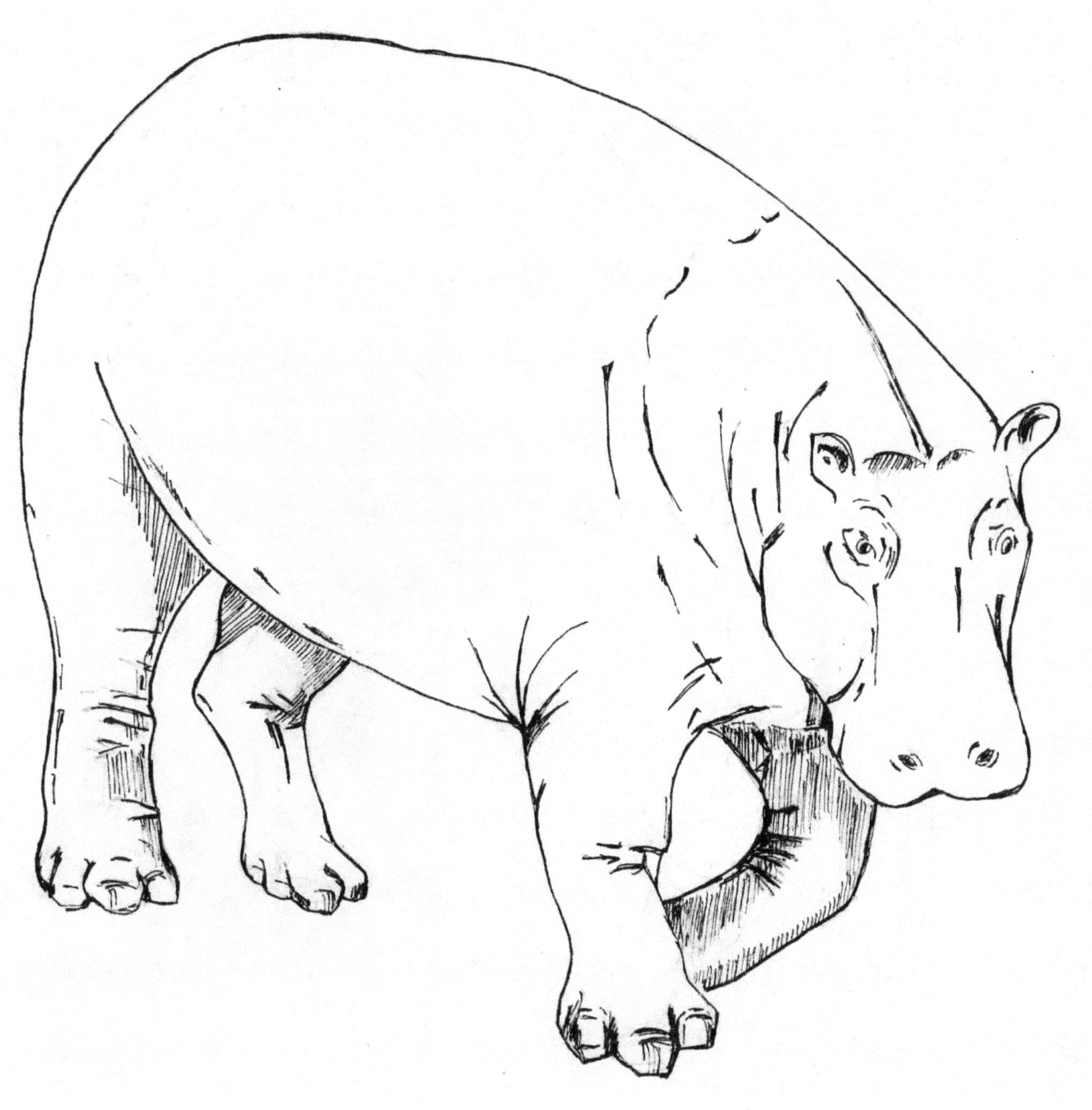

HORSE

As I have shown in the beginning of this book on the "Shapes" page. These drawings are made up with circles, rectangles, triangles and more. Start making this horse by drawing a circle for the head then follow up with the rest of the body.

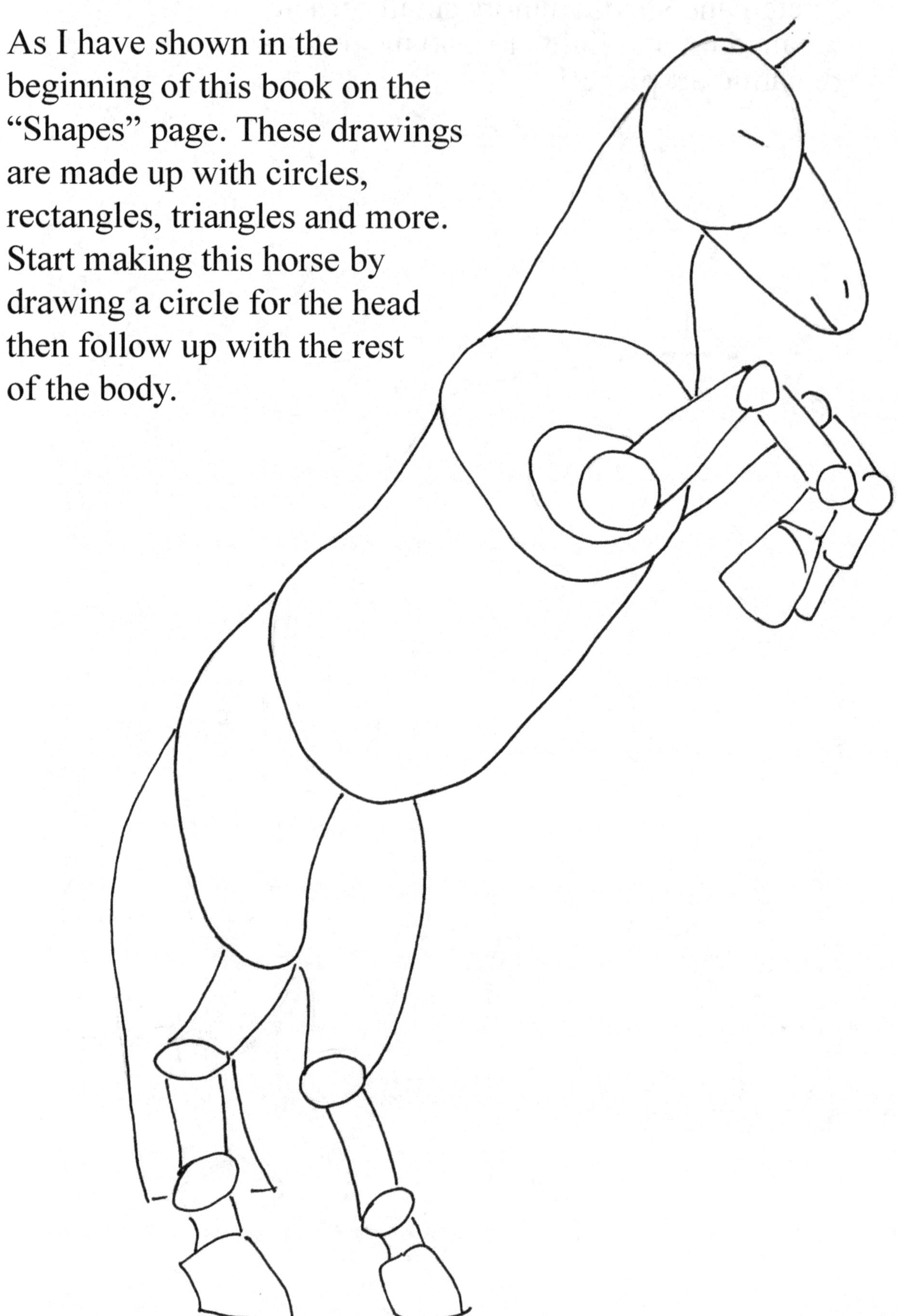

et's begin shaping the head, face, ears
eck and the legs of the Horse.

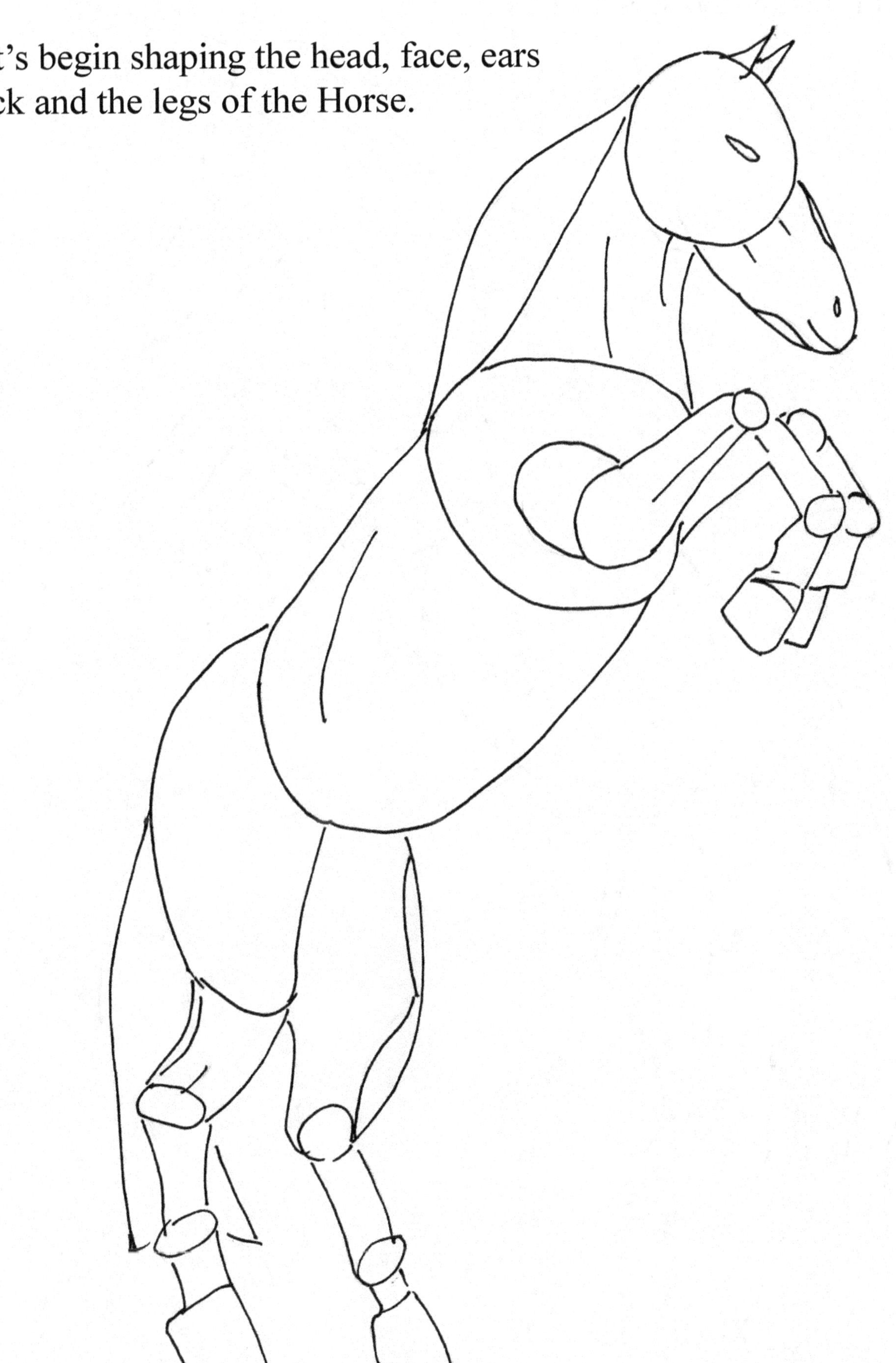

Erase all guidelines and add more
lines for details and structure.

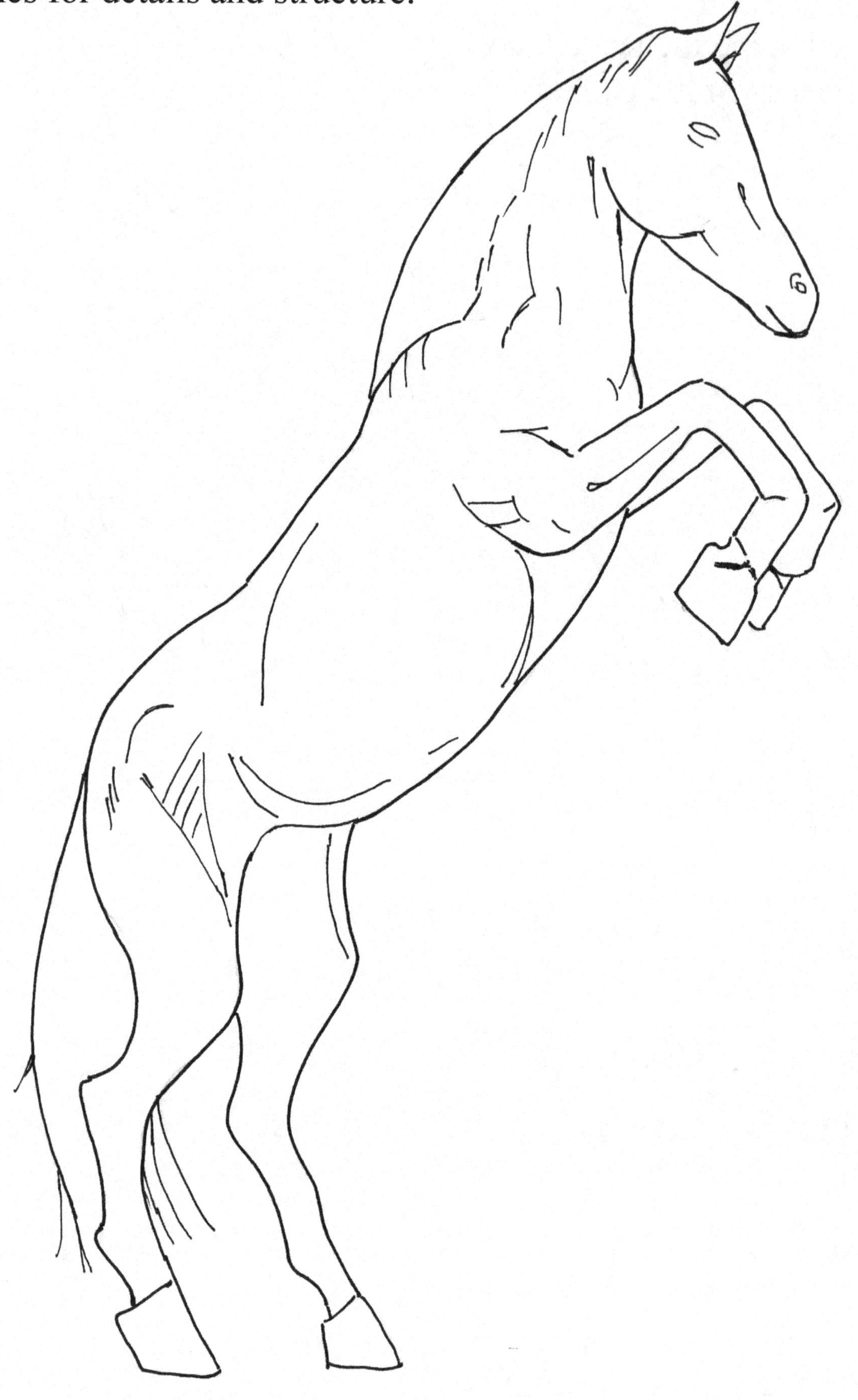

Sketch and shade in more small
lines to create dark and light tones
to make for a spectacular drawing.

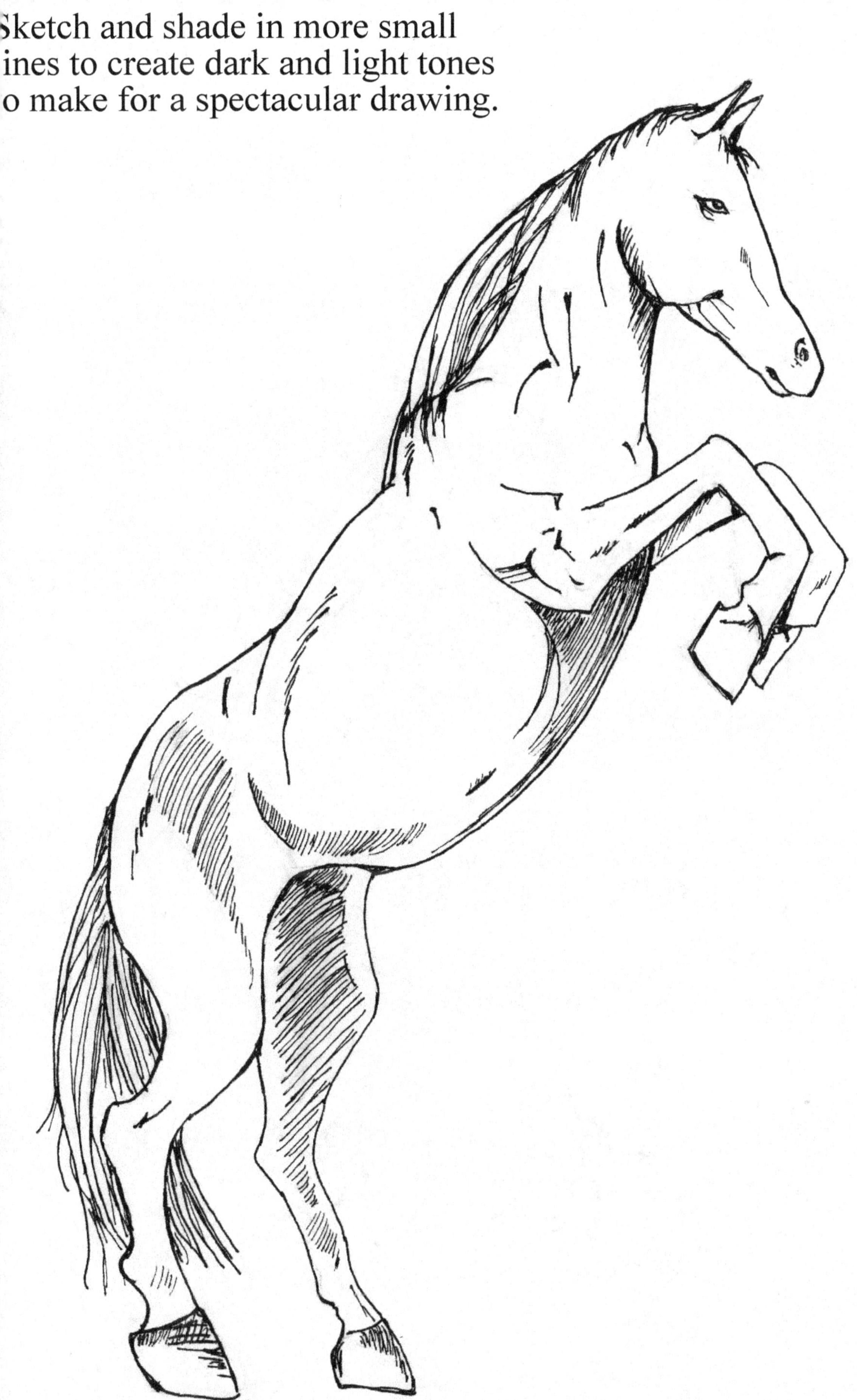

83

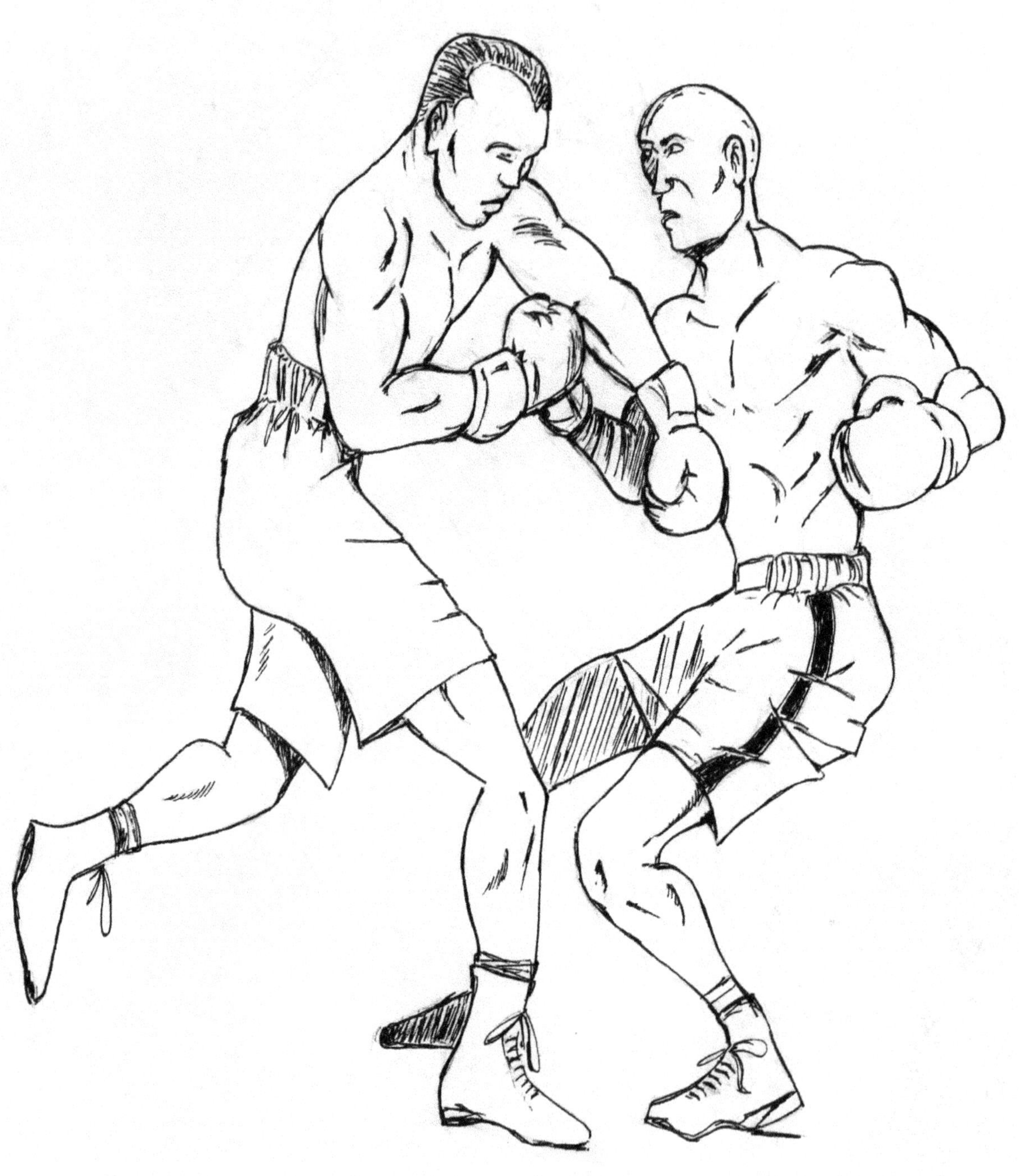

DRAWING SPORTS

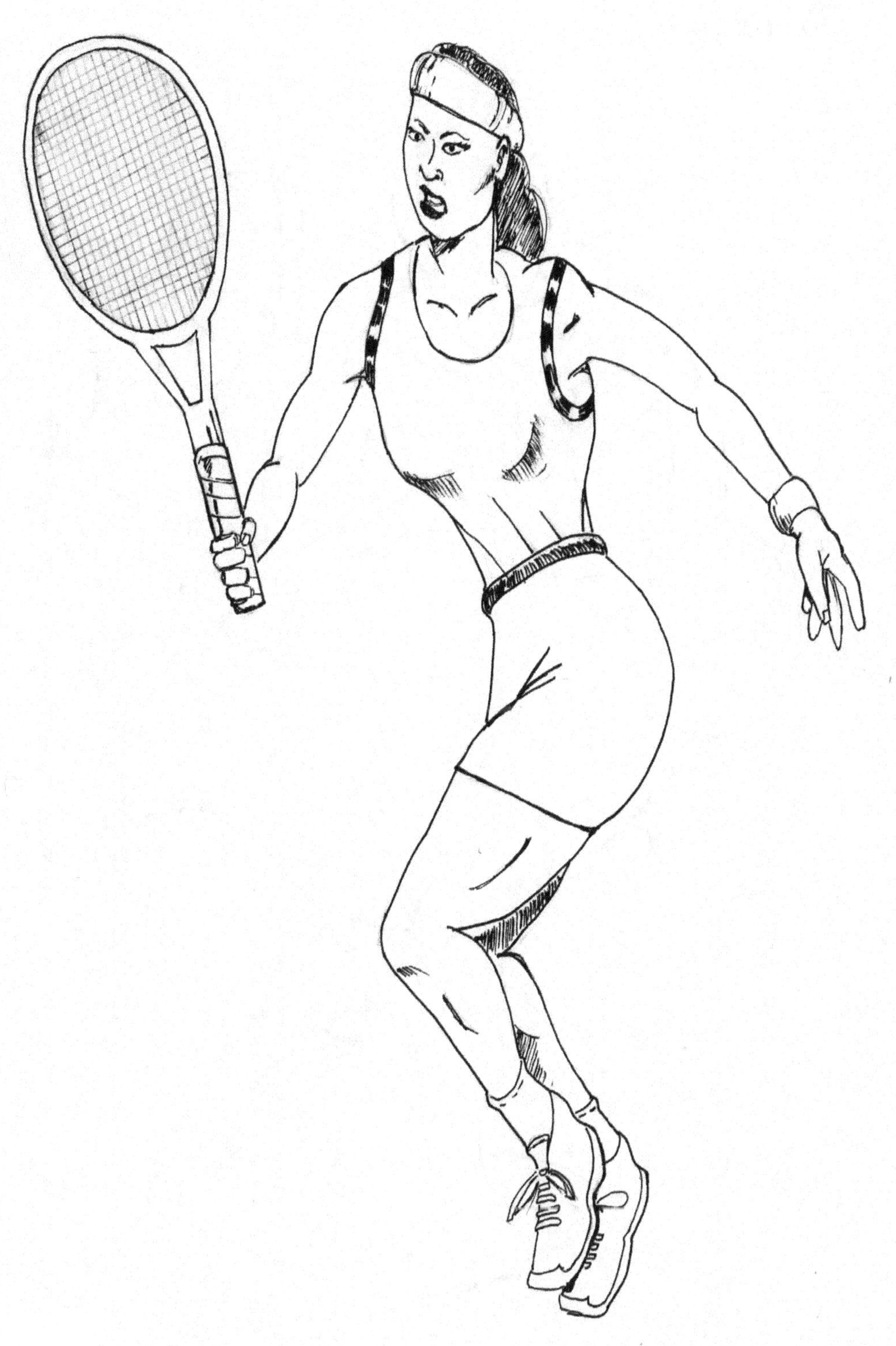

BOXERS

Draw these two human figures which consist mainly of oval and rectangle shapes. Start with the figure on the left, then proceed to draw guidelines for the head. Next draw in the neck, shoulder and torso. Work your way down to the legs and feet. Then start drawing the figure on the right.

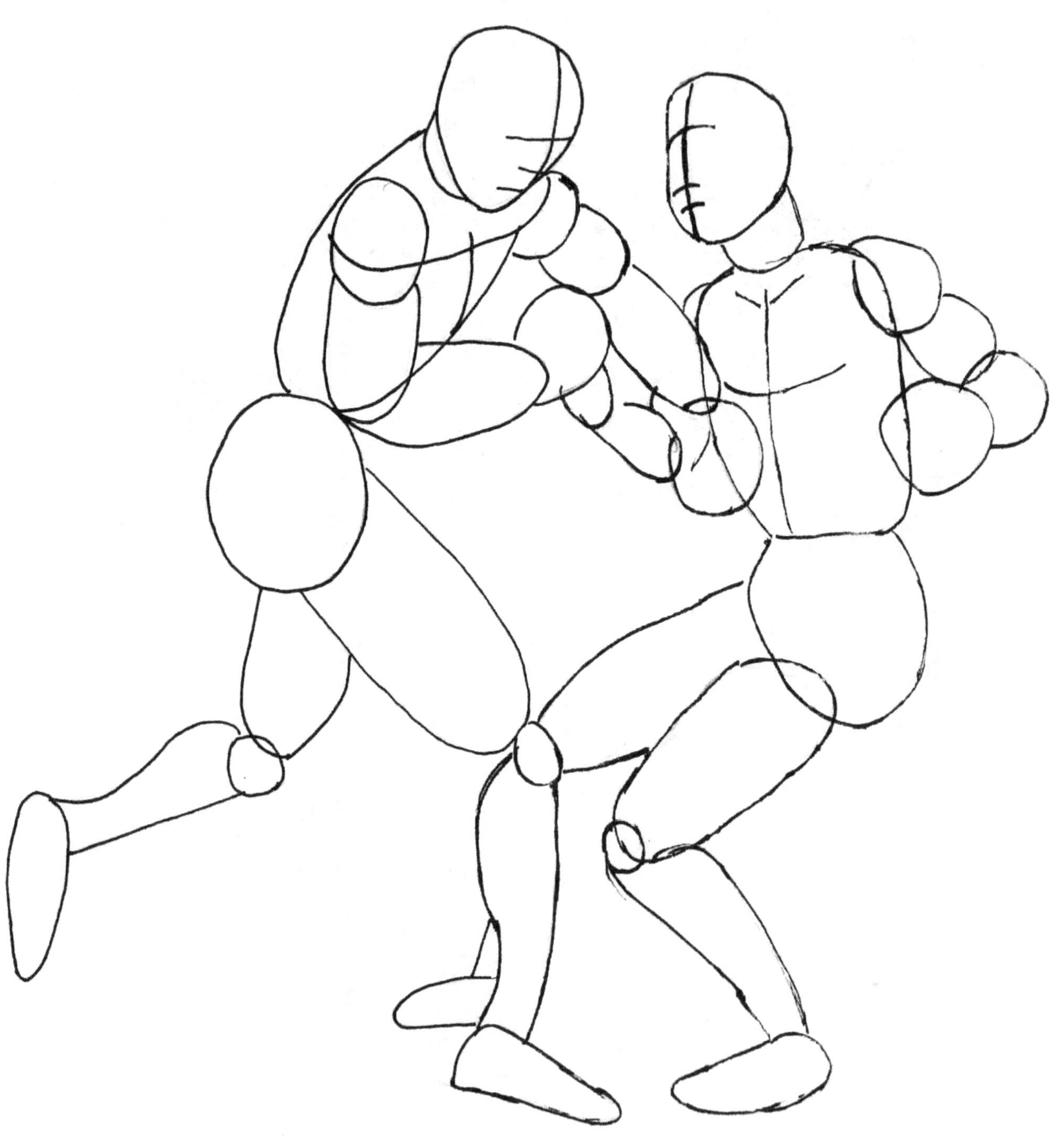

Let's form the face on both boxers as well as the boxing gloves, shape the arms, and the torso.

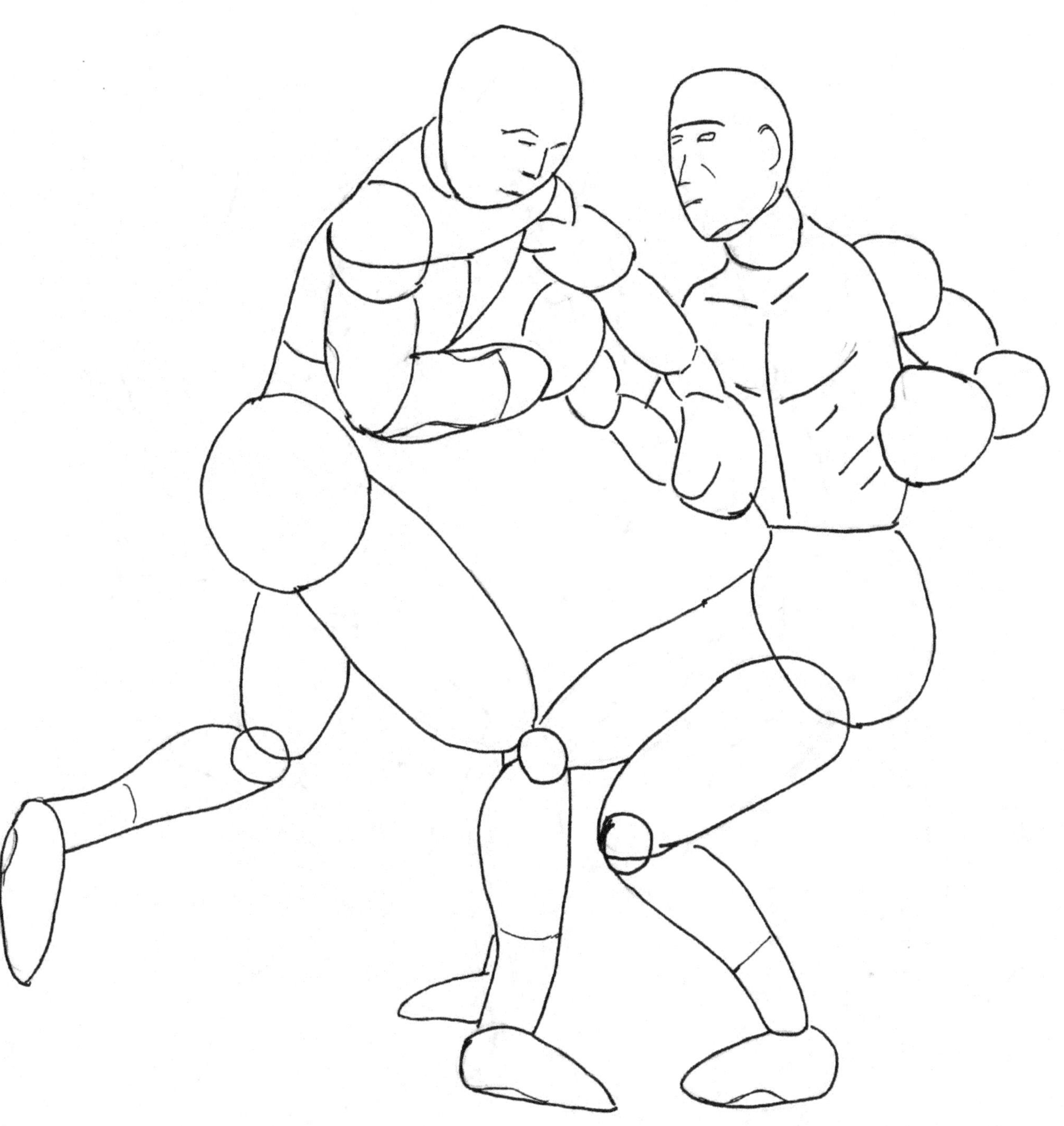

Erase all the guidelines and then draw more
lines for details and structure for both boxers.

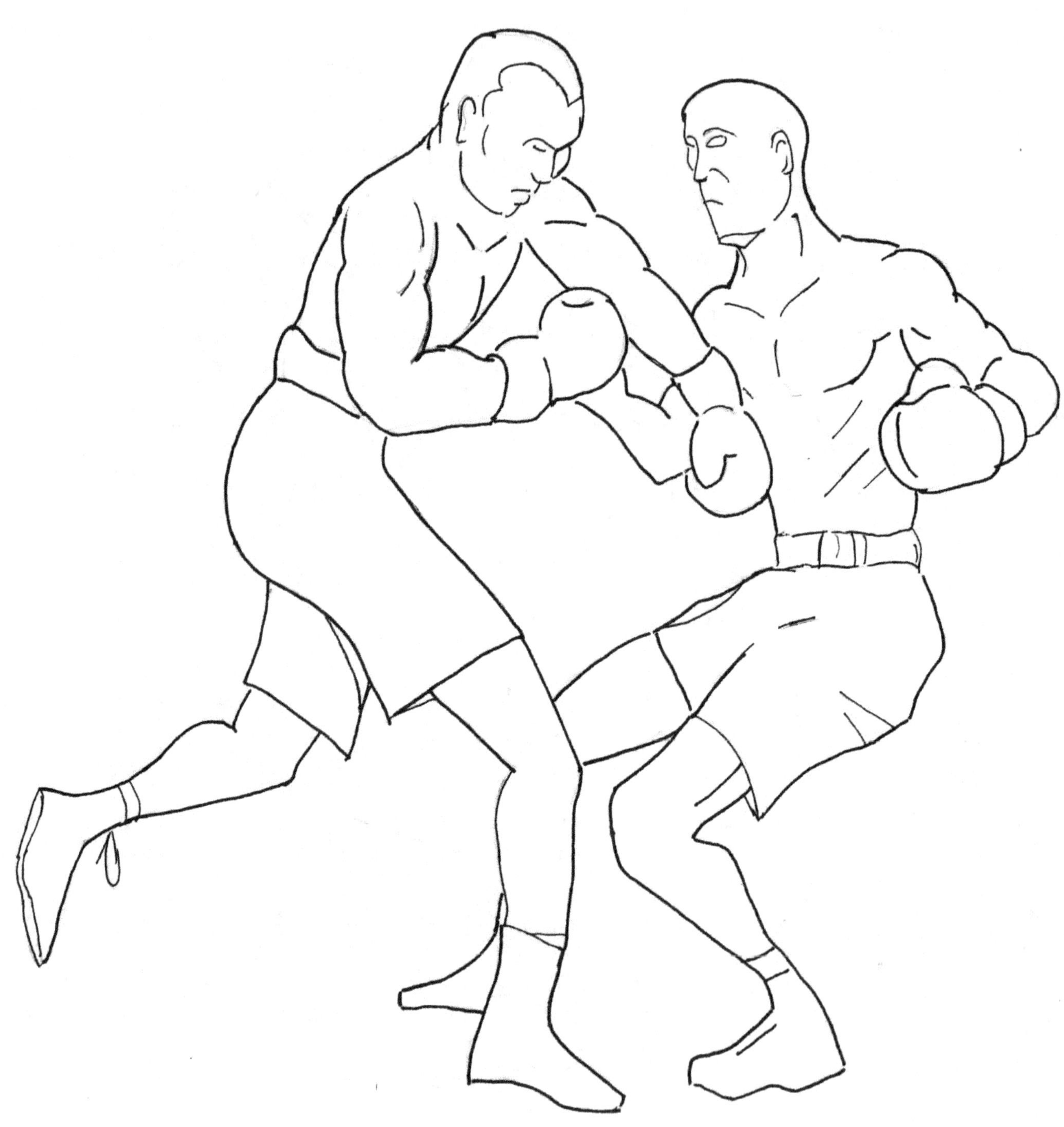

Now, let's draw in the black strip on the balded headed boxer's trunks, add the lights, darks and shadows to both boxers and you're done! What a picture!

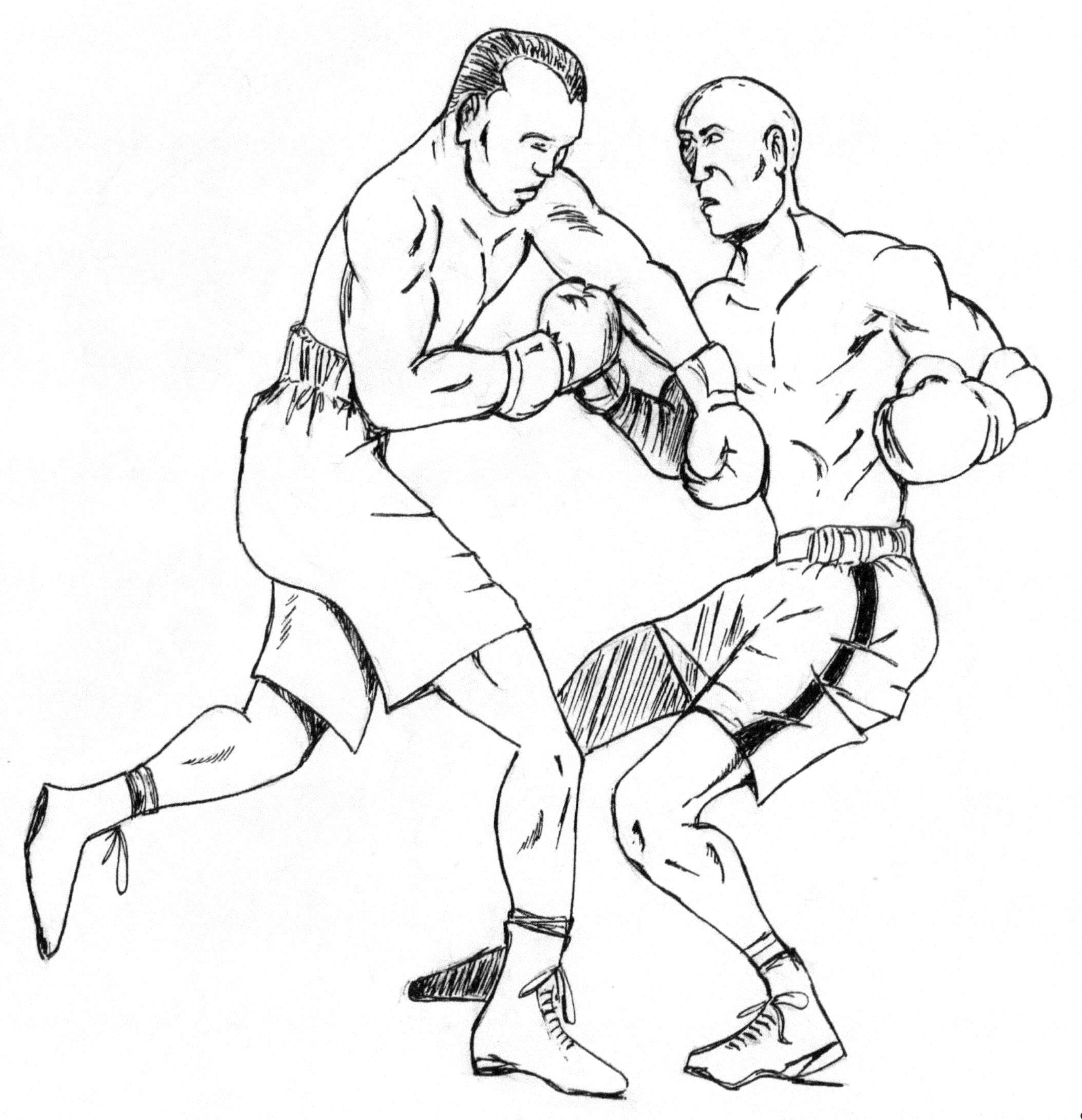

TENNIS LADY

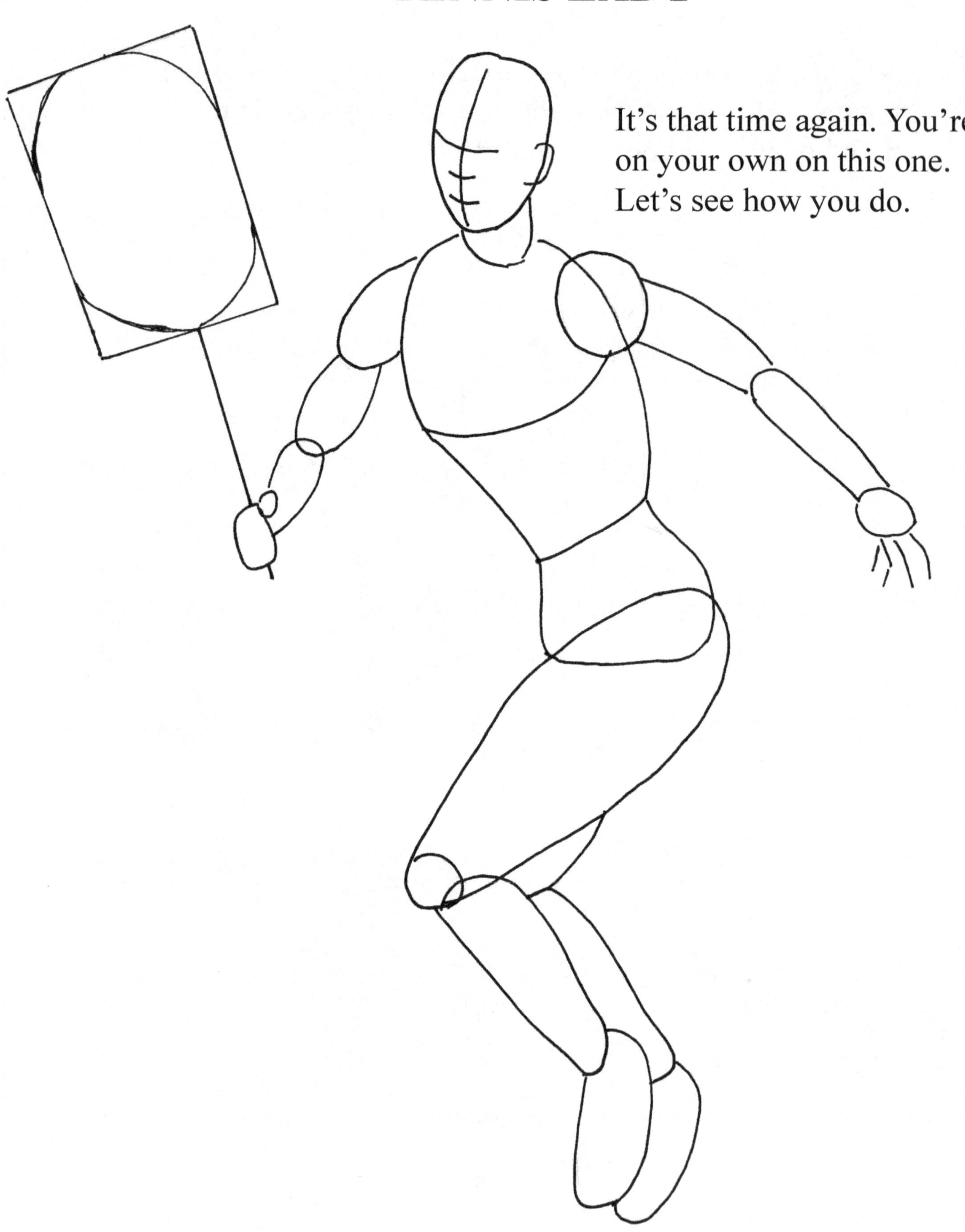

It's that time again. You're on your own on this one. Let's see how you do.

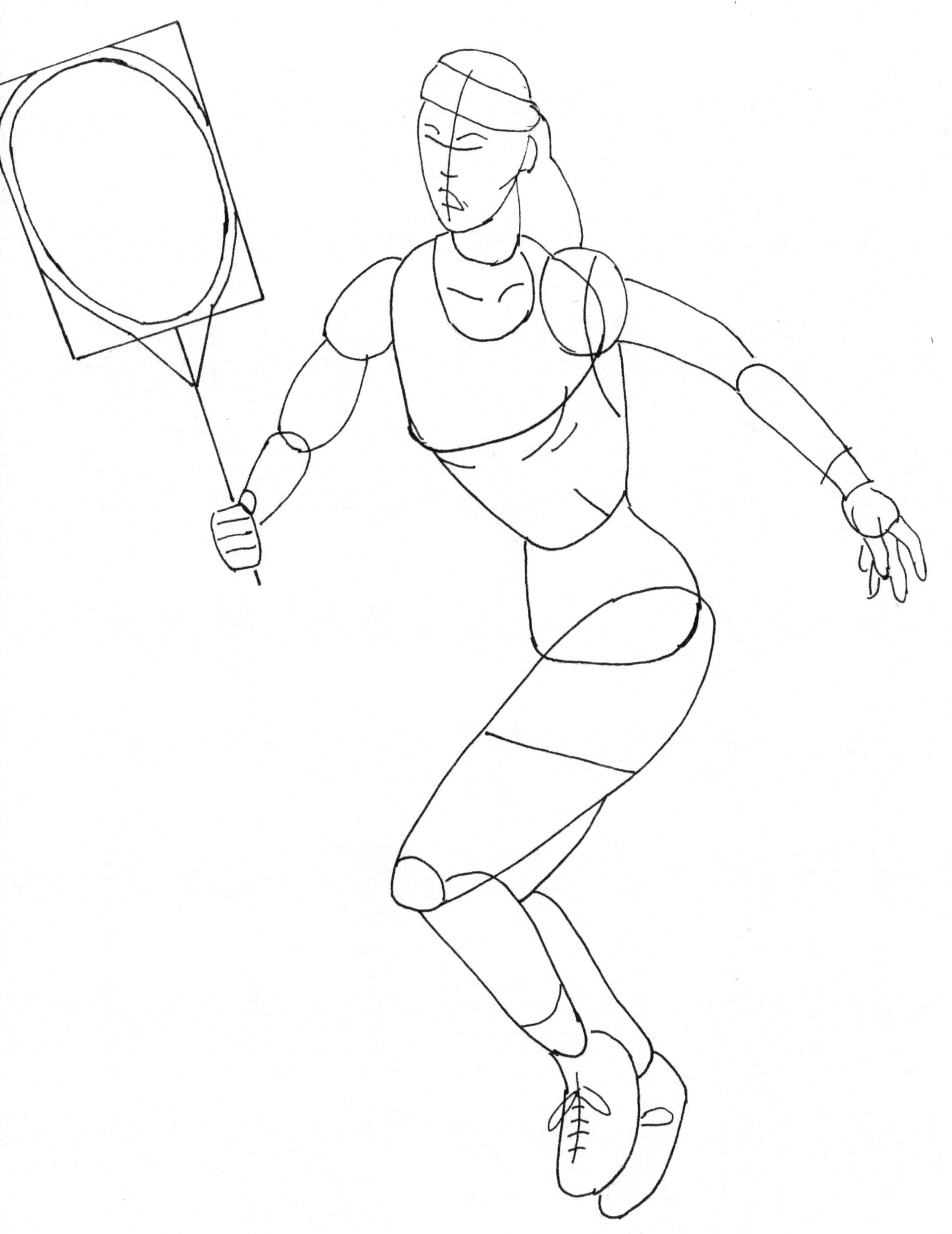

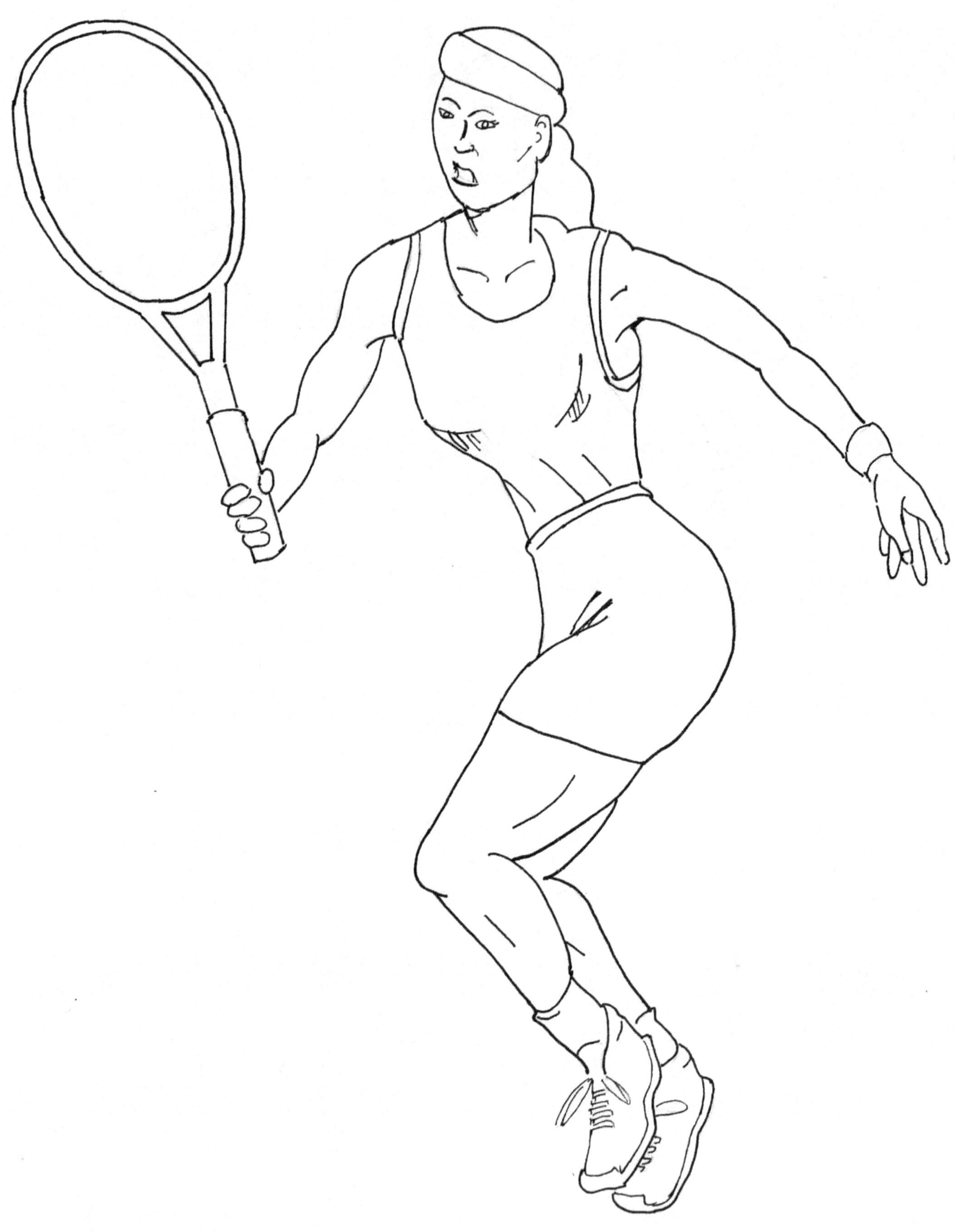

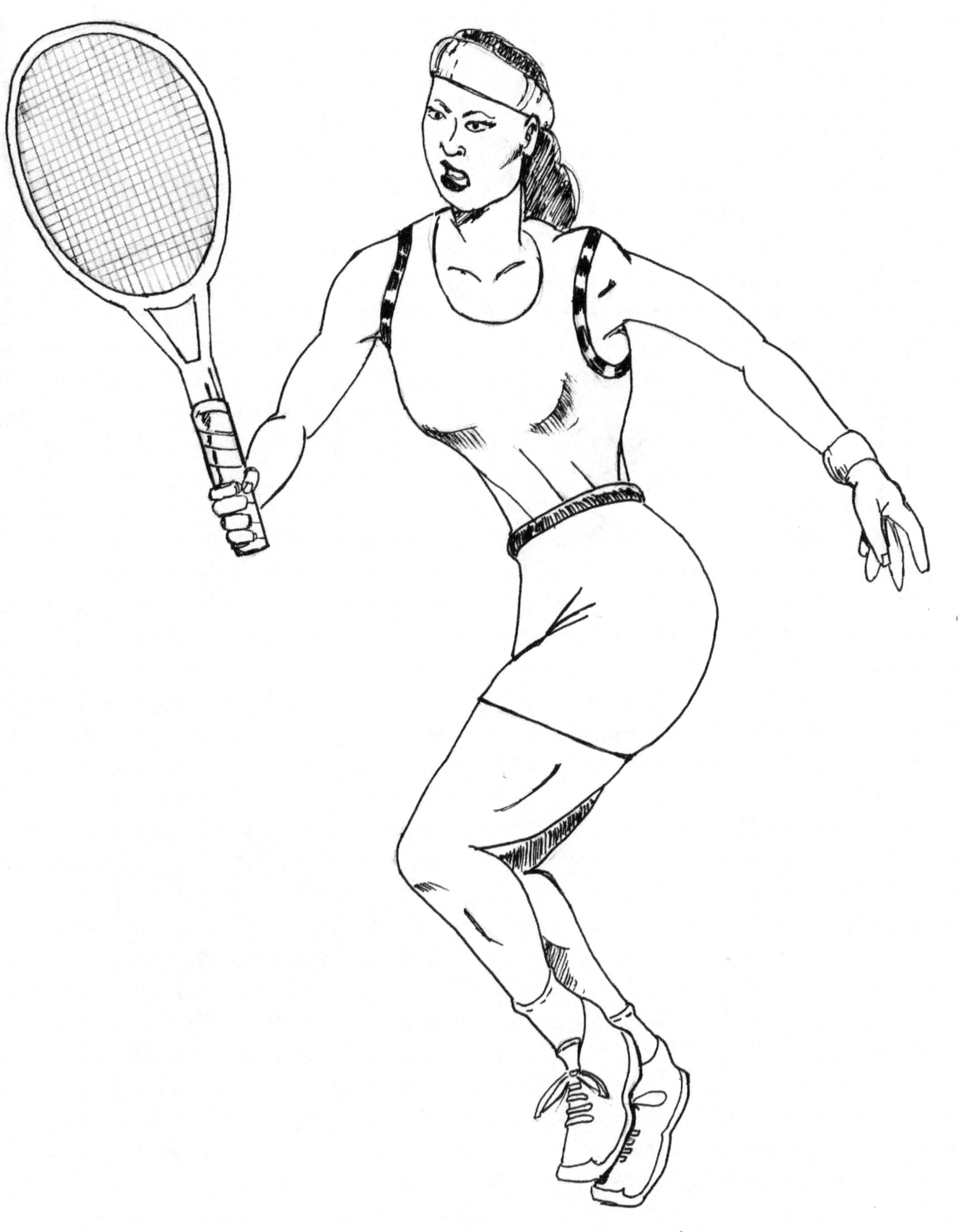

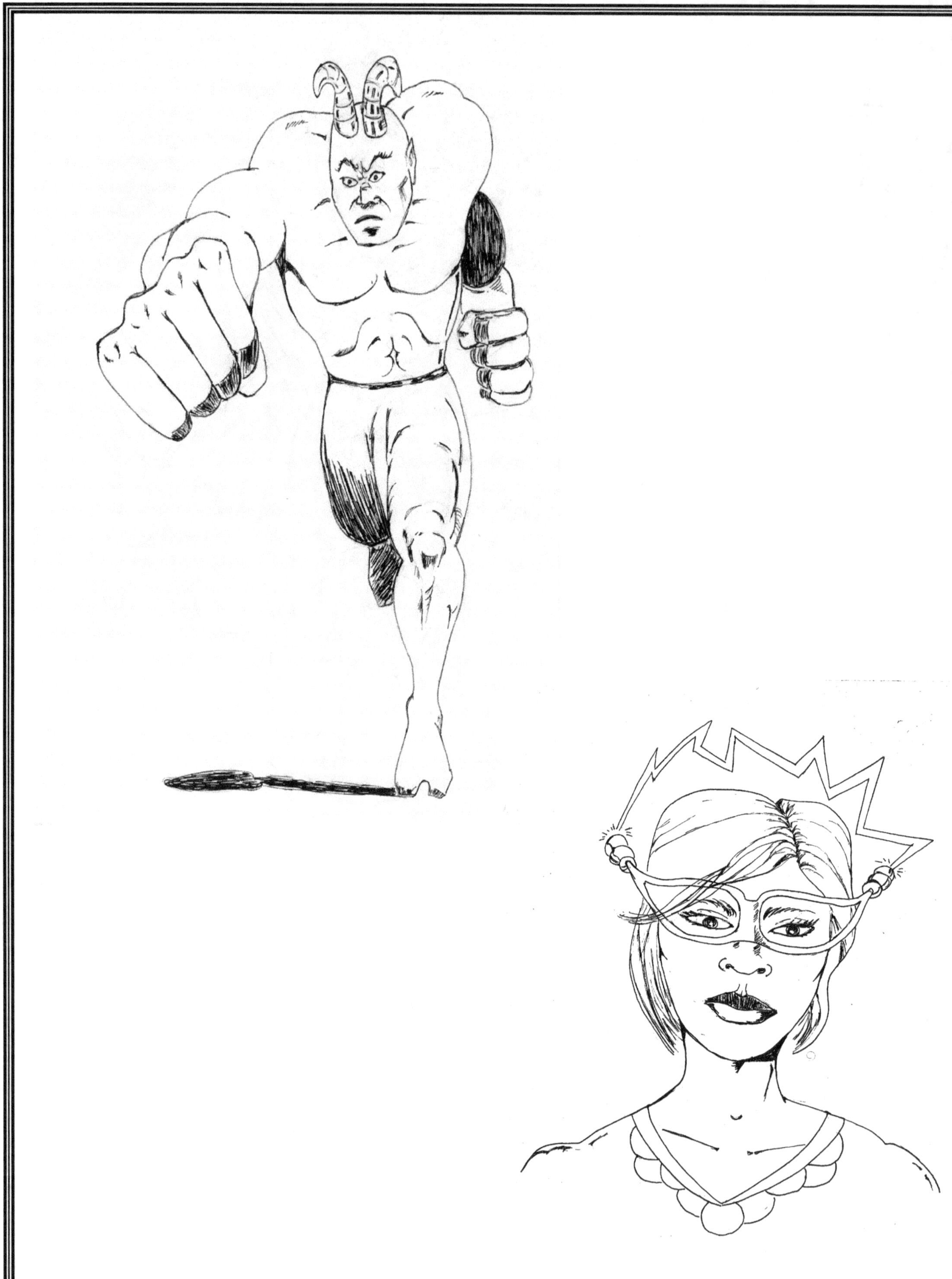

DRAWING SUPERCHARACTERS

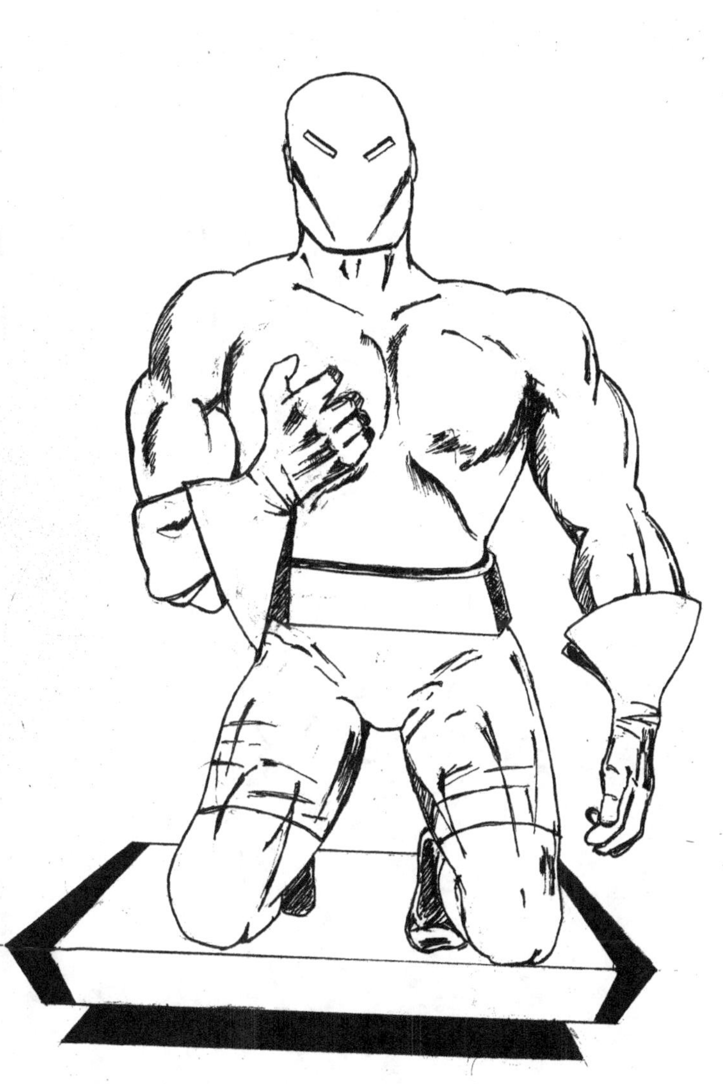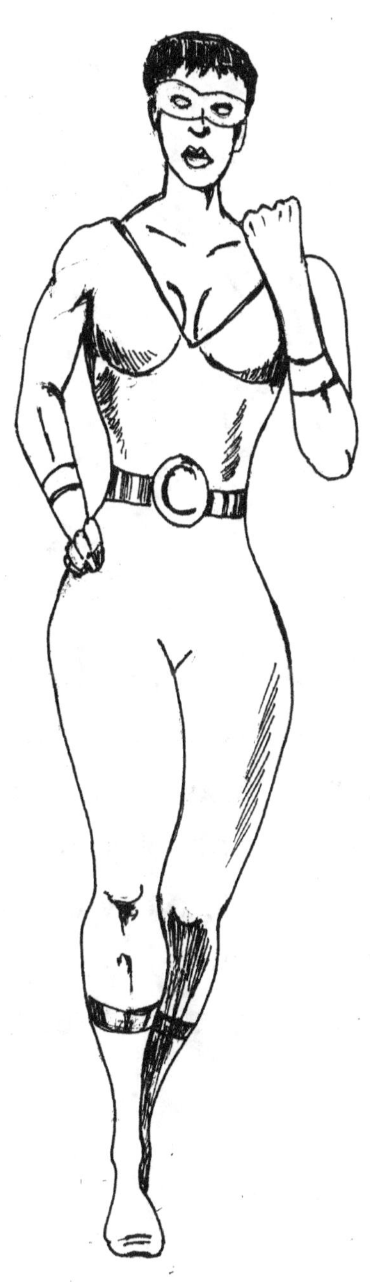

RAM-MAN

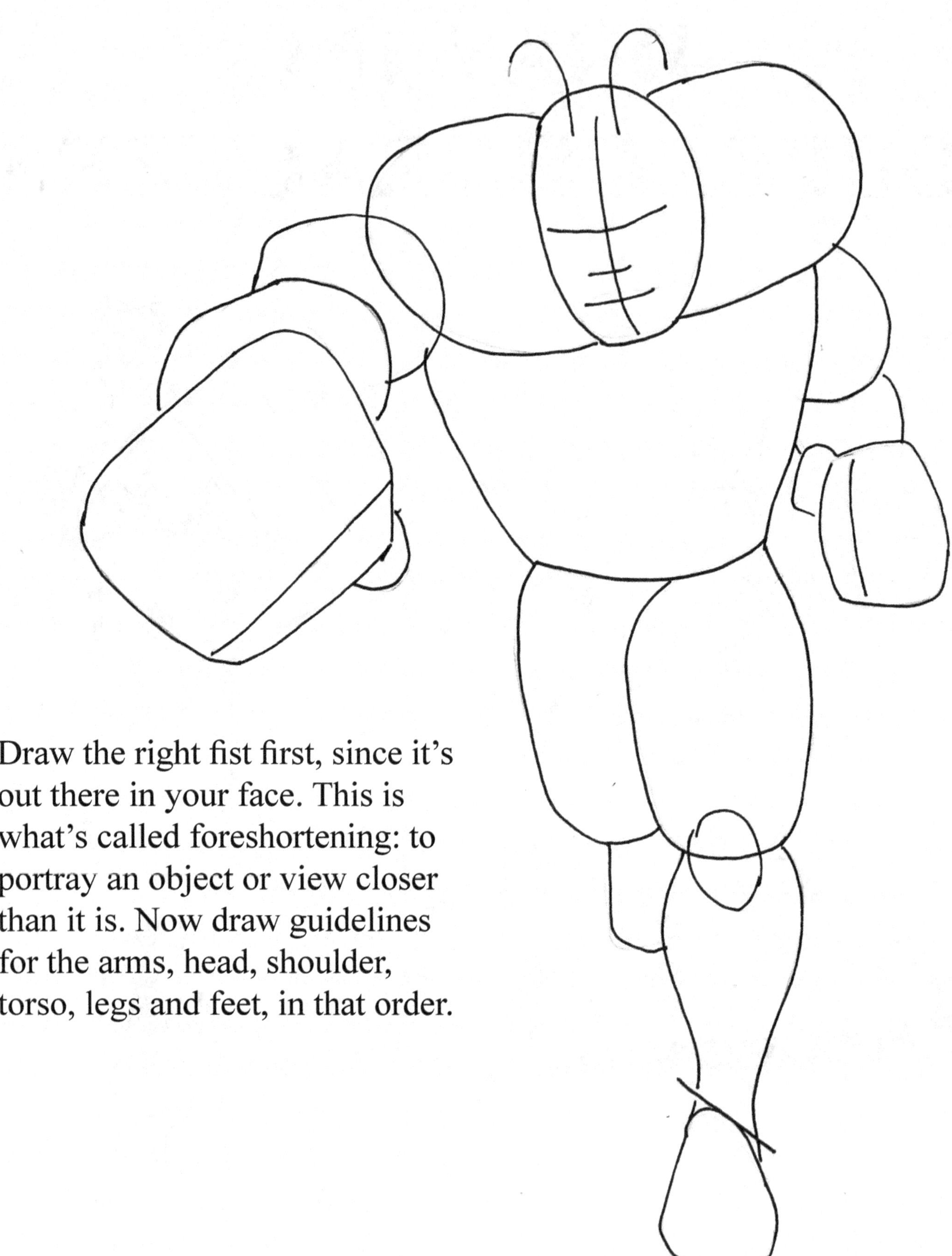

Draw the right fist first, since it's out there in your face. This is what's called foreshortening: to portray an object or view closer than it is. Now draw guidelines for the arms, head, shoulder, torso, legs and feet, in that order.

Put in more details by
drawing the horns, eyes,
nose, mouth, chest, rib cage,
fists, ankles and feet.

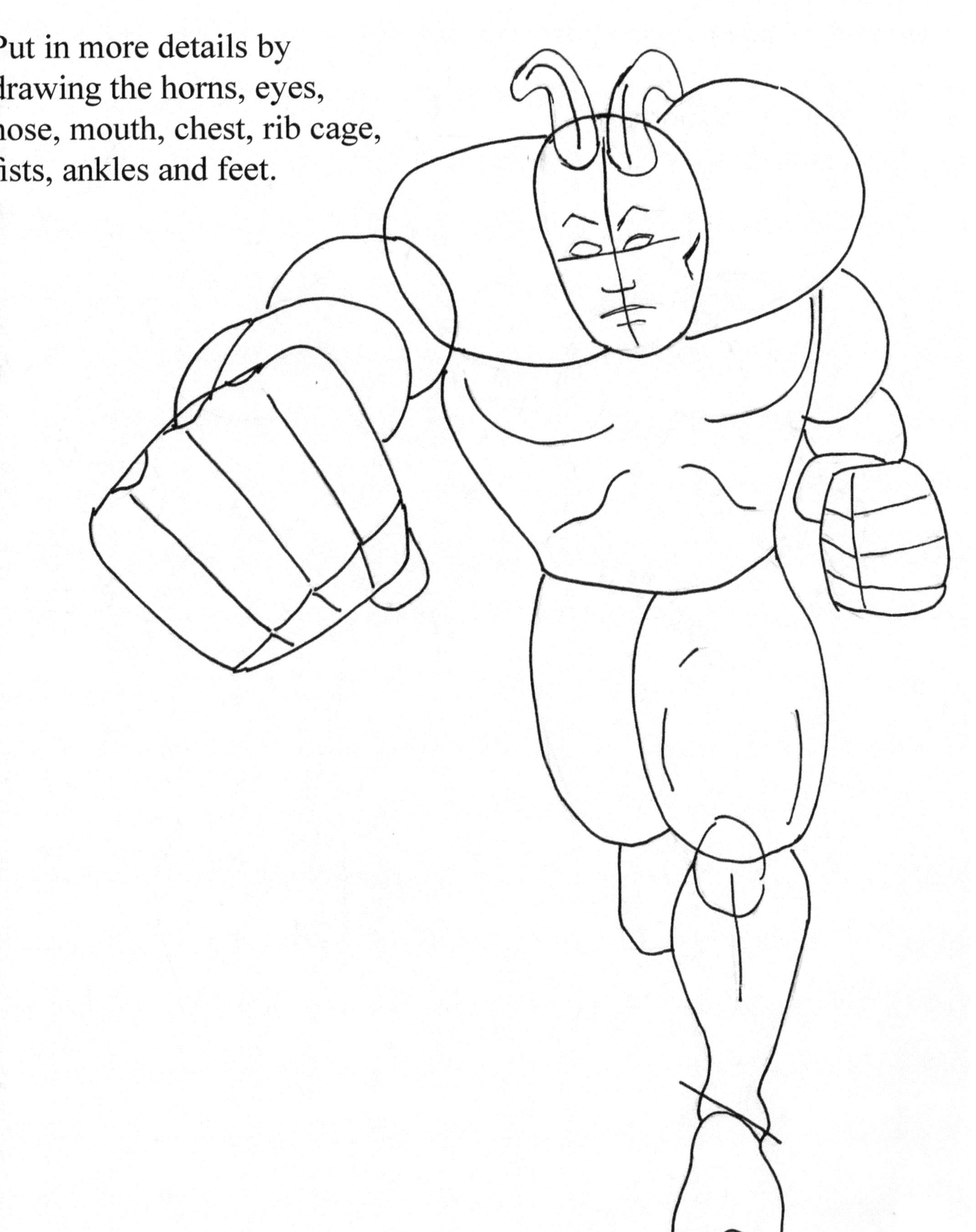

Erase all the guidelines and draw in more details to your entire drawing. I wouldn't grab this guy by the horns.

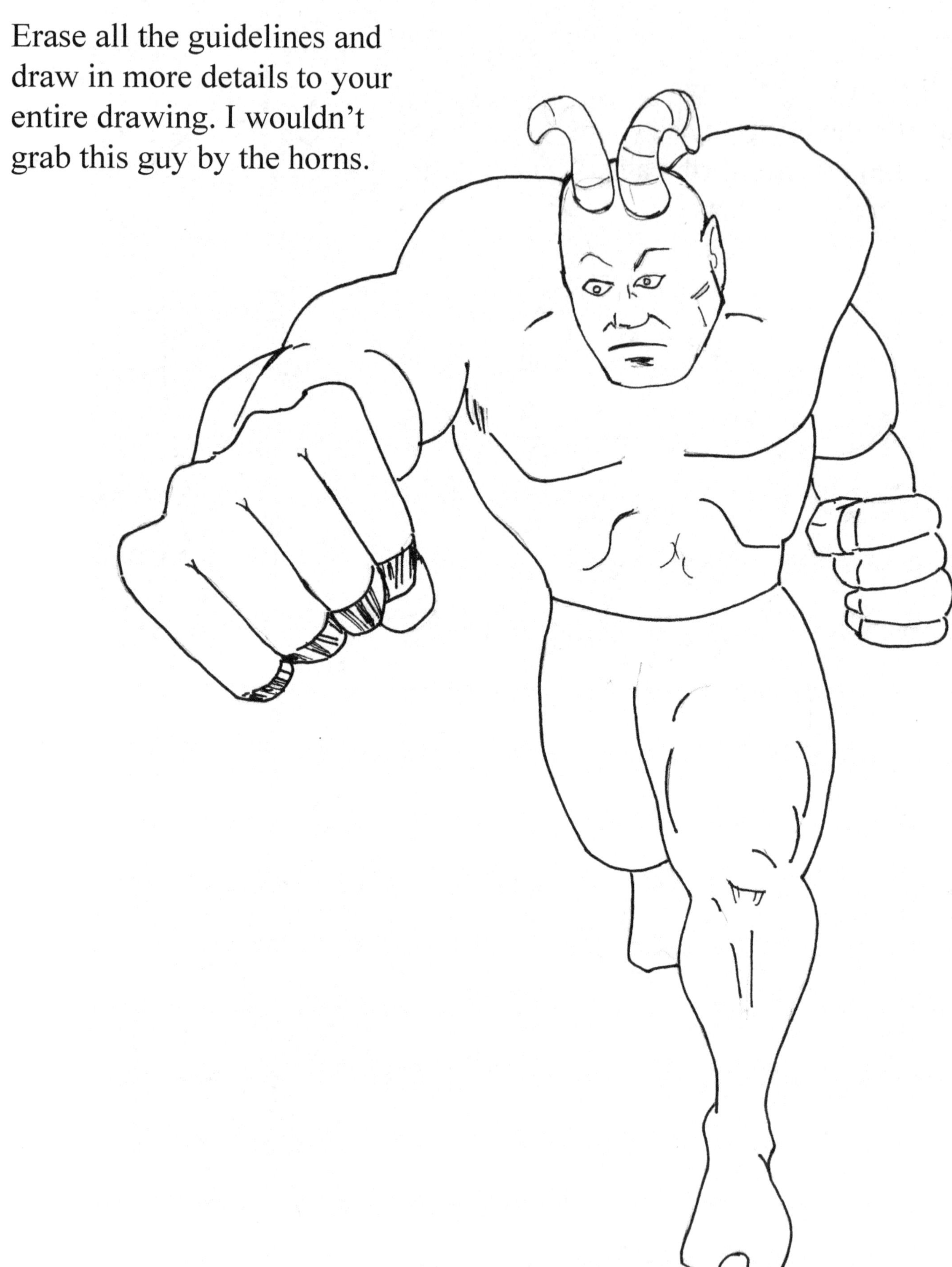

Sketch in details of the horns, fist, torso, and the rest of the body. Shade in your dark and light areas to complete your awesome artwork.

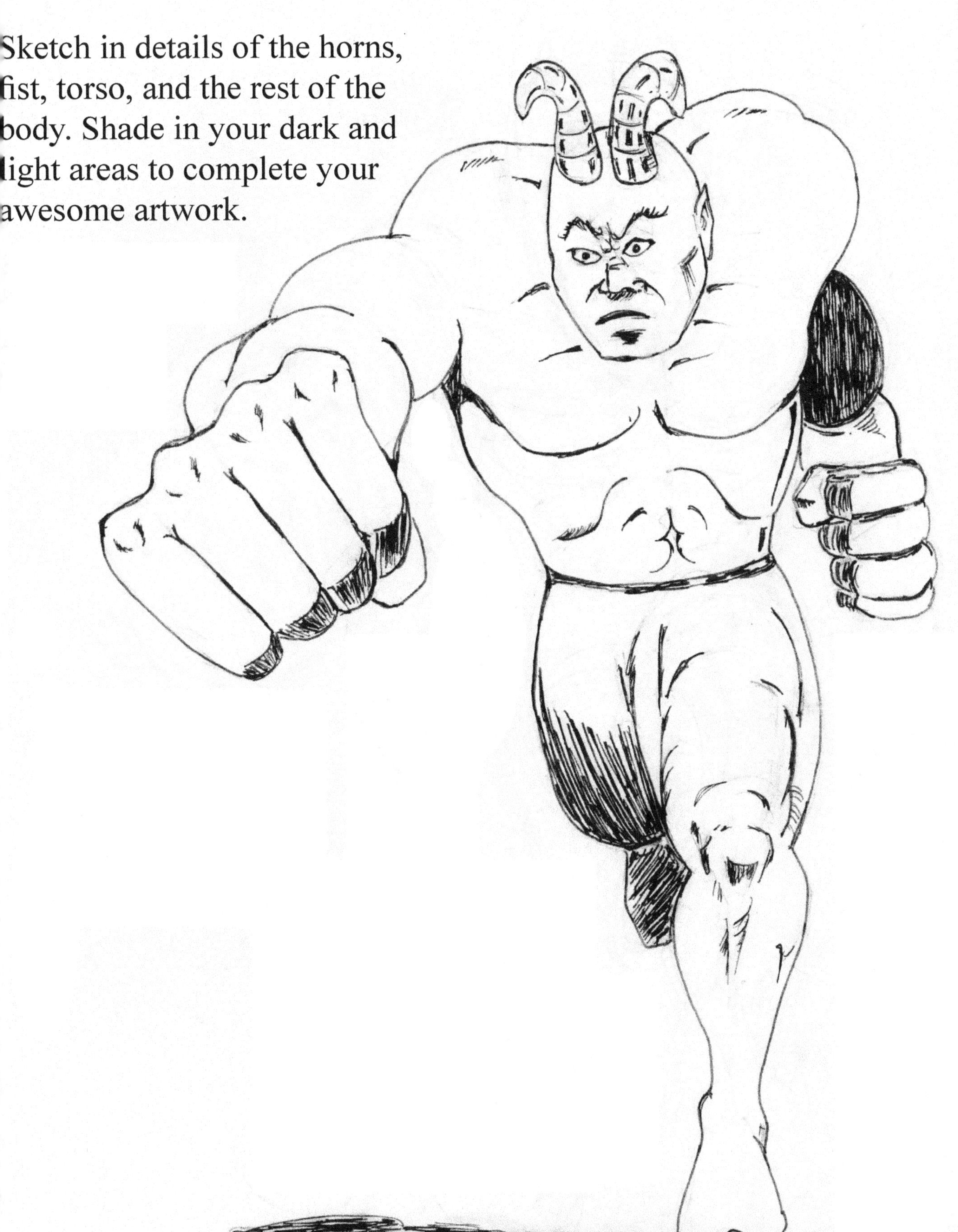

SPACE EYEGLASS LADY

Draw a egg type form for the head, then place guidelines to indicate where the eyes, nose and mouth will be drawn.

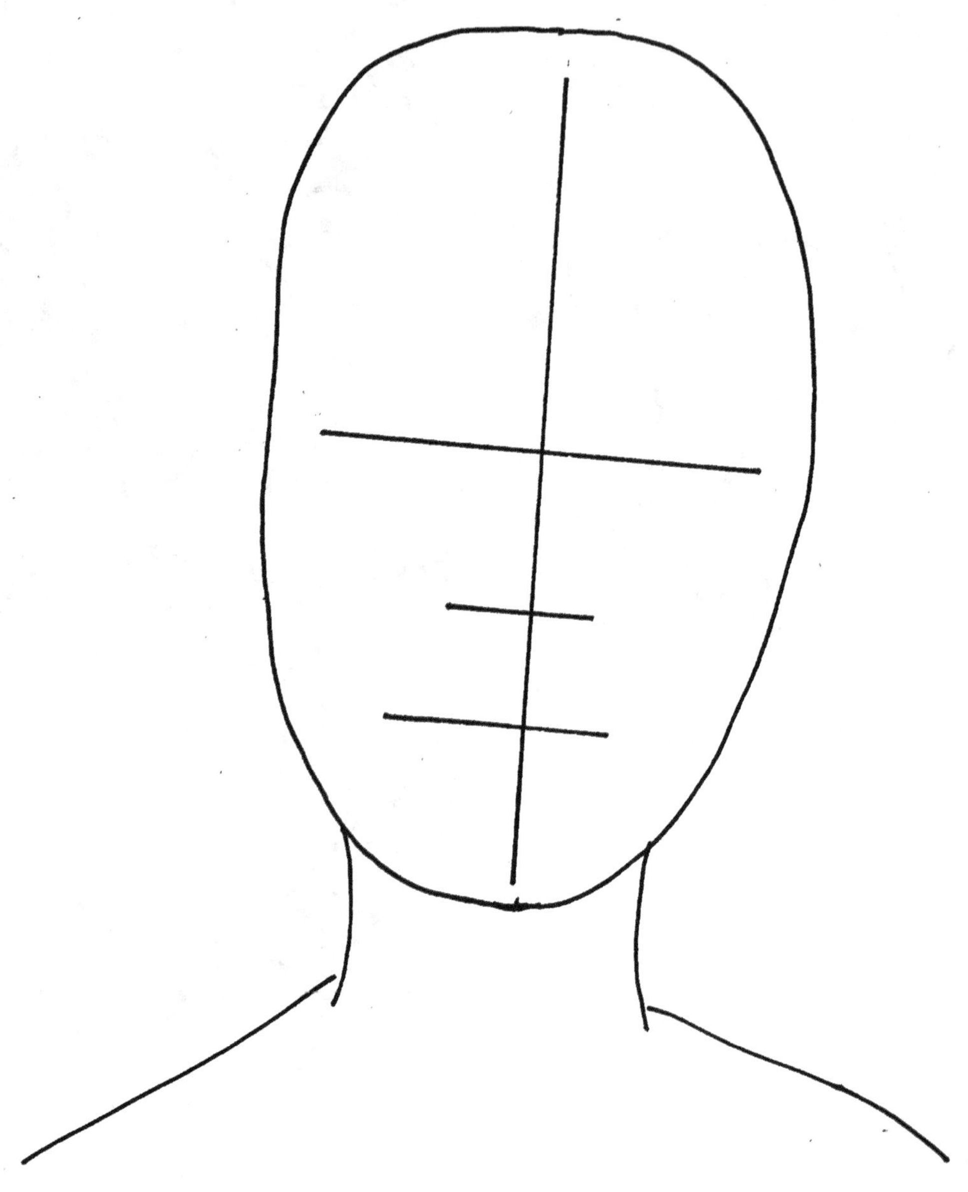

Now let's sketch guidelines for the hair, space glasses, and give more details to the eyes, nose, and mouth. Draw the neck and partial shoulders.

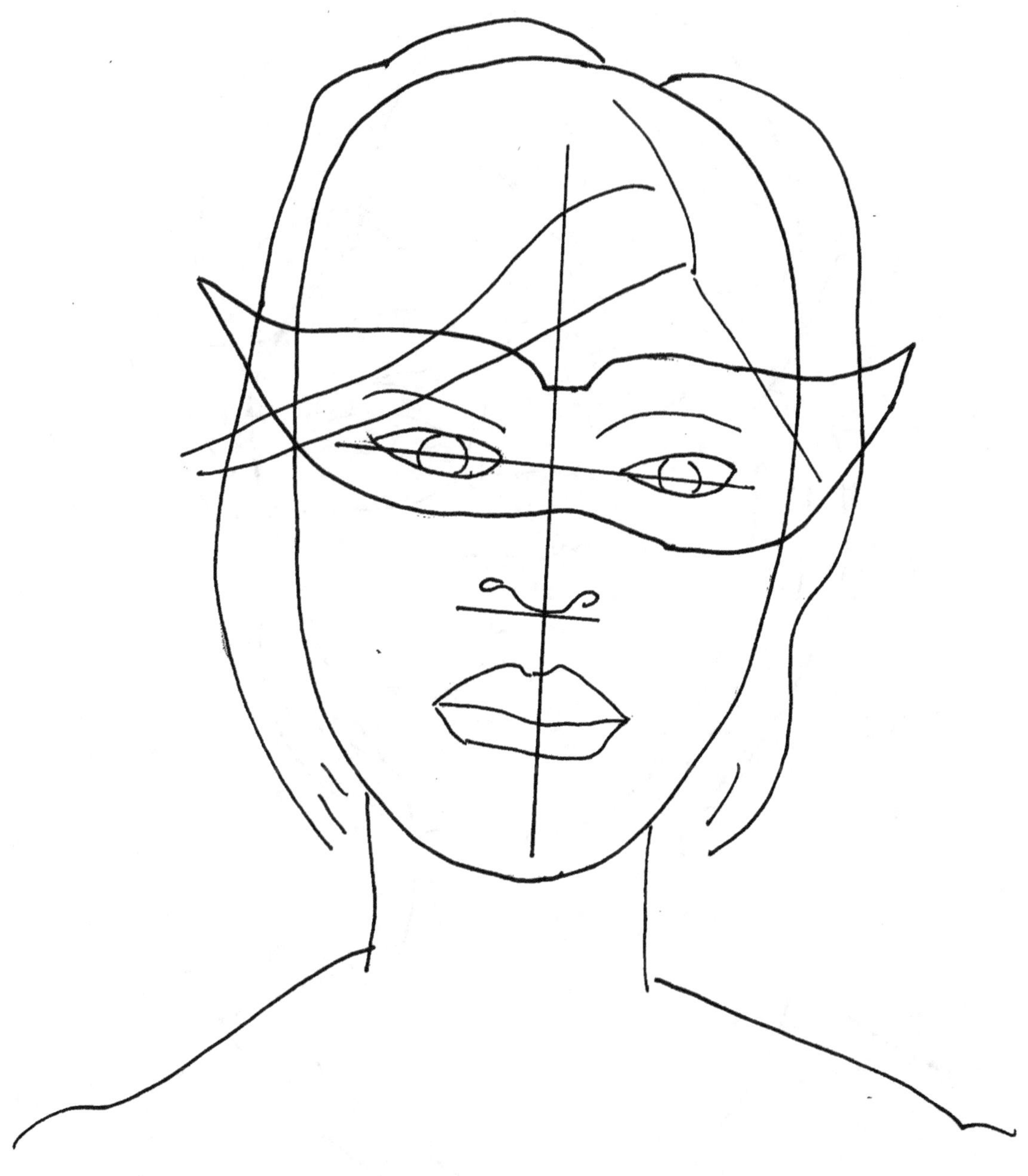

Erase all guidelines. Sketch in more details for the hair,
space glasses, draw necklace design on her neck line

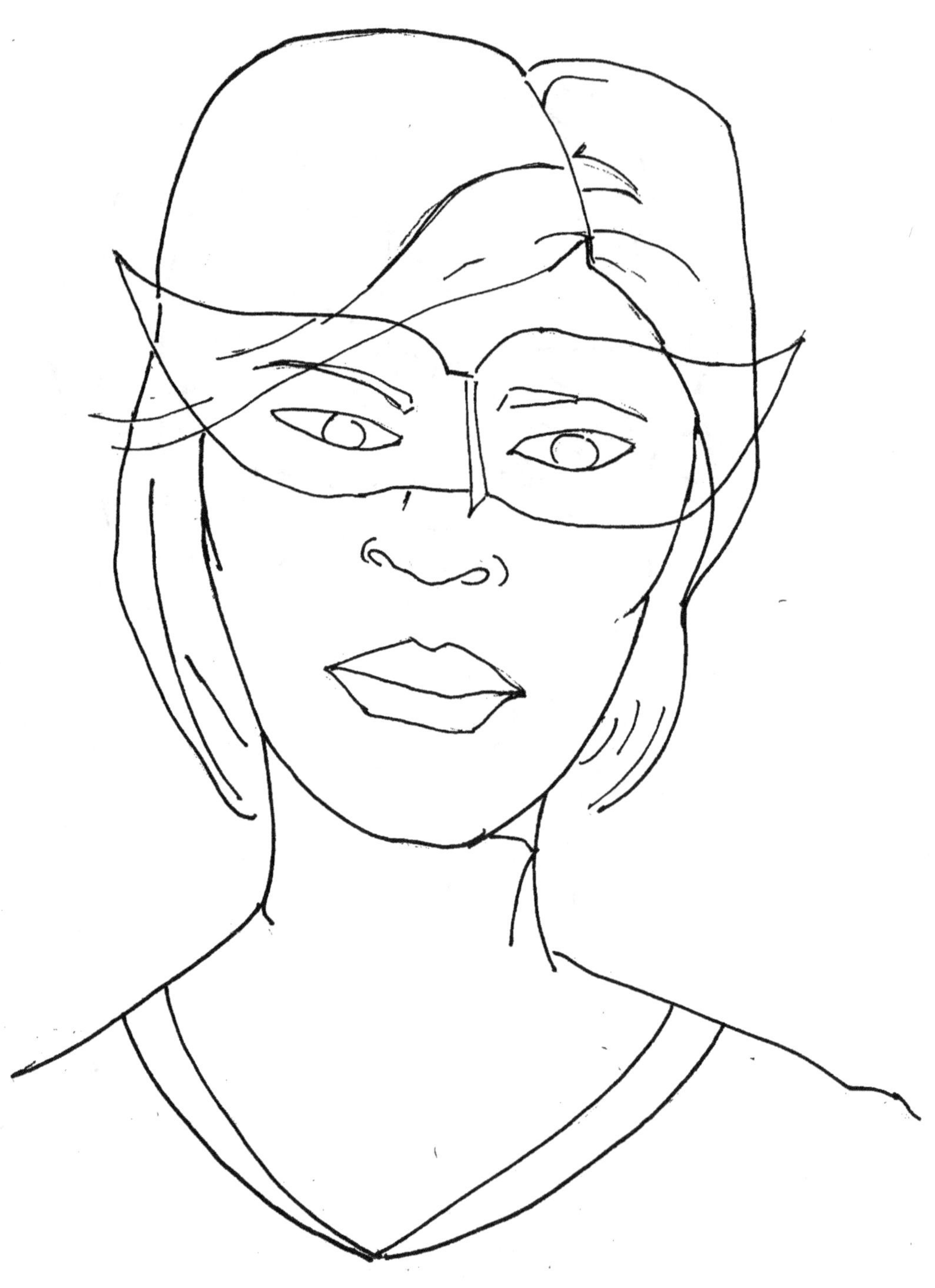

Shade in the lights and darks in her face, hair and neck areas. I added a gadget to the space glasses with lightning circulating. Here is the electrifying picture.

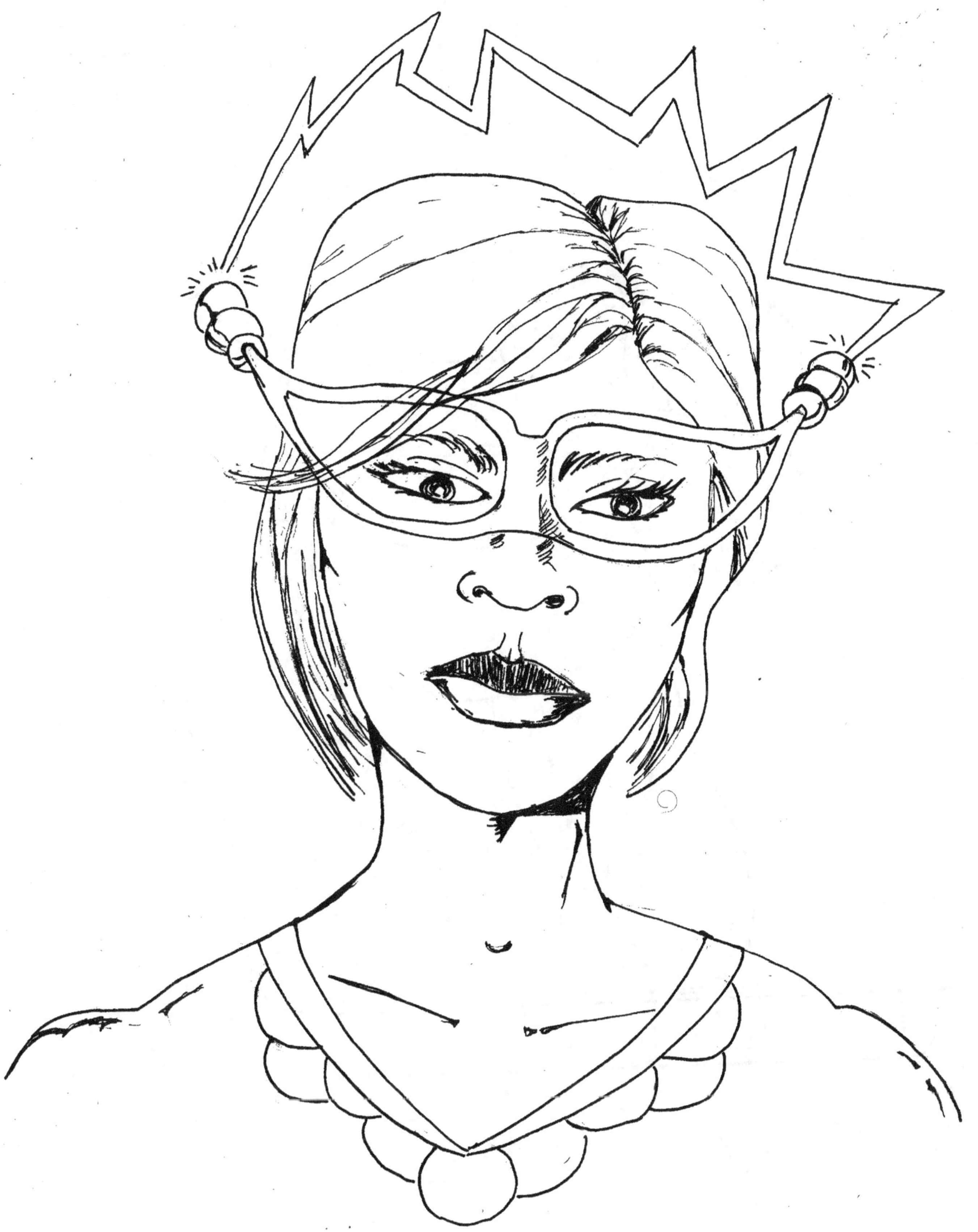

METAL RIDER

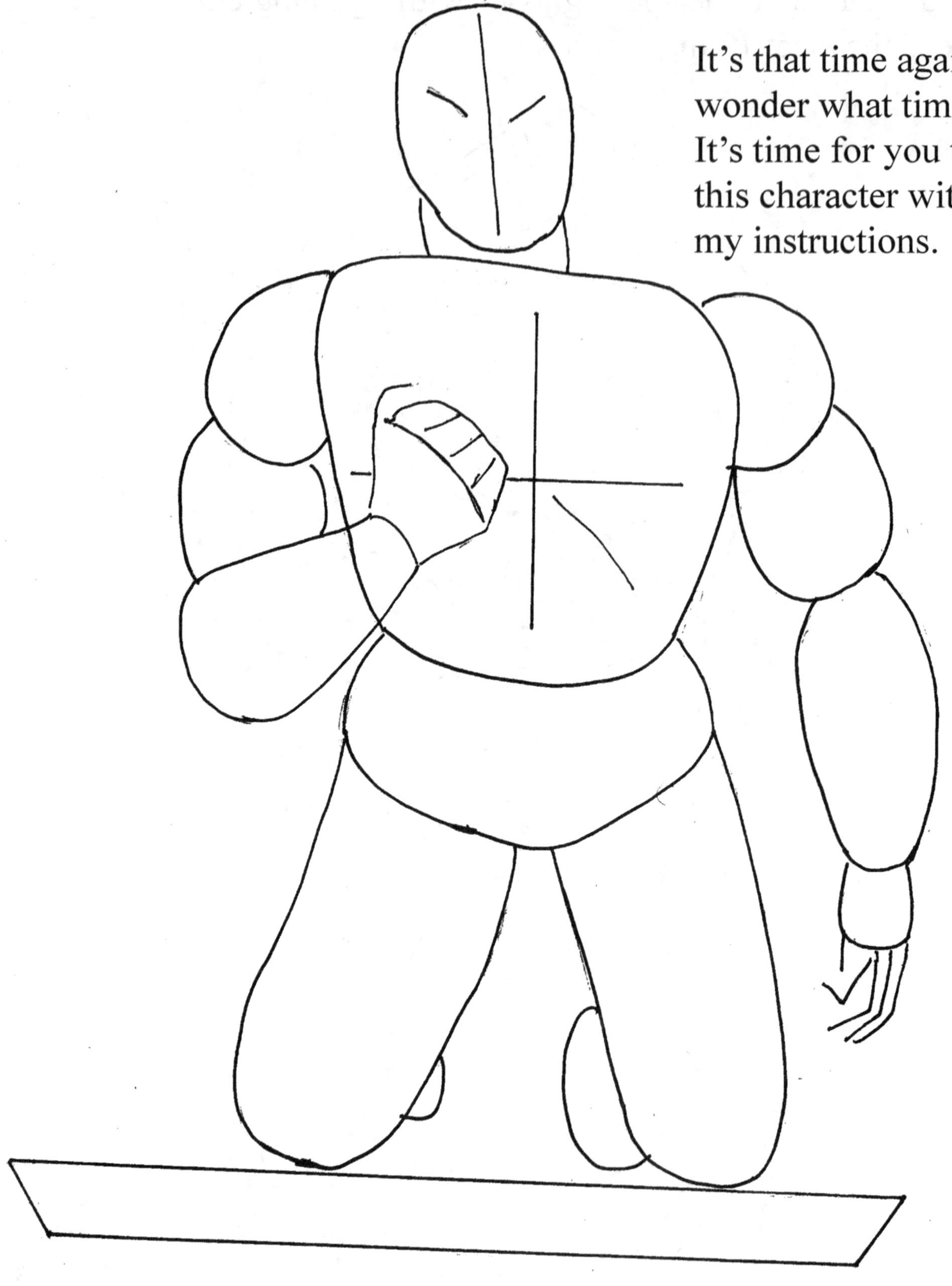

It's that time again. You wonder what time is it? It's time for you to draw this character without my instructions.

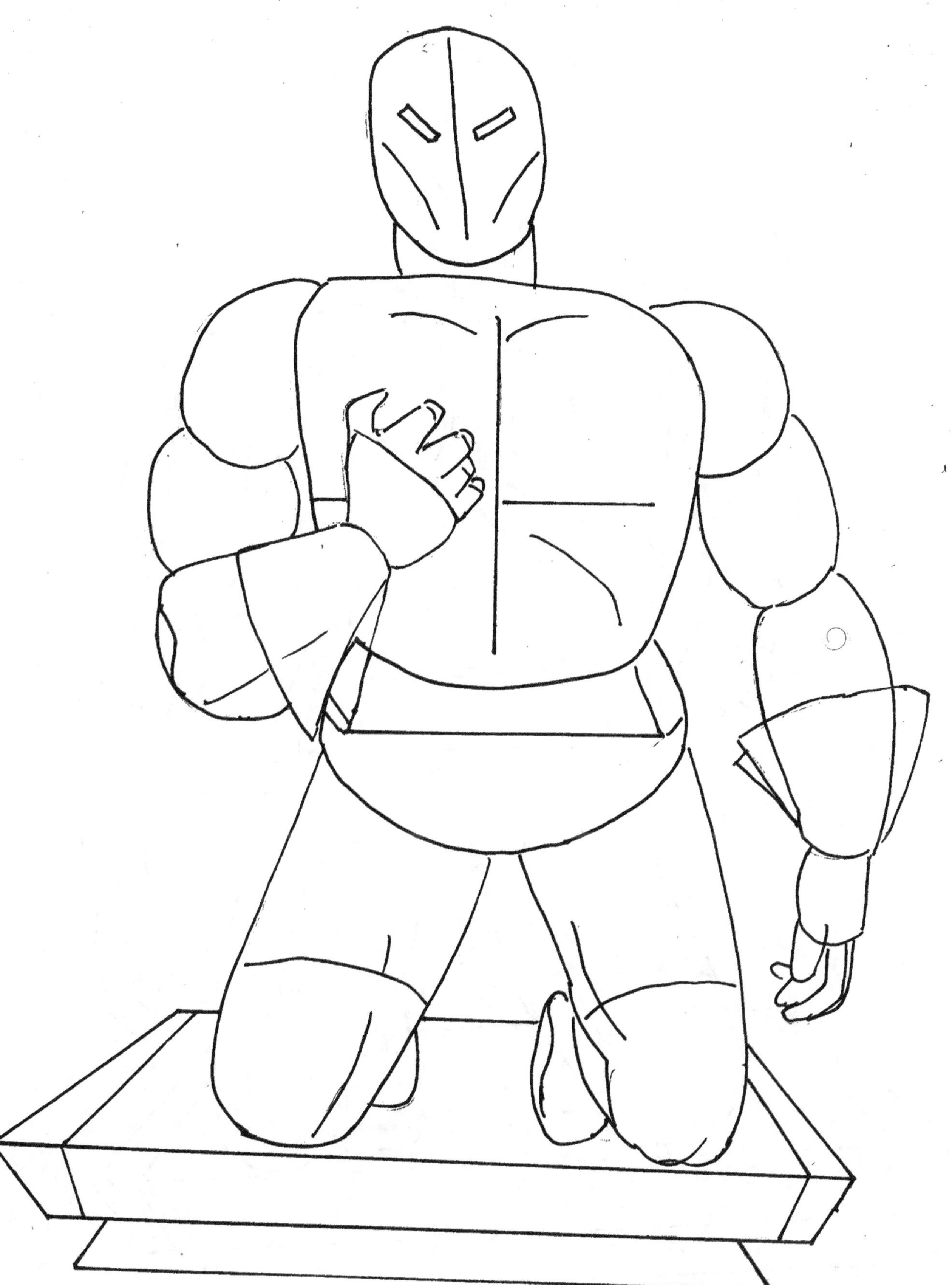

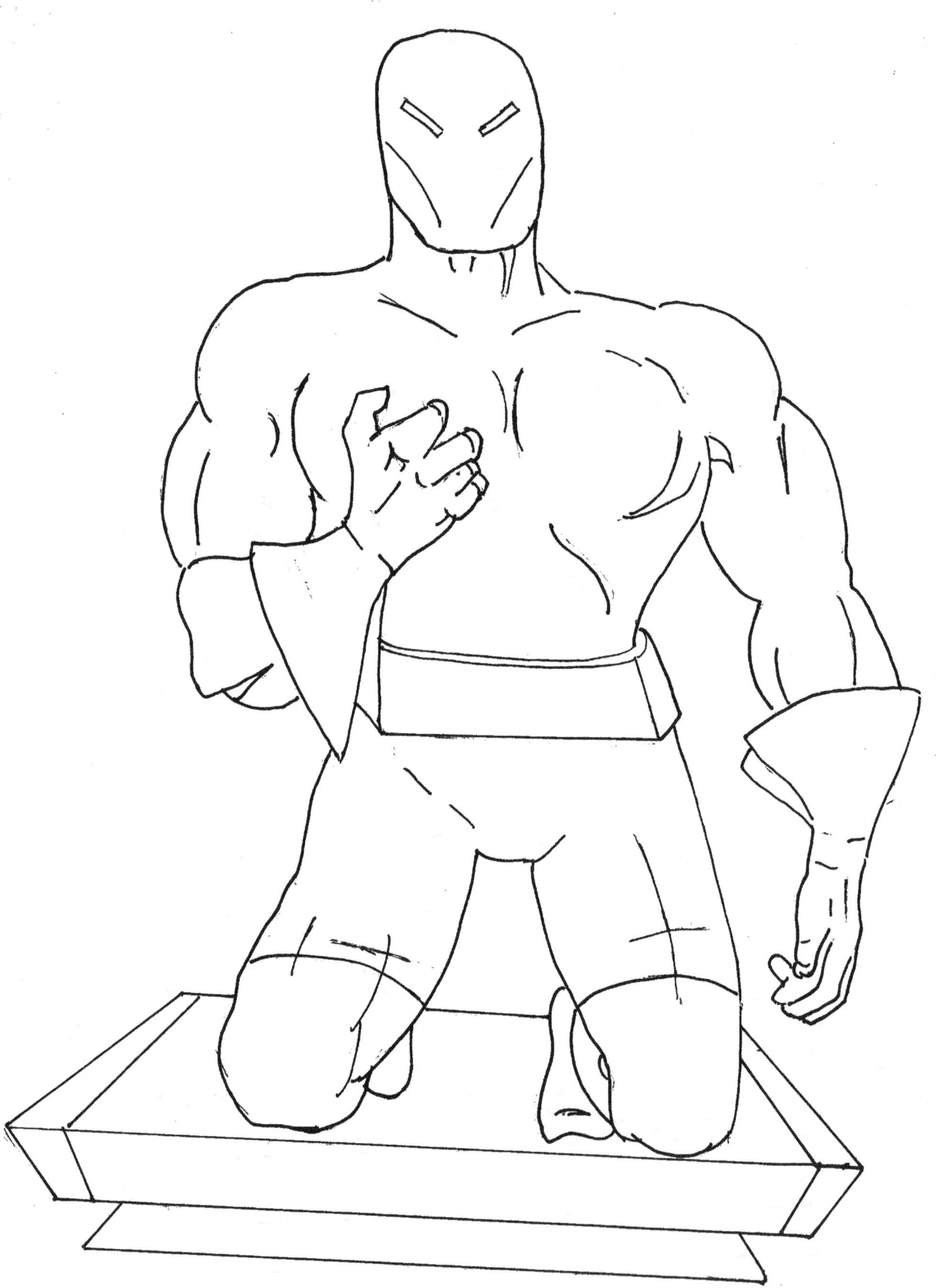

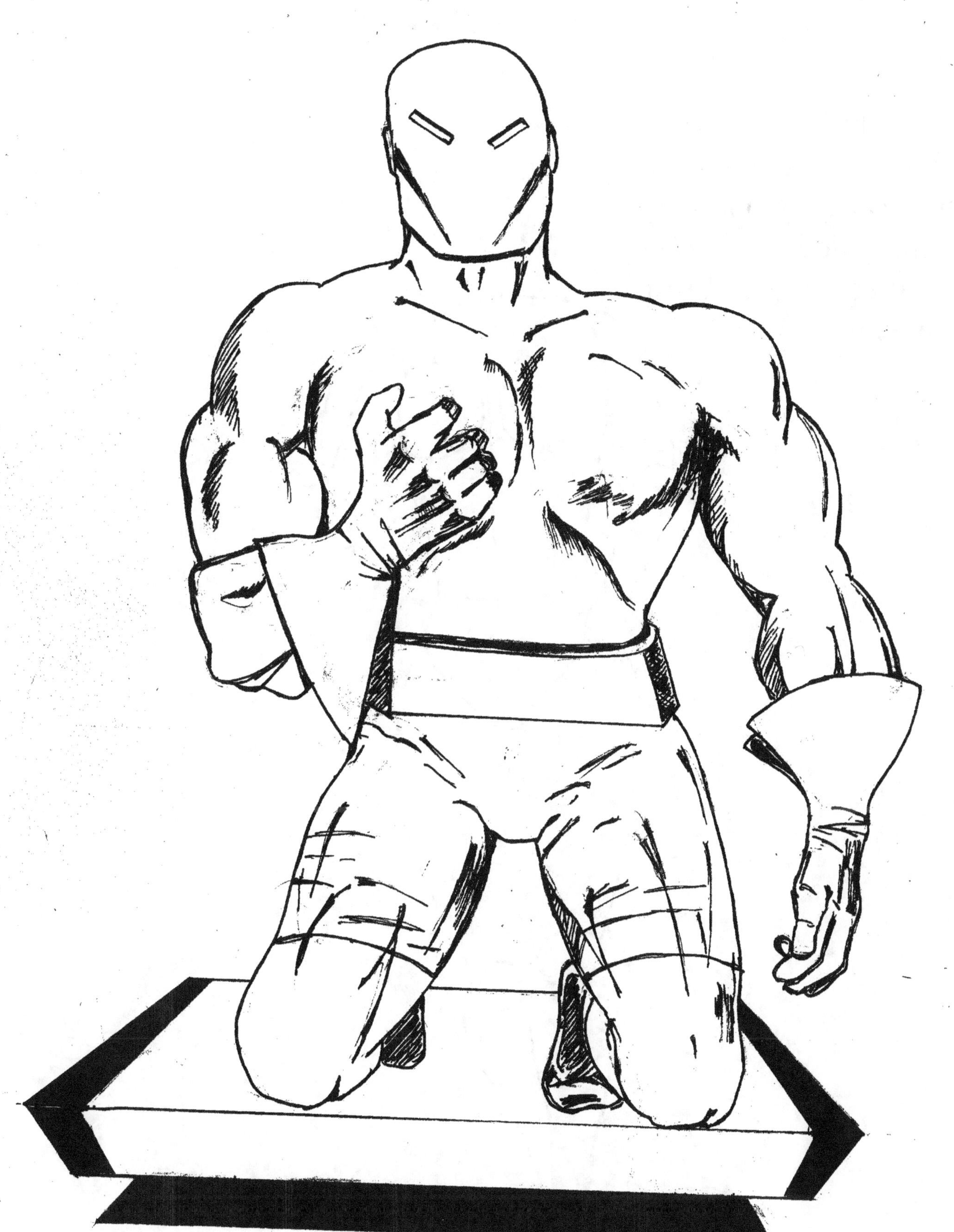

C-LADY

As usual let's begin with the head on the C-Lady to start your drawing. Continue drawing guidelines for the neck, torso, arms and rest of the body.

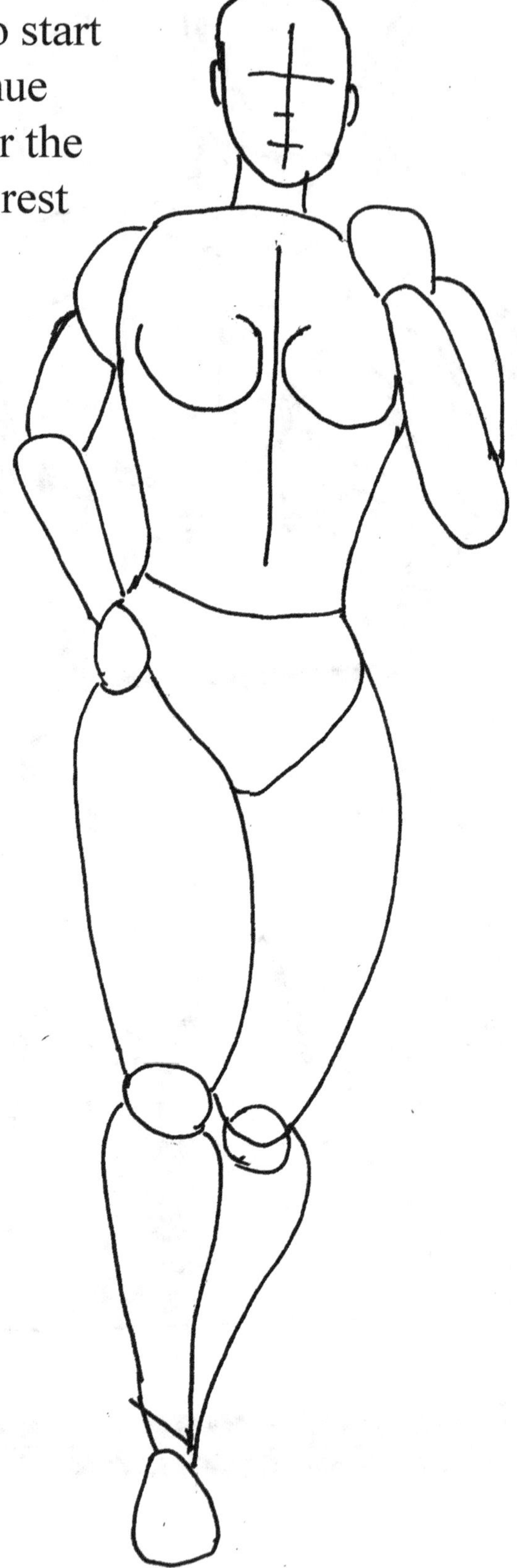

Along the guidelines, sketch in the hair, eyes, nose, and mouth. Then proceed with the rest of the body.

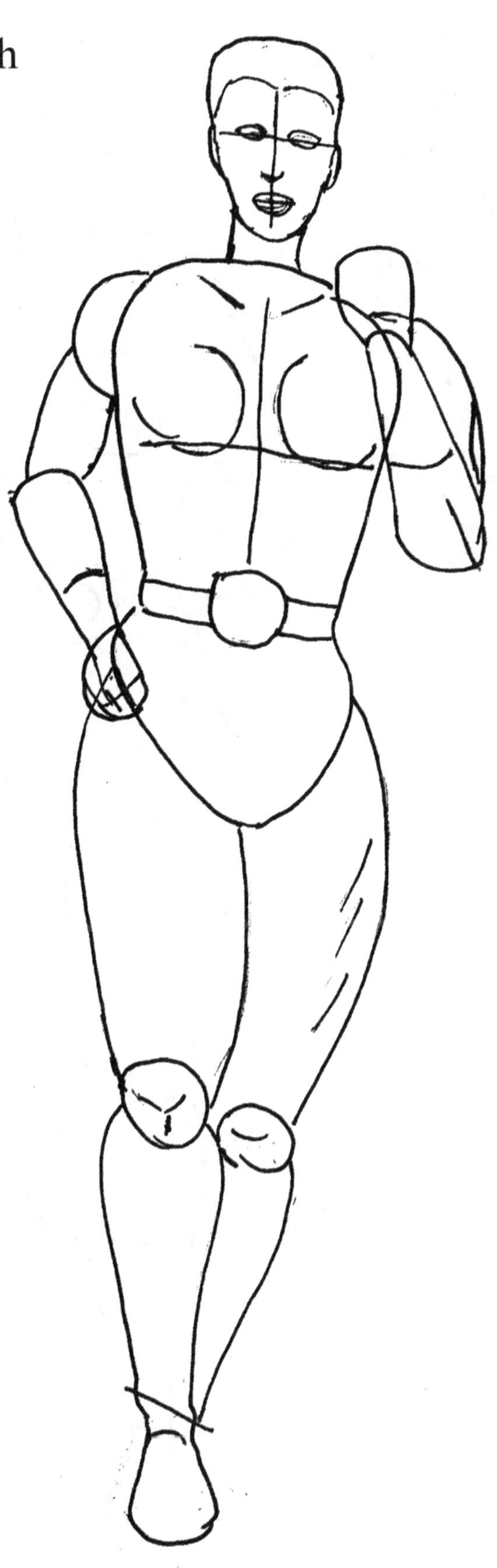

To bring this drawing
to a close. You need
to erase all guidelines
and start to indicate
where the details will
be applied.

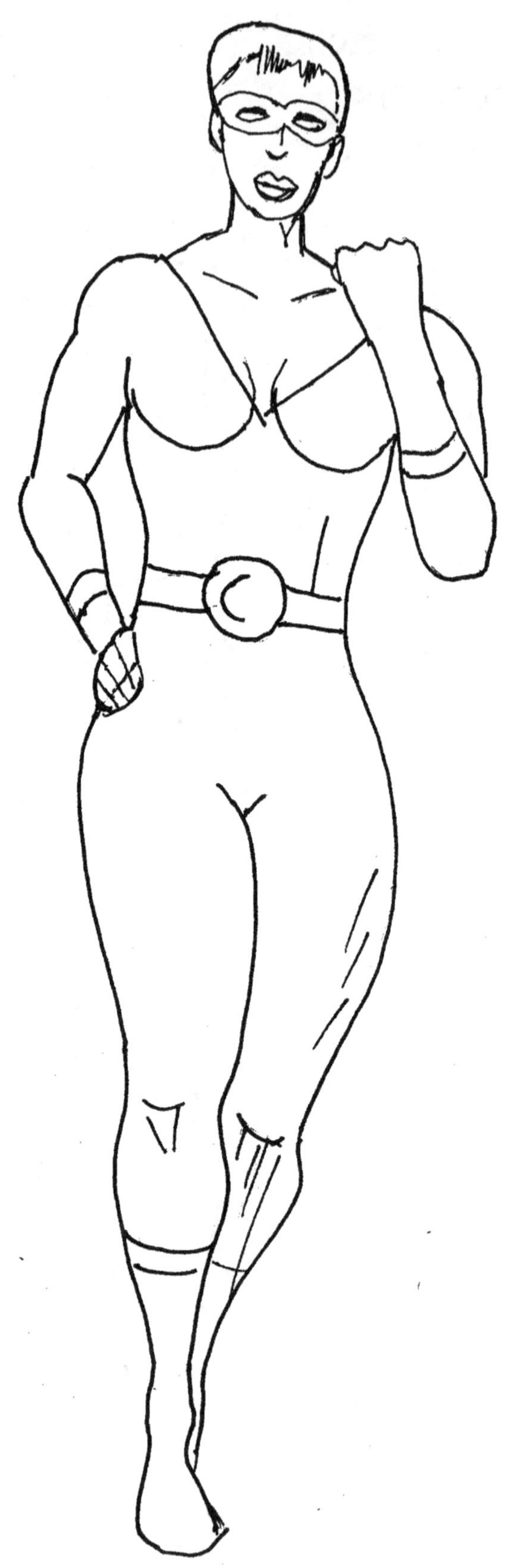

Once you apply the
details and you sketch
in the lights and darks
so it's neat. Now what
you have is your
masterpiece complete.

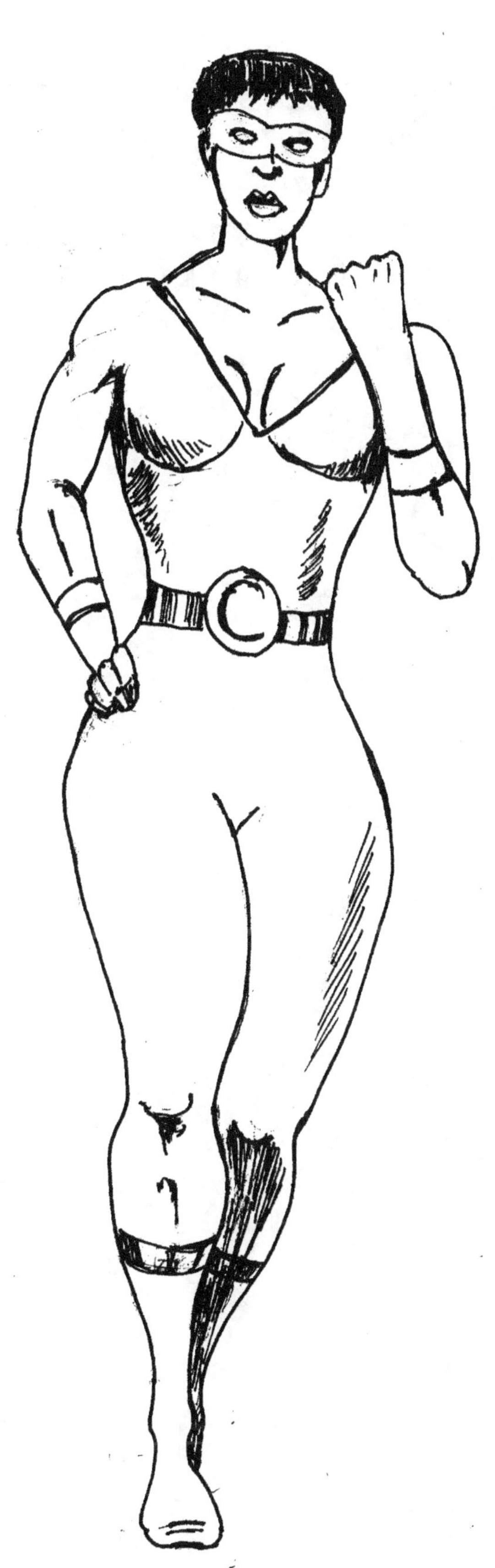

Ain't Nothing To It, But To Do It!!

FANTASY DRAWING

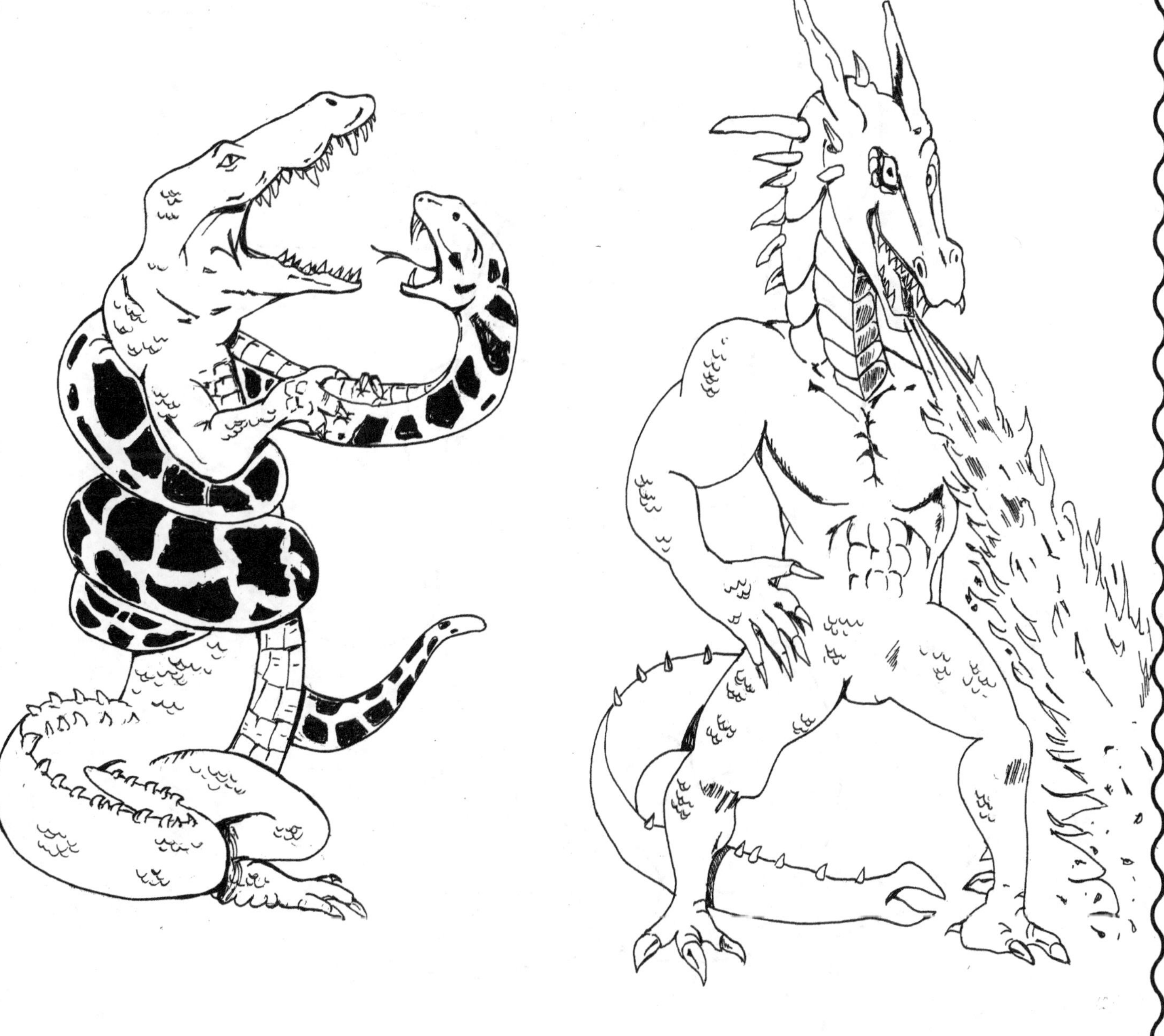

ALLIGATOR VS. SNAKE

Draw the alligator first
starting with the head.
Then draw the snake
with one long line
of his body wrapped
around the alligator

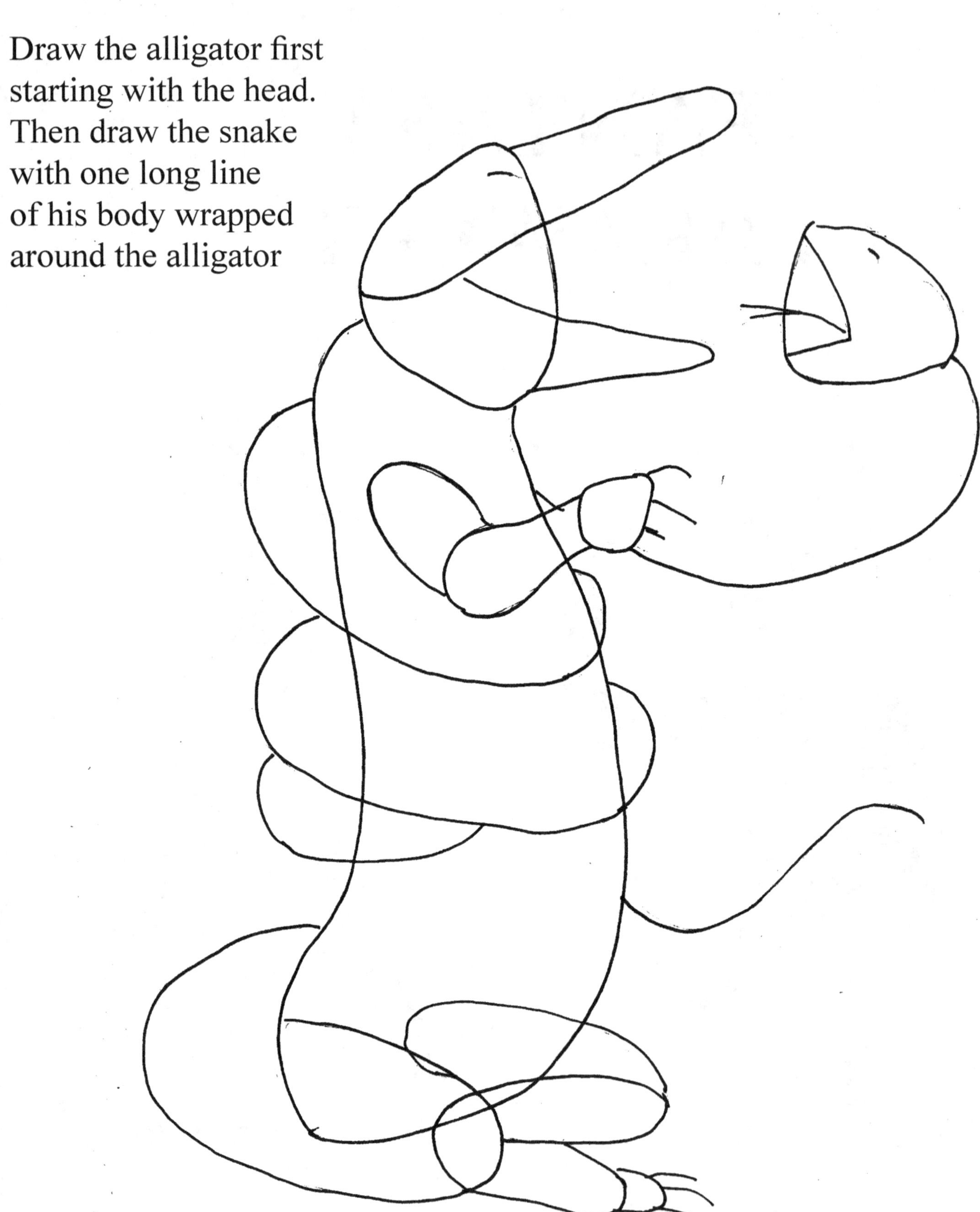

Sketch in details on the alligator's head and
tail. As well as drawing another long line to
fill out the snakes's body and head.

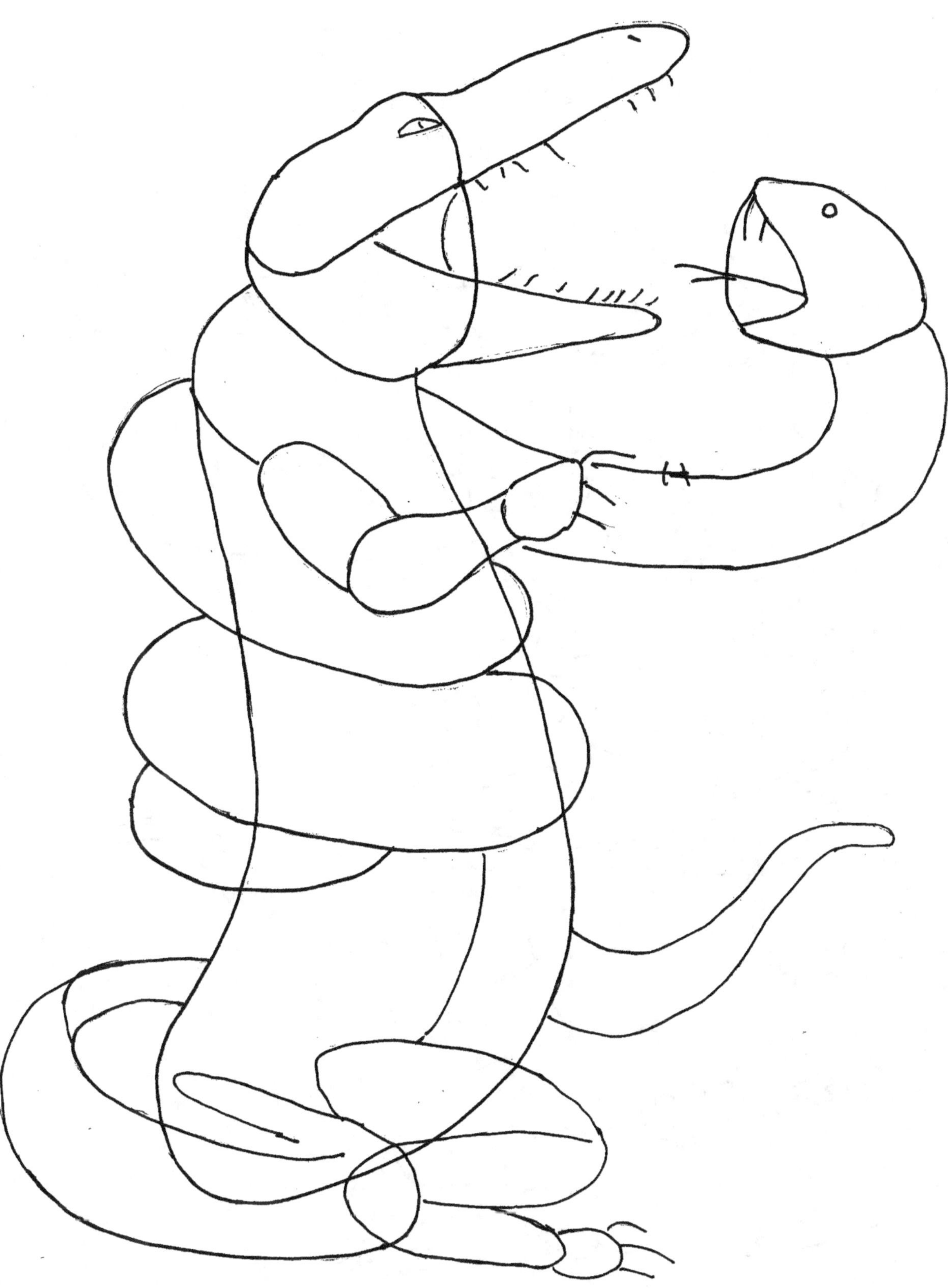

Erase all guidelines, then draw more details on the alligator's face, body, legs and tail. Sketch in more details on the snake's head with the body skin texture formation.

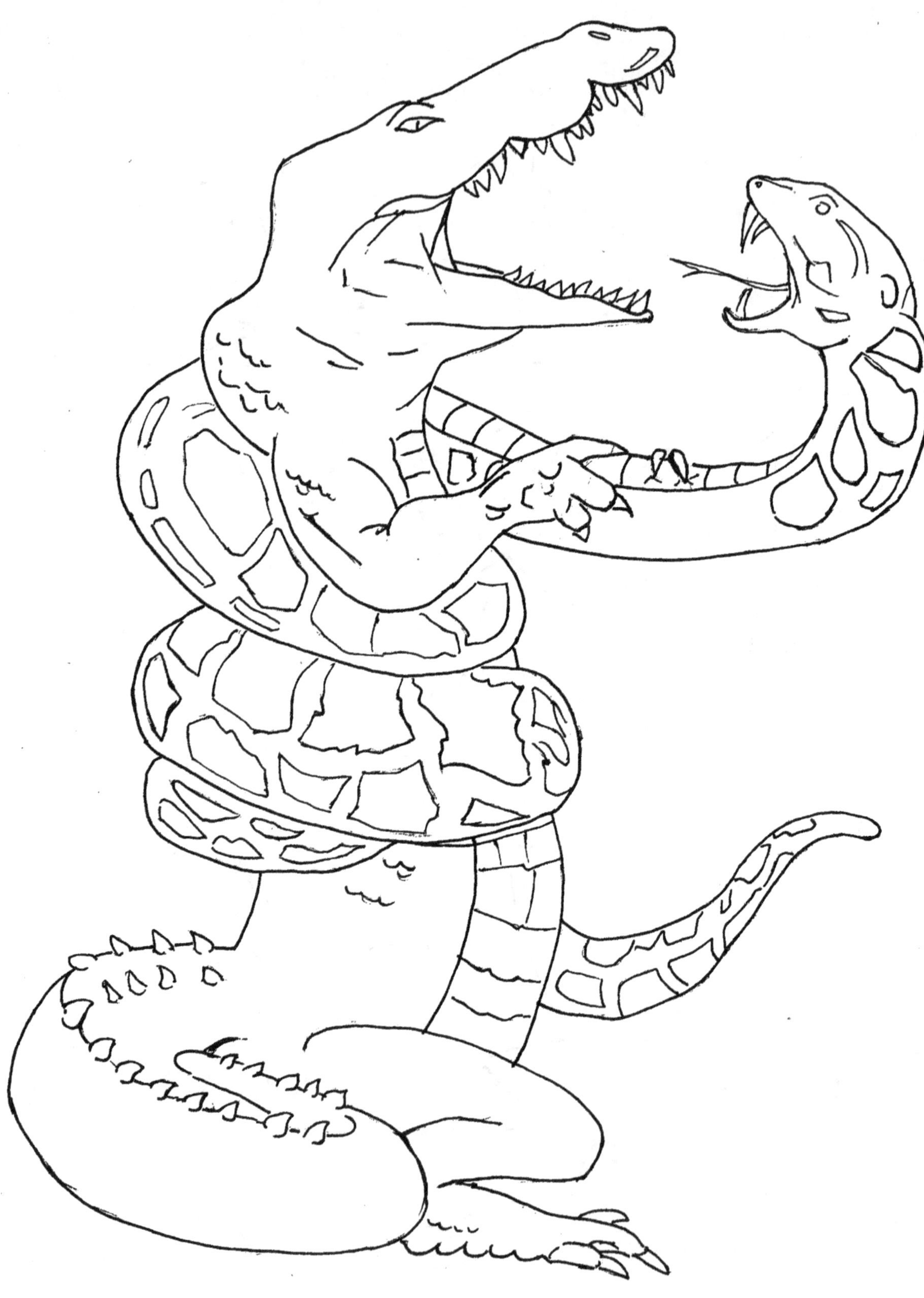

Carefully with your marker sketch in the shades of
darks and lights to complete this fantasy work of art.

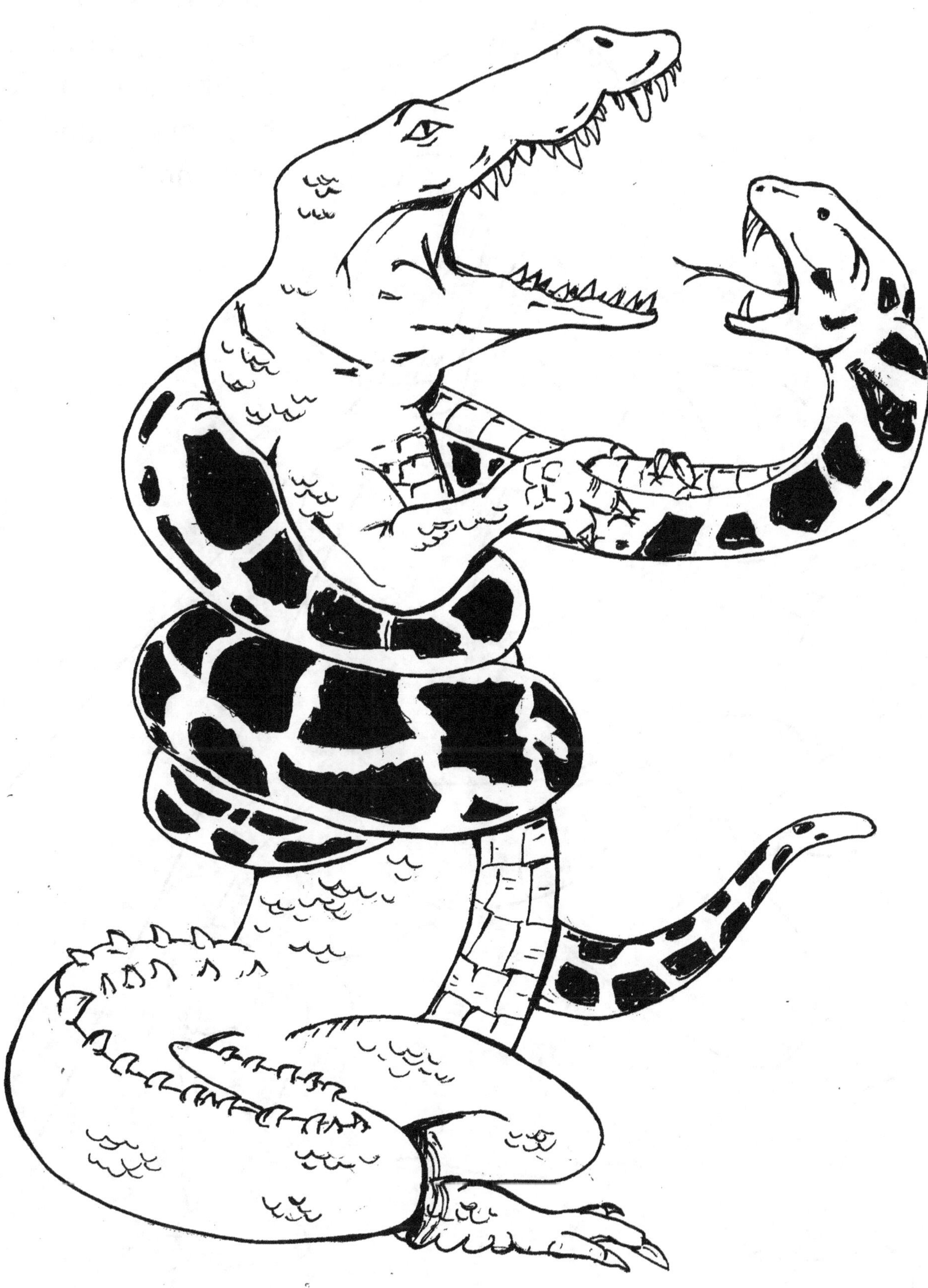

117

MAN-DRAGON

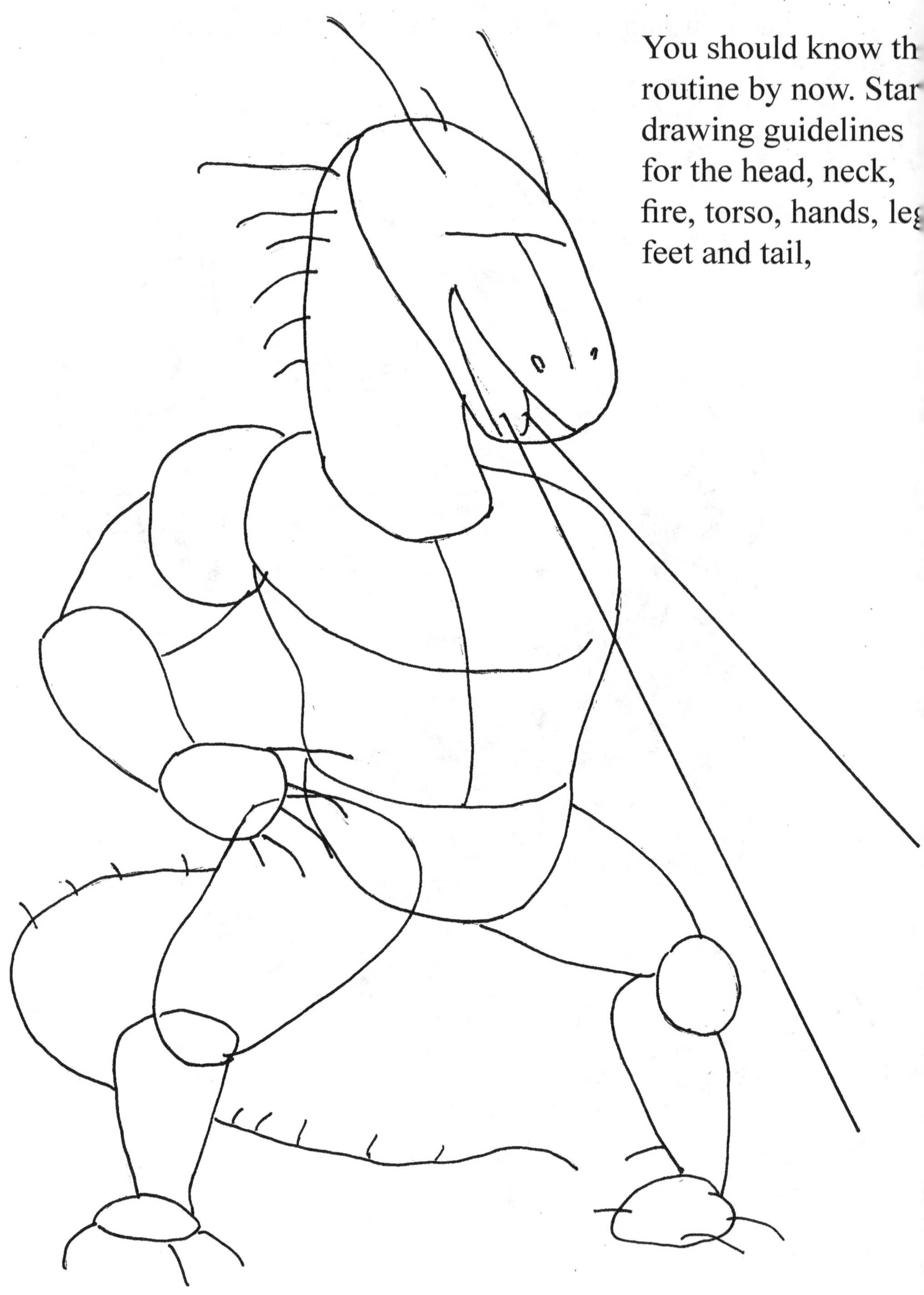

You should know th[e] routine by now. Star[t] drawing guidelines for the head, neck, fire, torso, hands, leg[s] feet and tail,

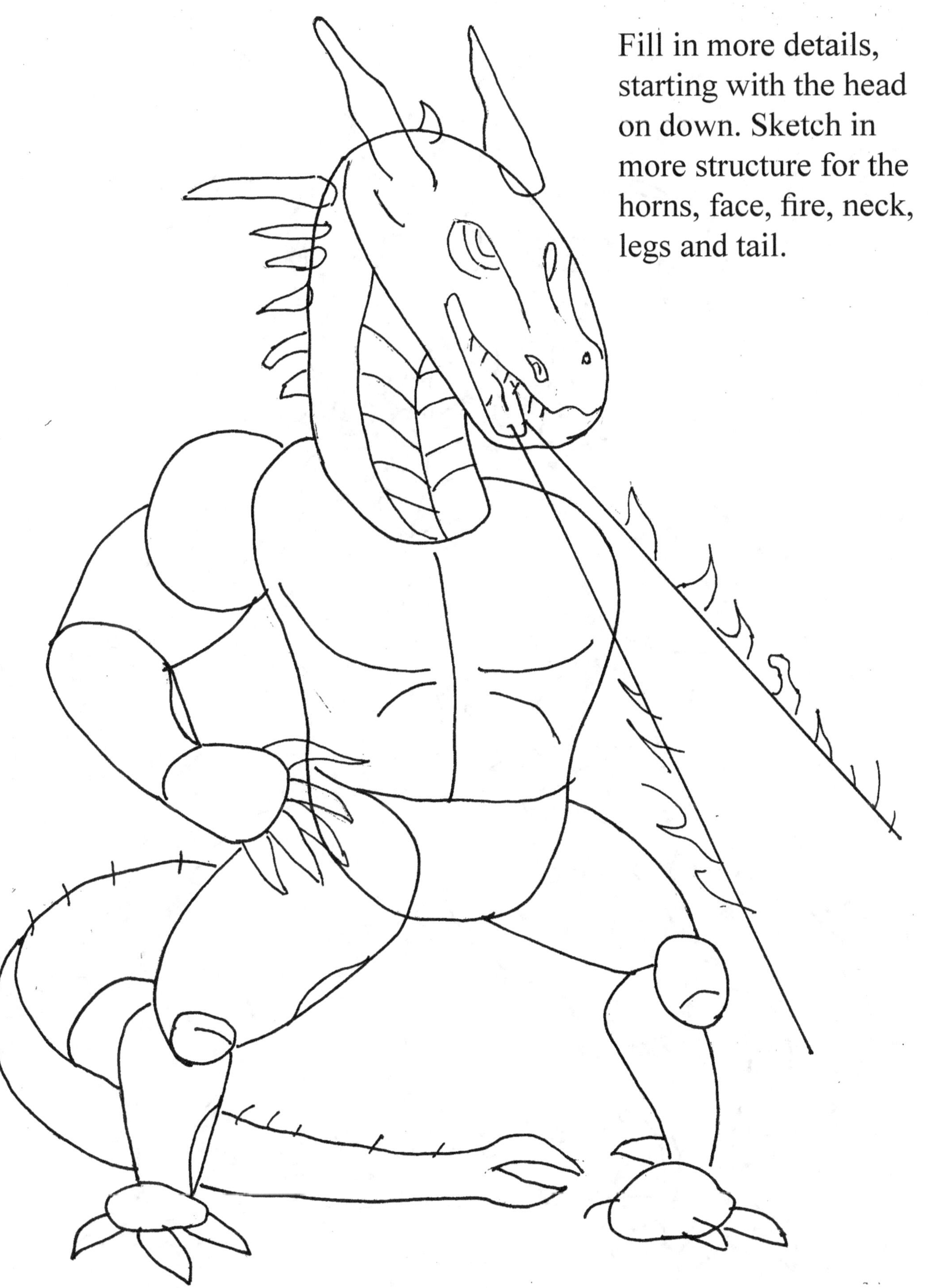

Fill in more details, starting with the head on down. Sketch in more structure for the horns, face, fire, neck, legs and tail.

Here's a more defined drawing with all the guidelines erased. Now draw structure lines to present a more refined picture.

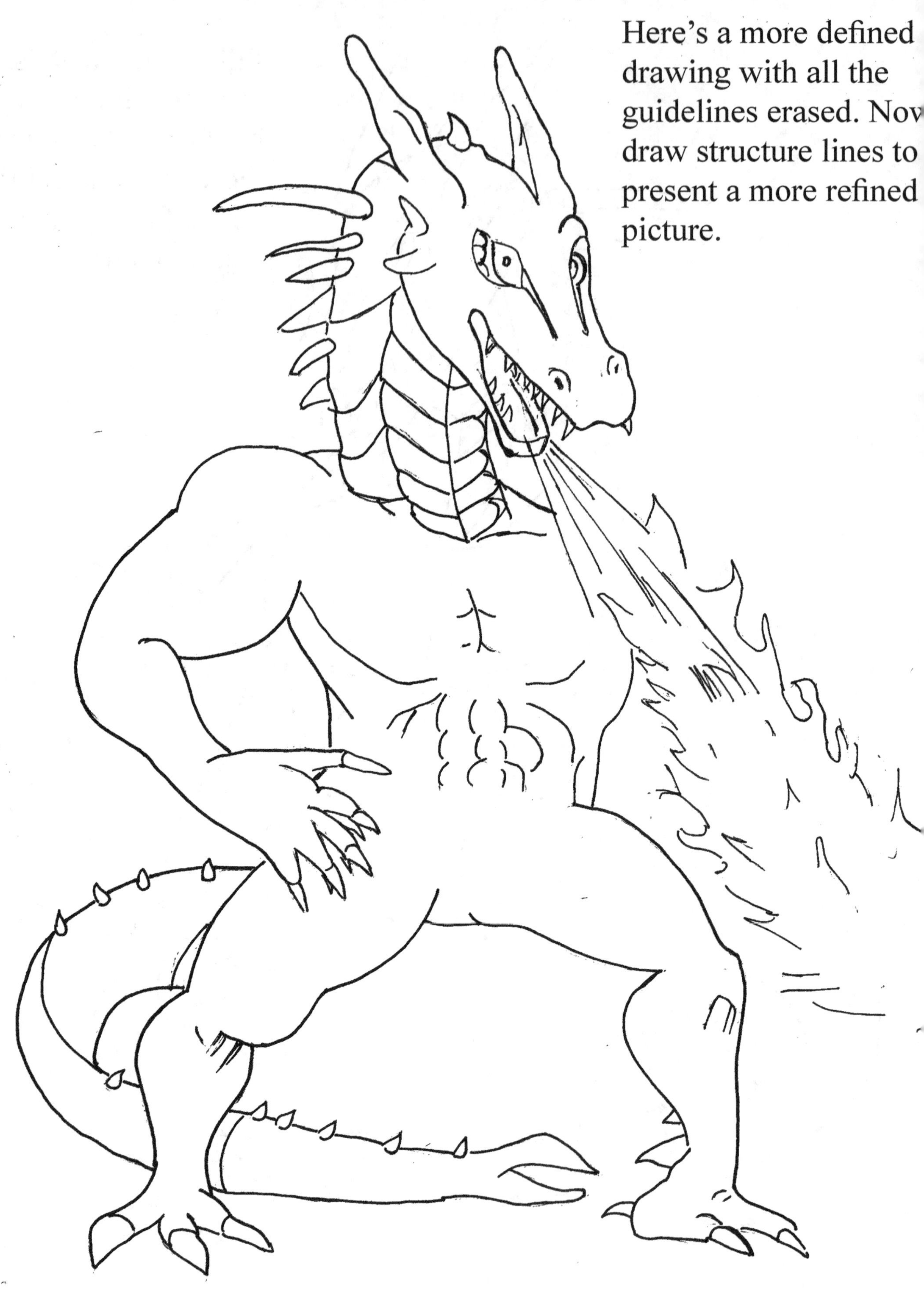

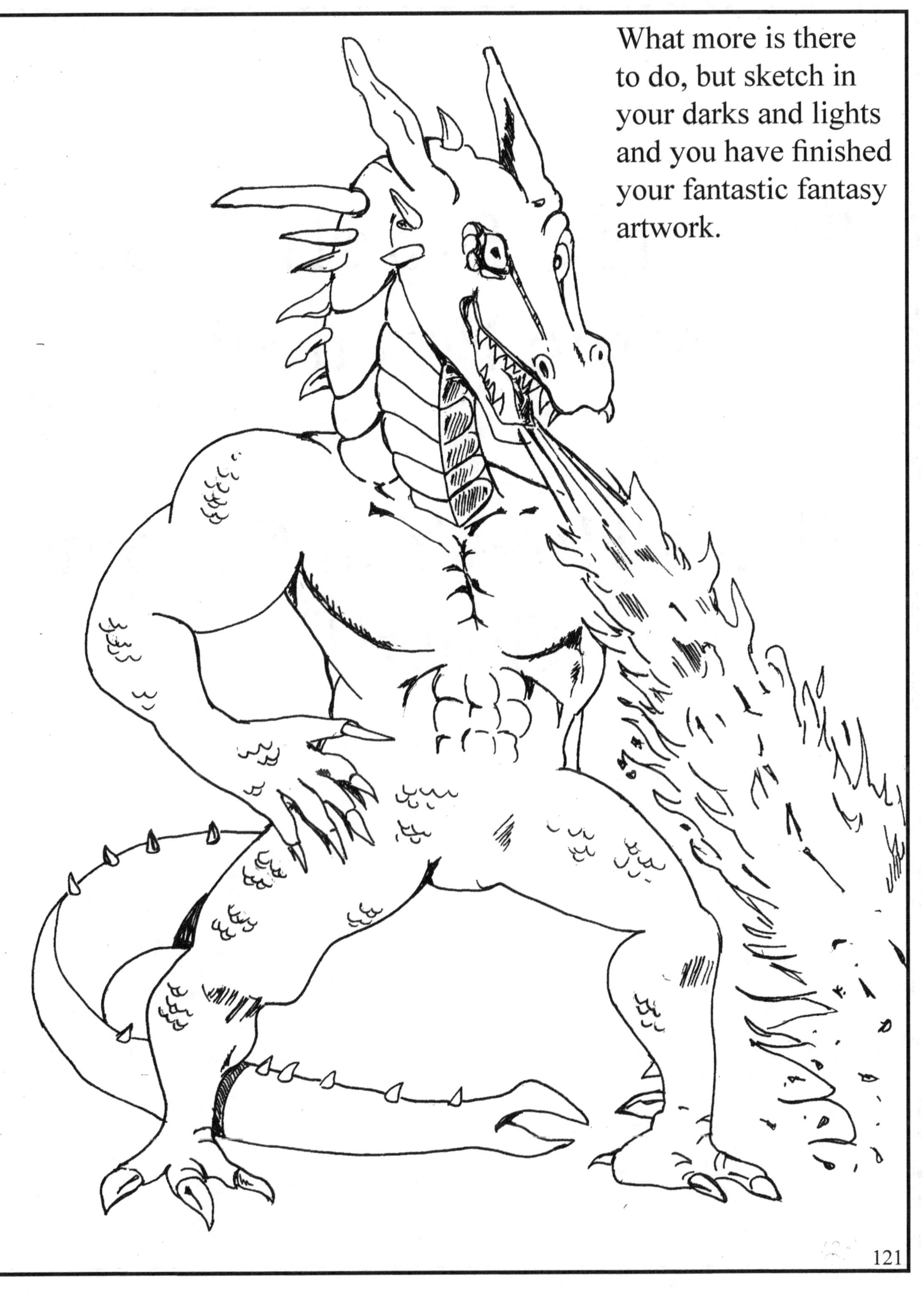

What more is there
to do, but sketch in
your darks and lights
and you have finished
your fantastic fantasy
artwork.

Practice, Practice, and More Practice!!

That's How You Become Great!!

COVER LADY

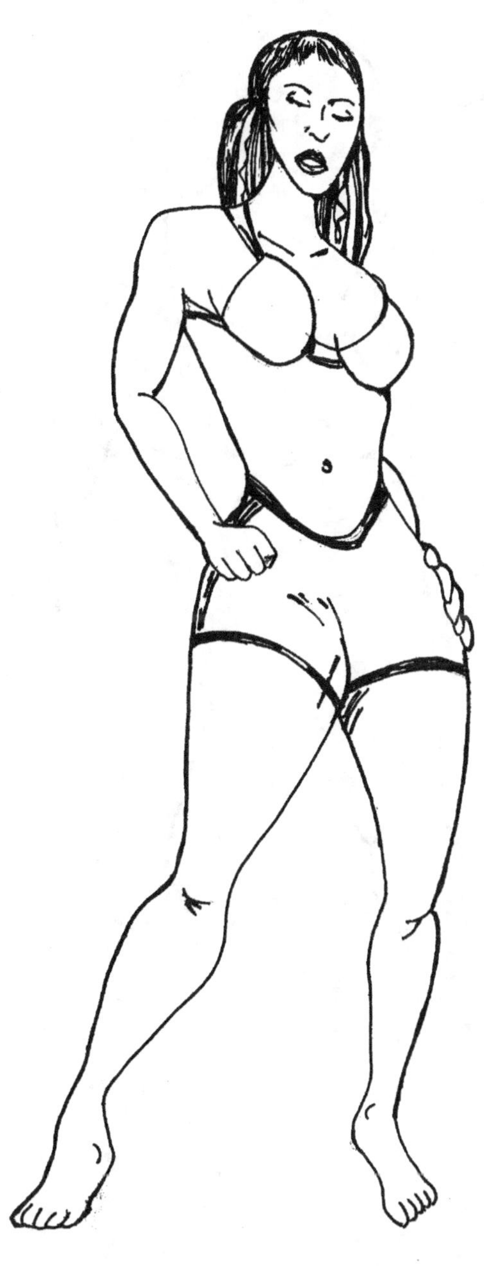

COVER LADY

Last but not least, let's finish
this book with our beautiful
Cover Lady.

You know where to start,
so let's get started!

You know what to do next.

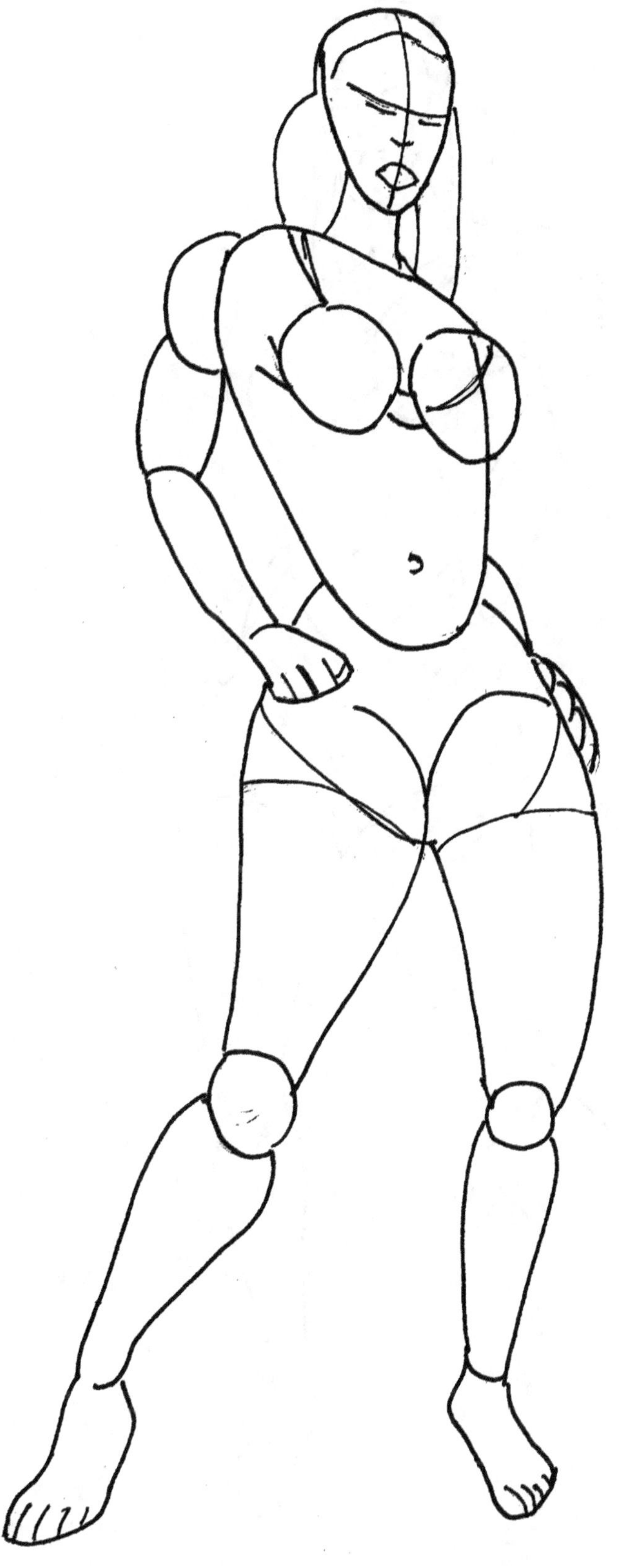

What lines did you have to erase and add to get this picture?

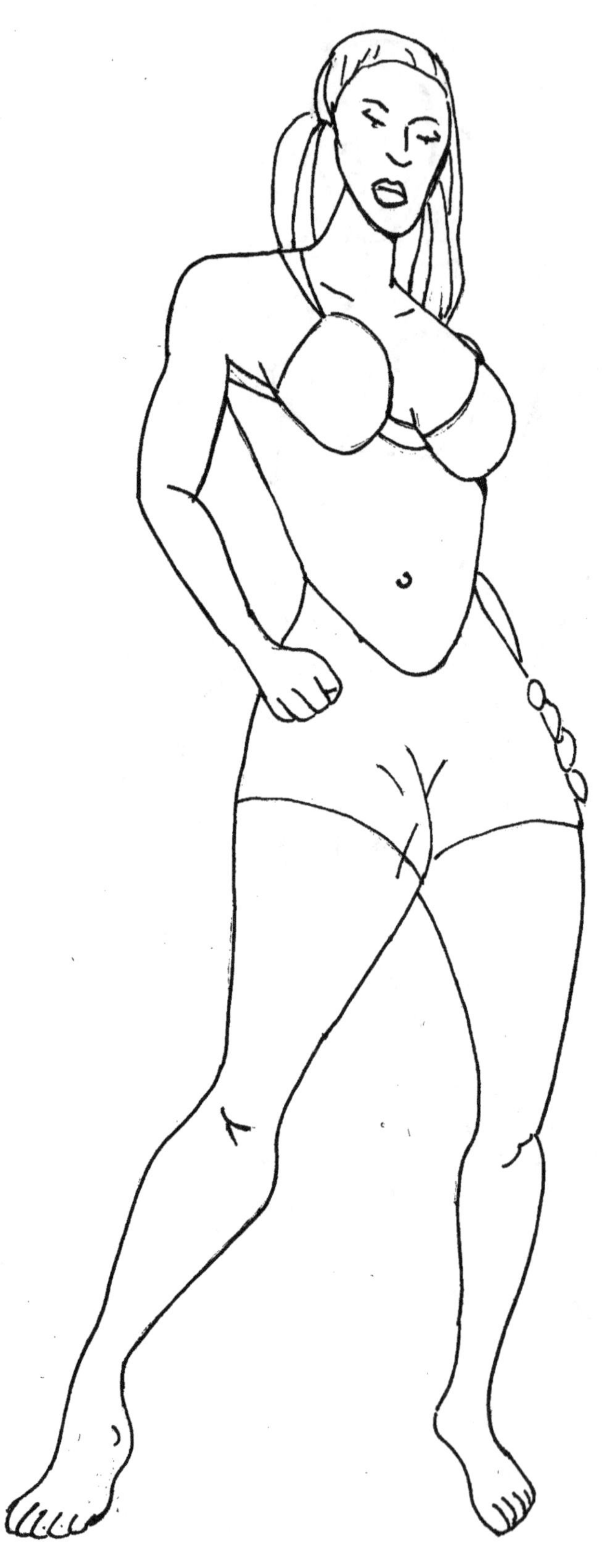

After applying the finishing touches. This is what you have...A
beautiful woman, and that's no jive. That's why I named her
Sadie....The Cover Lady.

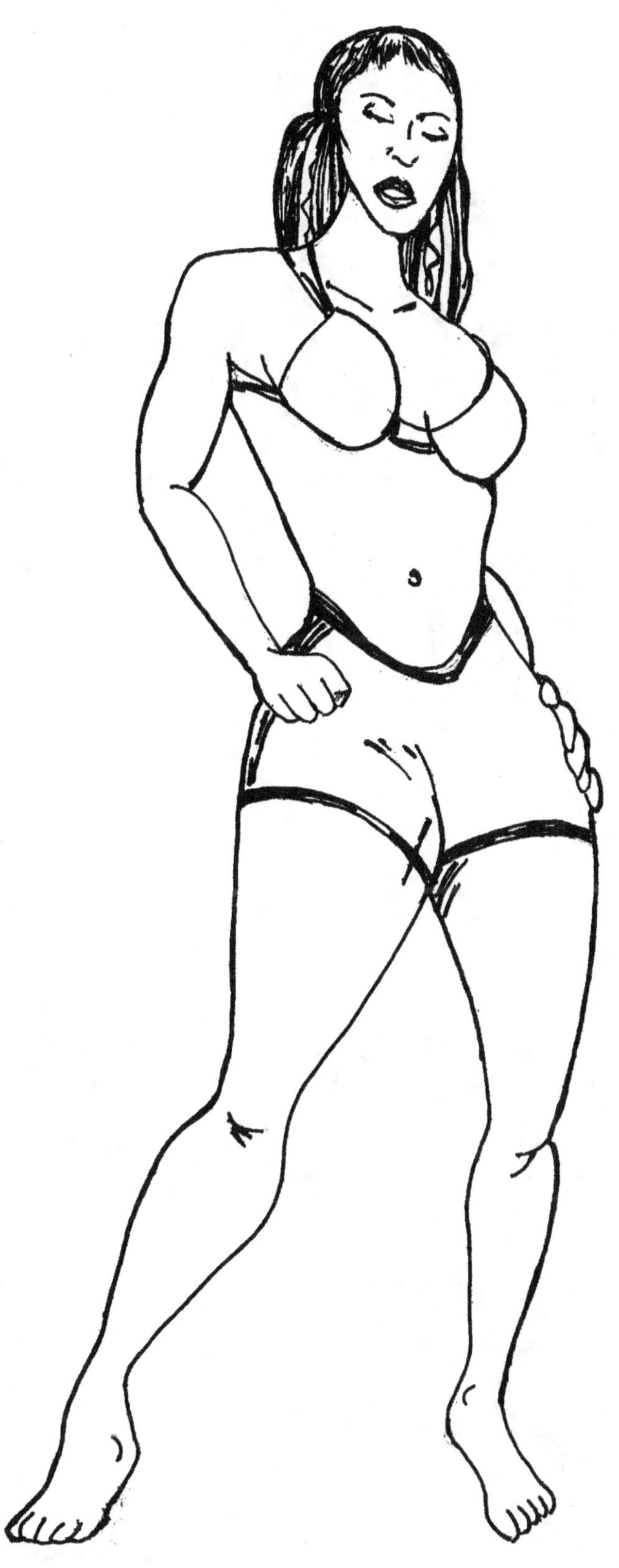

PHELPS PUBLISHING
Collage of Art

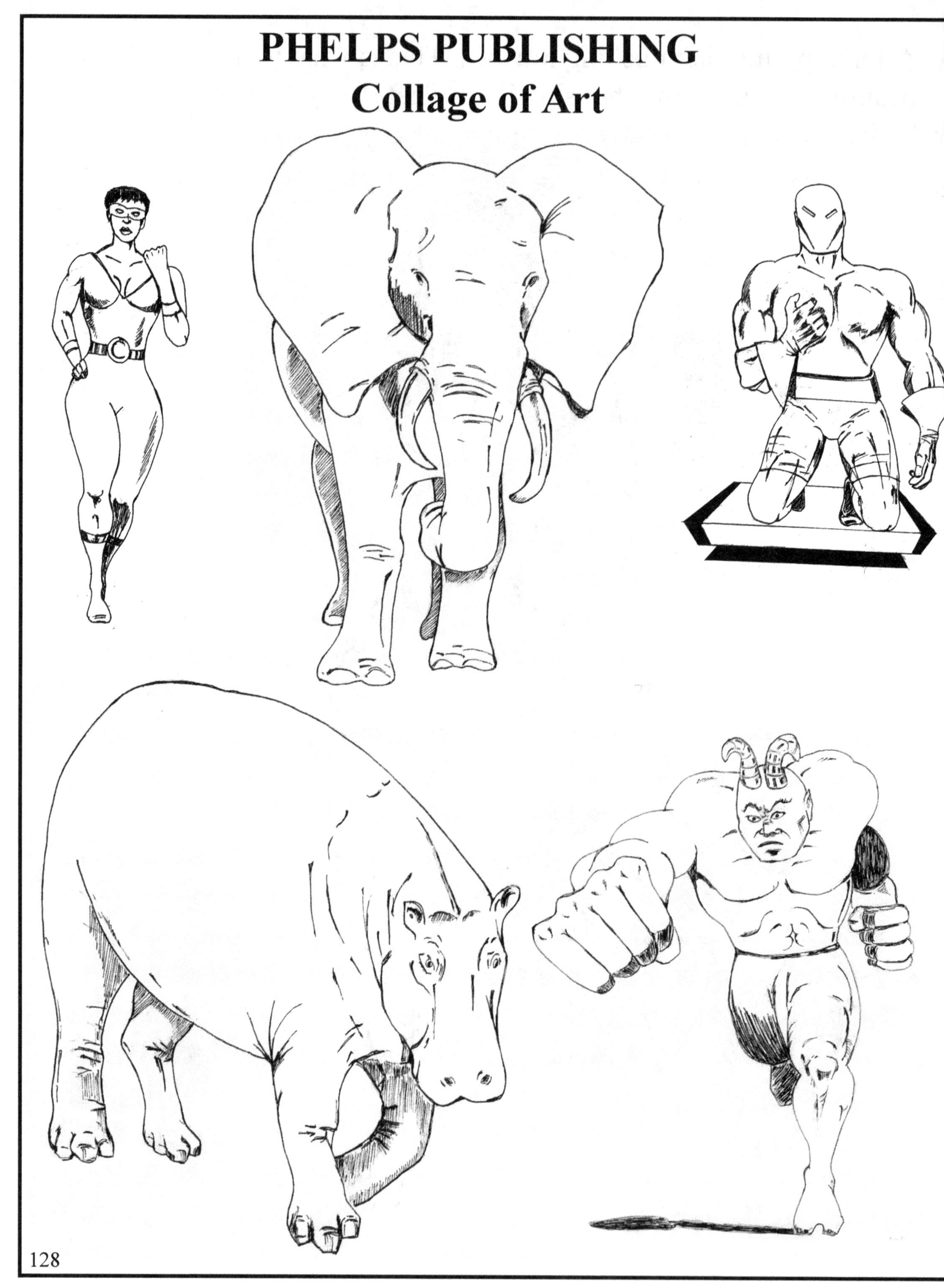

PHELPS PUBLISHING
Book Showcase

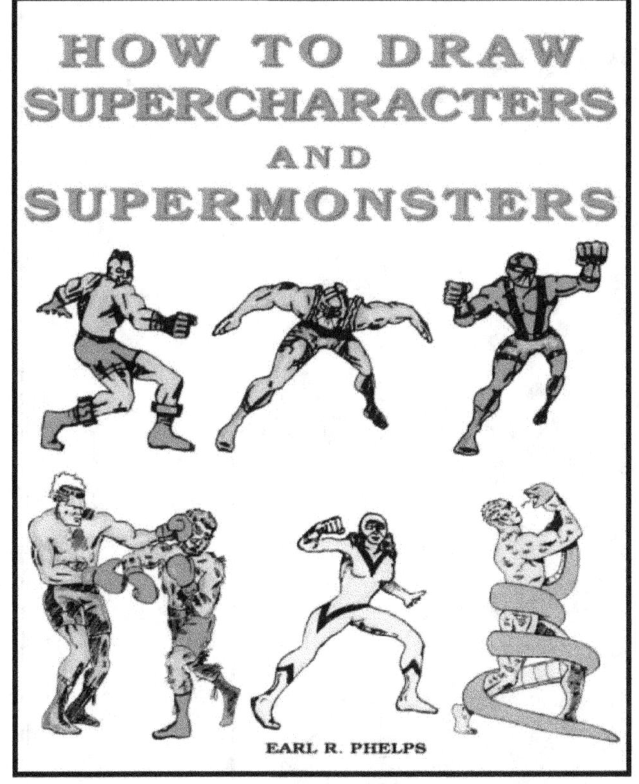

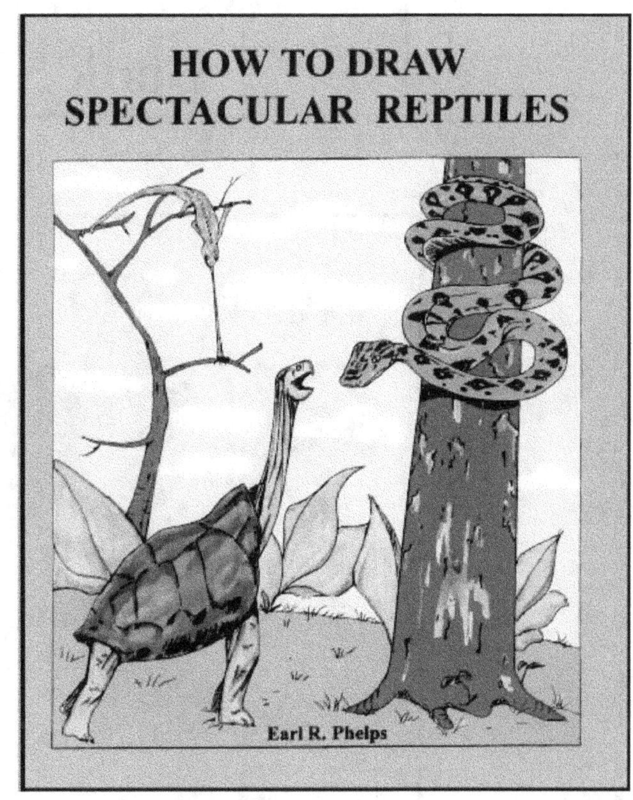

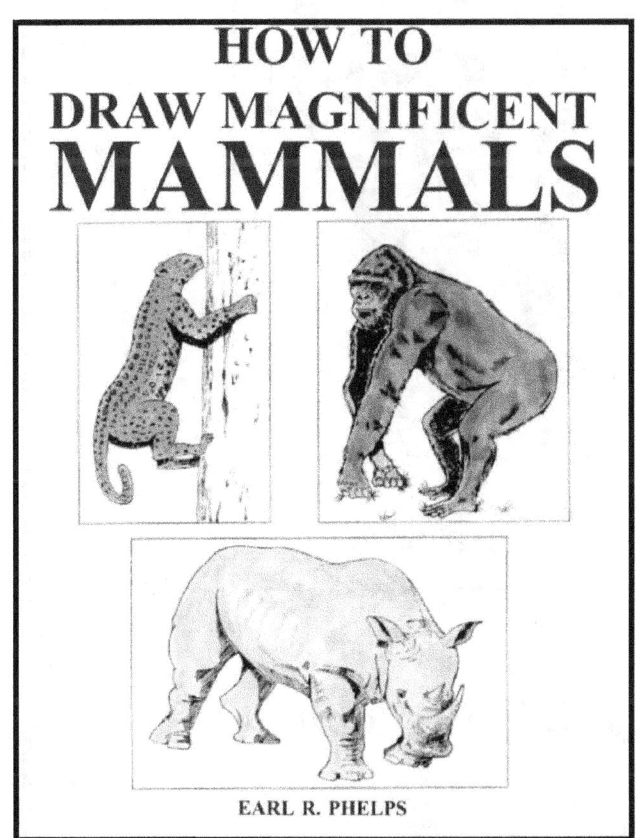

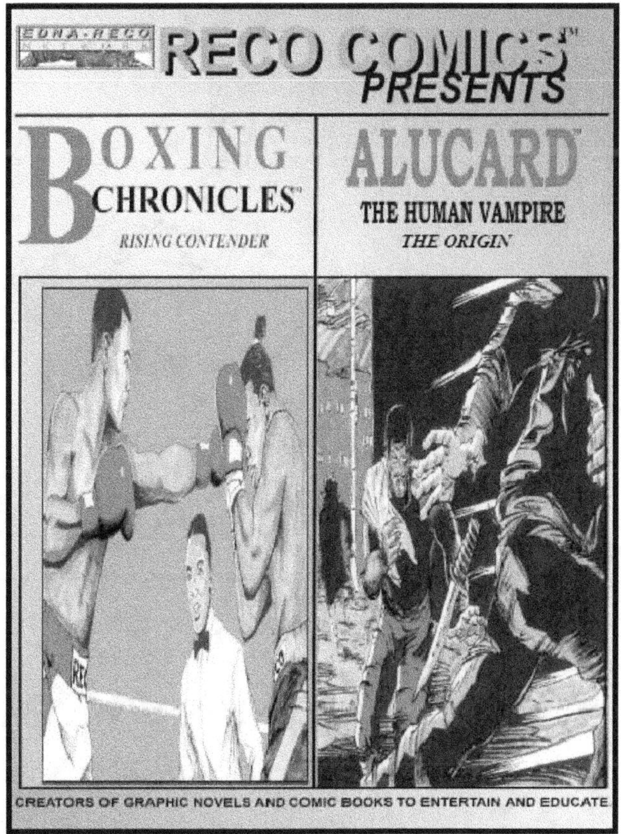

https://www.phelpspublishing.com/